HOME GROWN LEGACY

LIFE, LADDERS AND LEARNINGS IN THE WORLD OF HOME IMPROVEMENT

ERIK DARDAS

With all my heart to:
First and foremost, my wife and best friend Pam, without whose love and support I would not be here today. I thank God every day that you hung in there with me.
Jackie, our daughter and our greatest collaboration. I am so proud of you.
My mother and father, Ken and Julie, for courageously making life's most difficult decisions and setting me up for success.
My in-laws, Jack and Barb, for loving and supporting me as if I was your own son.
Our friends throughout the United States, who treated us like family when we were new to an area and felt all alone.

FREE GIFT FOR MY READERS!

As a way of saying "Thank-You" to my Readers I have a special gift for you.

Top 10 Lessons I Learned from climbing the corporate ladder at Home Depot for over 30 years!

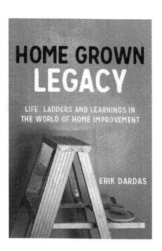

CONNECT WITH ME ON MY FACEBOOK PAGE TO RECEIVE YOUR FREE GIFT:

https://www.facebook.com/ErikDardasAuthor/

"When things are working, look out the window at those who contributed. When things are not working, look in the mirror."

— MARSHALL GOLDSMITH

FOREWORD

I am a Dardas through and through, orange blood and all. The smell of lumber, paint and fertilizer are easily recalled by my brain because my father loved taking me to work. In his own way, this was him showing me his world and what he was proud of in his life. Therefore, walking into a Home Depot store will always put a familiar smile on my face.

Although I no longer get to call my father to the front of the store over the intercom system, the quantity and quality of his accomplishments plus his being the living embodiment of the slogan, "You can do it. We can help™," only serves as a reminder of the piece of the empire that my father helped to build and rule with a steady hand. This book is evidence that real leadership is best built from the ground up.

—Jackie Dardas

INTRODUCTION

April 1997

"So, Dardas, you think you're bigger than my company?"

Home Depot co-founder Arthur Blank's pointed question aggra-vated my queasy stomach as my professional life flashed before my eyes. There I sat on the plush couch of his executive office next to Vern Joslyn, my Regional Vice-President, after flying down to Atlanta from Philly that morning. Under normal conditions, going to the home office was a good thing: you met with peers, attended training classes, and interacted with employees you only saw in person a few times a year. Over the course of my then 13-year career with the company, I'd developed wonderful relationships and was well-known by many of the folks at headquarters.

But on this sunny, hot, and humid day the circumstances surrounding my unexpected visit were entirely different – all because of an ego-driven decision I'd made. Now, thanks to my failure to deliver on a requested action by my superiors, I'd placed my career, my family, my legacy, and my livelihood in jeopardy.

"What have I done?" I thought to myself. I took a deep breath and prayed for the right words to come out of my mouth in response to Arthur's question. One that would somehow keep me employed when he had every justification to fire my sorry tuchis.

Without hesitation I replied, "Arthur, I'm embarrassed to be here, but the only thing I can say is that I would not do anything to intentionally disrupt your company or not adhere to a policy, given all you and Bernie and this company have done for me. More importantly – and don't take this the wrong way – I would not do anything to intentionally embarrass and downgrade the name of Dardas at the Home Depot. I have been beside myself for two weeks, knowing I was being investigated. But I can tell you, if you ask anybody who knows how I've been performing while this was going on, they would say they thought I was up for a promotion, based on my attitude and behaviors. That's what I tried to do the whole time, continue to perform in my job as if nothing negative was going on."

Arthur, Vern, and Steve from Human Resources listened attentively, then asked more questions about the incident to get a full understanding of what had taken place. After about 20 minutes, Arthur told me to go back out and take a seat while they evaluated everything and made their decision. As instructed, I left the room and sat down in the lobby, where I prayed harder than I had over the past two weeks and engaged in some serious soul-searching while awaiting my fate.

My thoughts led me back to another place and time, where I relived the moment that had made an indelible impression on a young man searching for greater career fulfillment. In truth, on a superficial level, I needed a part-time job to supplement my income from my full-time position with a Pompano Beach, Florida computer company. Since my father worked for Home Depot, having relocated the family to Florida from Pennsylvania years before to don the orange apron, it only made sense to apply there.

But I was totally unprepared for what happened once I walked through the sliding glass doors.

The intoxicating energy of the place blew me away. From the

smells of lumber and paint, to the sight of enthusiastic employees hustling to serve their customers, forklifts racing through the aisles and the pulsating music emanating from the PA system, every element of the Home Depot atmosphere created an impact that would soon lead to my decision to quit my job in the tech field. I was going to join the world of retail in what would become the world's largest home improvement chain.

So, where did all it go wrong? How did the young guy with so much promise and potential – not to mention a family legacy to live up to – screw this up so bad?

I promise to share all the details of what went down back in 1997 later in the book, but let's just say it marked a turning point in my career and provided yet another huge opportunity for my own personal and professional growth. For now, whether you are a man or a woman; whether you're entry-level or management; whether you work in retail or another profession; or whether you have a college degree or a high school diploma, I invite you to join me in the retelling of my life, ladders and learnings in the world of home improvement. It's my hope that my screw-ups, successes, and challenges will assist you in being the best version of yourself, doing the things that most fulfill you, and having whatever brings purpose, meaning, and joy to your life.

Time waits for no man or woman, so let's get going!

—Erik

IN THE BEGINNING

"Choose your battles wisely because you're not going to win all of them. In fact, if you fight ten battles, you're probably going to lose eight or nine. I know you; you're going to want to fight all ten. But when you fight ten battles, you can't allocate the right resources to win the one that means the most to you."

— KEN DARDAS

As a kid growing up in Bay City Michigan, I had no idea how much my father's sage advice would impact me and my career at the Home Depot, or that I'd ever come to appreciate my old man's knowledge, gleaned from his own highly successful retail career. God forbid, I'd ever follow in his footsteps, seeing how hard he had to work and the hours he had to put in. My dream was to play pro ball, so naturally back then, I was all about sports – football, basketball, and baseball. In fact, I held such a crystal-clear vision in my mind of my career in the pros, by the time I got to high school I was already practicing my autograph. My wife Pam always said I should have been a doctor with my wonderful cursive!

Like many kids in my age group, I idolized Cincinnati Reds catcher Johnny Bench. As a matter of fact, I can still name every starting player on one of the greatest teams of all time, "The Big Red Machine," a legendary force in major league baseball that made an unforgettable impact on the entire profession. Being a pitcher on my Little League and high school baseball teams gave me the opportunity to learn some important, early lessons about the relationship between the pitcher and the catcher, surrounding yourself with good people, and working together as a team to achieve a common goal.

Competition was another athletic lesson I learned in high school that would have far-reaching ramifications throughout my business career. When not playing the other sports, I loved to play tennis, with my best friend at the time, Lynn Voisey – who was so much better at it than I was. We played together regularly, enjoying the esprit de corps and the workout this vigorous sport provided. At first, Lynn loved it just a bit more because he won all the time; however, I would not give up and neither would he. As time went on, I noticed I was getting better and better, and our matches were getting closer and closer, much to Lynn's chagrin. When we reached a point when circumstances prohibited us from playing together anymore, we were nearly at the same skill level. Later in life, the lesson proved its worth: instead of fearing someone who is better than you, or feeling defeated by a situation, embrace the proper mindset and commitment to turn the matter in your favor.

Of course, it was impossible for me to understand the influence these experiences would have on my future career but combined with the work ethic my parents instilled in me, they would sustain me through the inevitable highs and lows that come with building a legacy and a personal brand.

I'm the eldest of three children in a Christian family of five, born to my parents when they were just eighteen years old. Since both worked extended hours in their respective professions, they required me to do chores around the house, including vacuuming, dusting, mowing the lawn and taking out the trash – not exactly fun for a kid who would have rather spent all his time on the baseball diamond, football field or basketball court. In fact, I'd have rather run ten suicides on a basketball court than dust, which was my least favorite chore of all. Regardless, the renowned Midwestern work ethic infused my daily life from the time I could walk and talk.

And it didn't just involve sports practices and household responsibilities. At the impressionable age of ten, a friend and I started our own snow shoveling business, which solidified in my mind the value of a job well done, thanks to one neighbor who employed our services. Unknown to me, he had supervised our efforts from the window of his warm living room until we'd cleared the driveway. When it was time to pay us, he handed more cash to my friend than me.

"Young man, do you know why I'm giving you less money?" he asked. Without waiting for my response, he continued, "When I watched from the window, I noticed your friend did most of the work." Now, you won't be surprised to hear that I was pretty upset at first. I didn't know whether to cry or shovel the snow back into his driveway. Nevertheless, this incident impressed the value of a work ethic on me. I now understood the concept of being rewarded for working hard and appreciated the excellent life lesson. And you can bet that never, *ever* happened to me again, no matter what I was doing!

From these humble beginnings, positive influences surrounded me and built the foundation for my personal and professional success. Aside from my parents (and wise neighbors), my grandparents on both sides played a vital role in my early life. Despite their stature, sometimes I found them easier to talk to than my mom and dad, and truly enjoyed great relationships with them. One of my most treasured (though distant) memories involves my paternal grandmother teaching me to tie my shoes. However, she didn't "spare the rod" when discipline was called for, because I clearly remember her forcing me to eat soap as a punishment for using curse words. The apple didn't fall far from the tree because my parents kept a wooden paddle with my brother's and my name carved into it above the refrigerator.

Being the eldest had its perks in this regard; of the three of us, my brother, sister, and me, I spent the most time with my grandparents, especially the summer of 1979, before my senior year in high school, which marked the beginning of a course that would ultimately change my life. My father, who'd been a manager with J.C. Penney's, had recently resigned from the iconic department store to accept an hourly position as a sales associate with a promising new Atlanta-based home improvement retail chain that had recently expanded into Florida. While Mom and Dad searched for a new home for us in the town of Tamarac, I split time between both sets of grandparents' houses in Michigan. One of my favorite memories of this time involves my maternal grandmother, a very cool lady with whom I stayed up late watching *Fernwood Tonight*, while she drank a beer and we laughed until we cried.

In retail, if you're willing to relocate at your company's request, your chances of being promoted to higher levels increase significantly. That's the reality for members of management who want to climb the ladder. When my dad was still at Penney's he'd moved us from Bay City Michigan to Youngstown Ohio to Hickory (now known as Hermitage) Pennsylvania to advance his career. In Hickory, I attended high school and got my first "real" job at Ponderosa Steak House after school. When I arrived for my shift in the late afternoon, all the day's dirty dishes, glasses and silverware would be stacked up and waiting for me in two or three bus carts. I'd wash them as fast as I possibly could, wanting to do the best job I was capable of. Later, I'll describe some important lessons learned from my days at Ponderosa, but for now, let's just say that my experience there proved to be another rung on the ladder – one for which I'll always be grateful. It's also a big part of the reason why I emphatically recommend that parents require their teenage kids to get a part-time job, regardless of the family's economic status, something I'll discuss in more detail.

In high school, I was happily involved in sports, had the girlfriend of my dreams, and was engaged in productive, part-time work. When my father accepted the ground-floor position with a growing company named Home Depot in Fort Lauderdale Florida right before my senior year, I assumed my parents would allow me to complete my senior year and graduate with my friends, then join the family. But I soon discovered he had other ideas. "The family stays together," he advised me sternly, ignoring my teenaged angst and plaintive pleas.

Like it or not, my only choice was to obey orders. But with every fiber of my being, I resented having to move and attend a new high school where I didn't know anyone. To make matters worse, in what felt like a bad omen, the week we moved to Florida a hurricane hit. The entire ordeal of moving created so much social anxiety for me, I stopped playing my beloved sports and, thanks to my introverted nature and self-esteem issues, my fear of speaking in front of the class intensified. If someone had told me back then that a manager at a future job would help me overcome my fear of public speaking years later in a surprising way, I would have told them they were crazy. But I'll get to that in a bit.

To my surprise, in Florida students were dismissed after lunchtime, which gave me more flexible hours to work my part-time job at Publix, the famed southern supermarket where I started as a bag boy. Still viewed as the #1 grocery chain in the southeast, at Publix I strengthened the foundation of the work ethic that began in my childhood. From the moment I walked in, there was an energy about the place I would only experience again when I became a part-time sales associate at Home Depot. I learned at the outset you established respect at Publix by how fast and hard you worked, and the quality of the customer service you provided. The expectation was that you sprinted as fast as you could to gather and clear carts. From the furthest points of the parking lot when you gathered them up, you raced – you didn't stroll – to the front of the store. Employees even held contests to determine who could complete this task in the shortest amount of time, and though there were some near misses with customers, cars, and fellow employees, it was fun for the customers to watch us hustle. Keep in mind, there were no mechanical cart pushers back then, so all we had to assist us was our own human "horsepower." Good thing we were all in shape back then, not sitting around playing video games on our smartphones. Prior to the influx of technology with its countless apps, PONG was our only option. No wonder most of us engaged in physical recreation!

When it came to bagging groceries, the challenge was who could bag them the fastest and best without crushing the eggs, bread, and other perishable items. In my job at Publix, I cleared a ton of carts, bagged more groceries than I can count, and learned that to survive, you had to move through your tasks with speed and efficiency. Publix and Home Depot shared a similar culture and values. Both cultivated a laser-focus on the customer and exhibited a remarkable energy and pace that has helped them achieve long-term success. As for household chores? Yes, I still had to do them, though in the warm, tropical climate they involved year-round yard work in addition to the required housework. So, while my parents toiled at their jobs, they expected my brother and me to take care of things at home in exchange for an allowance.

Despite my shyness, I befriended a girl named Jaime at my Coral Springs High School, who introduced me to her boyfriend, Lee, with whom I also became great friends. After graduation, he set me up with a job at Modular Computer Systems (ModComp), a Pompano Beach-based company, while I attended classes at RETS Tech Center at night. It came with an assembly-line mentality and involved mostly sitting, with very little physical activity. The job was redundant, not a good fit for me at all. Although the company and position offered upward mobility, I just wasn't wired (pardon the pun) for the tech industry. However, even though I didn't love it, I still worked hard and took pride in what I did.

Now, don't get me wrong: I wasn't *all* work and no play. As a resident of Fort Lauderdale, also known as "Fort Liquor-dale," drinking, partying with friends, and weekends at the beach were also part of my agenda. Yet, this jampacked schedule of work and play left me – and my bank account – unfulfilled. I was sick of living paycheck-to-paycheck. When my dad heard I was looking to make more money, he recommended applying for a part-time job at Home Depot. I don't know if he was trying to help or just wanted me to move out of his house, but he offered some powerful advice:

"You learn as much from the people who are doing things wrong as you do from those who are doing it right."

I didn't know it then but adhering to this philosophy would help me through every phase of my career.

As I mentioned in my introduction, the frenetic energy of Home Depot impressed me from the second the sliding glass doors opened to reveal the sight of forklifts racing around, employees running, and rock 'n roll music providing a backdrop for the electric atmosphere. In sharp contrast to my computer job, I was mesmerized by the dynamism and physical activity, just as I was at Publix.

When I started as a part-time sales associate, I pushed myself harder because I didn't want anybody to think I was getting special treatment as a "legacy" employee. Every night and weekend, I stayed until closing and cleaned everything up – often until two or three a.m. – and went home filthy. I'm not kidding when I say I had concrete dust in my ears and up my nose. We could not go home until we had an inspection walk, so when you thought your job was done, you called for a manager over the PA system to walk you. That meant there were multiple occasions when I only had time to go home, shower and change before heading to my day job at ModComp. All I can say is, thank God for strong coffee!

The one time I complained about the hours, my manager looked at me and asked, "Dardas, do you want this job, or do you just want the *other* job?" At that point, I was only at Home Depot to make extra money, so I sucked it up and did what I had to do – I worked my tail off until they told me I could go home. Working two jobs meant that I often missed out on good times with my friends and going to events on nights and weekends, like the Winterfest Boat Parade or the Rocky Horror Picture Show. It felt like a tremendous sacrifice, but I was beginning to understand the long-term return on investment (ROI).

But a funny thing happened over the next several months: I fell in love with the place, the environment, the attitude, the people, and the entire concept, even as I grappled with nagging thoughts like, *Do I need to go back to school? Should I follow through on my career at ModComp?* Eventually, I resigned from both ModComp and Home Depot to attend school – which only lasted for one semester. After I left, I missed Home Depot terribly. In my heart, I knew I belonged there. When I decided to return in less than a year from the time I'd started as a part-time associate, I felt fortunate to wear the orange apron full-time.

"This is it," I declared to myself. My 33-year career had officially begun.

"There are no secrets to success. It is the result of preparation, hard work, and learning from failure." – Colin Powell

In July 1984, I earned a promotion to department supervisor, which was truly unique because I had never served in any type of supervisory capacity. Up until then, I'd only done things where I was responsible for myself, whether participating in sports or hobbies or making my own personal effort to perform well in a job role.

I accepted this new challenge to manage the garden department – which came with an earth-shattering 50-cent increase to $6.75 per hour – with enthusiasm. Within Home Depot, there are 11 merchandising departments. Garden was (as it remains today), the highest revenue-producing department in the company. It became a living, breathing training course for me – possibly even better than a four-year business degree. In this role, I accrued real-world experience instead of learning theory in a classroom. Looking back, it was probably the most significant position I had because it laid out foundations that carried me through the rest of my career.

Per Home Depot's structure, I had direct oversight of the department. At that time, a department supervisor was responsible for customer service, scheduling personnel, ordering all merchandise, training personnel, stocking shelves, and coordinating all trucks and deliveries. Those were the major tasks. We were taught that at Home Depot, management-level responsibilities were greater than they were for higher-level management employees (and even officers in some cases) at other companies.

So, they handed me this department that encompassed two separate teams: Inside Garden Center that sold big-ticket items like power equipment, chemicals, BBQ's, etc., and Outside Garden Center that sold live goods and all related products like mulch and fertilizer. Within this setup, I had a relatively large team of over 20 associates.

From the get-go, I made a huge mistake. Following the promotion, my ego swelled to epic proportions (yes, I know, for all those who worked with me, that's probably hard to believe). After putting so much pressure on myself because of my dad and his vaunted reputation at Home Depot, and my decision to go full-time, I was consumed with pride. Forget that – I was downright full of myself and cocky. Okay, you know what? I'll just say it: I was a complete jerk. Prepare yourself now because this will be a common theme, since I went through this same scenario at every level I attained. And since I was so hard-headed, some lessons took longer to learn than others.

Enter Kate, a live goods specialist from the U.K. A tremendous associate with an acumen for plants and their care and survival, Kate was the leader of the team in place when I got the promotion. It was apparent to me early on that she was their earpiece. She had their trust and they looked to her for guidance during the transition between my predecessor and me. All they knew was that I was coming over from the adjacent department, Lumber and Building

9

Materials, whose employees were affectionately called "The Lumber Dogs," a title we accepted with pride because we did most of the heavy lifting and physical labor in the store. Because of the proximity of the two departments, we all knew each other. However, these associates viewed their new boss with skepticism because all they could see was that some guy who worked in Lumber was now promoted to supervisor of the Garden department. From the beginning, I knew I had to earn their trust, but I went about it in a completely bone-headed way.

A few paragraphs earlier, I mentioned some of the major tasks a department supervisor had to execute at Home Depot. If you will, take a little trip back to the Stone Age with me – you know, decades before technology revolutionized the retail industry (and our personal lives). All the ordering we had to do was on paper. Nothing was computerized. Nothing was automatic. There were no smartphones or other devices to scan UPC's. You had to do physical counts of the merchandise, the shelves, and the overhead, and write it down on paper. Then you had to dial the phone and call in that order, line-item by line- item. Next, you had to follow up on orders you'd already placed to get product in the door to fill the out-of-stocks. To describe it another way: imagine calling in an order for a vendor that had 500 items (such as PVC parts). It took multiple hours because you had to supply the model number and quantity for each one over the phone via voice, versus typing it on a computer keyboard and pressing the return key. Thanks to advancements in technology, the same task can now be accomplished in minutes.

In the pre-computerized era of business, is it any wonder my closest ally was my clipboard?

Thanks to Kate, I learned that to earn the trust of your people, you must be on the floor when you can, working with them and leading by example to help them understand who you are and what you represent. More than anything else, you must provide comfort relating to who you are, what your expectations are, and what they can expect from you.

People react differently to change, especially at a management level. In some cases, it can be downright uncomfortable. But I spent more time relating to my clipboard than I did to members of my team. And one memorable day, Kate was determined to set me straight. I recall walking out of the office area and onto the sales floor with my trusty clipboard in tow, and her meeting me at the intersection of the main aisle as it came into Garden.

"You and I need to talk," she announced. Kate was 5'3" but she spoke to me as if she were seven feet tall, with an unapologetic demeanor of authority.

"Okay, let's talk. What's going on?"

"You're losing the team, Erik." Now, to an athlete or coach those words are a death-knell.

"What do you mean, I'm losing the team? I just got here."

"Well, you *got* here but you haven't been *out* here."

"I'm losing the team? What am I doing?"

"It's what you're *not* doing. You haven't been out here on the sales floor with them. You haven't taken advantage of the opportunities to work side-by-side and talk to each person to get to know them better. They're frustrated. So, I'm coming to you and I'm telling you that you're going to have to do something quick." As the go-to person for the team, Kate and I had a good relationship. I took her words to heart.

Thanks to my laser-focus on learning the mechanics and functionality of the supervisor position, from paperwork to the systems we had in place back then, I'd lost sight of the forest for the trees. Lacking experience in managing employees, I thought I was doing the right thing by building a foundation underneath me first, while I was doing all the ordering, along with other operational responsibilities. If I was the kind of guy to shrug off mistakes, I'd tell you it wasn't ALL my fault; after all, you do not get a grace period at Home Depot. From the moment you accept a position, whether Garden Center Manager, Store Manager, District Manager – you are the owner of all that is good, bad and ugly within your area of supervision.

One of the first lessons I learned from my conversation with Kate was that a manager, coach, or leader at every level must find a way to be present with their team whenever and however possible. That dedication and effort will yield a return on investment (ROI) that is almost immeasurable because it affects countless other things that transpire within the realm of your business, your environment, or whatever you're doing.

After our chat, I immediately finished what I had to do, dropped my clipboard, and scheduled myself over the next couple weeks to work with each one of my direct reports. In those days, scheduling was done manually, with a three-part form where you wrote down everybody's names and shifts. Despite all the other paperwork I had to complete, I scheduled these meetings to enable me to spend quality individual time with every member of my team. For any millennial who is just entering the job market or starting a new position, at Home Depot, we operated according to a higher sense of urgency and commitment with no regard to the time required. Our top priority was to get the job done well and differentiate ourselves from our competition. This remains a strong lesson in today's world.

At the end of the two weeks, I went back to Kate: "Talk to me. What have you heard? What's been going on and how does the team feel?" She responded favorably and affirmed that they loved it, appreciated it, and felt so much better. "But, they're kind of going to wait and see," she cautioned.

"Well, what's the wait and see part?" I asked.

"They want to see if you're going to be consistent, that you're not going to lose them in the shuffle of the business and look at them as a number, but that you're going to continue to do what you did over the past couple of weeks when you can," she answered. This incident reminded me of my father's wisdom about learning as much from those who are doing things wrong as you do from those doing them right. What was my lesson here, aside from the fact that my dad really did know best when it came to life in the world of retail?

At every level in Home Depot, employees understood that you

had obligations, responsibilities and expectations to meet. At the same time whenever I've studied leaders at Home Depot and other companies or read about leaders through their books, I've discovered that the most successful ones at every rung of the management ladder have had their teams **with** them, not **for** them. In this case, my dad's quote applied specifically to leadership in that you could probably learn more from leaders and managers who do it *incorrectly* than you can from the ones who do it effectively. To be candid, not every leader at Home Depot was a great leader; not every manager was a great manager. But I learned from the poor ones and the exemplary ones to achieve my own standard of success. Let me be frank: despite Home Depot's remarkable success, the company has employed its share of non-productive leaders over the years, as we'll get into later.

Another practice I developed and applied throughout my career after this experience was that I always wanted to have a "Kate" with me at every level and location. Our forthright conversation and my subsequent actions taught me the importance of surrounding yourself with the most qualified, competent, and highest quality individuals. I wanted honest, constructive feedback from such reliable sources to keep a pulse on what was happening. I'd seen some leaders go down and be removed because they surrounded themselves with "yes" people who told them what they wanted to hear. If you surround yourself with those types of people, you'll never hear the true, honest, effective communication you need to optimize your business. You could use a sports analogy, where a coach loses the locker room and the team is suffering. I think that happens to leaders who don't keep all their senses engaged on what the perceptions are from their people. And I carried that with me at every rung of the ladder.

As I said, this was like a living management college course. When people ask me today what it was like to work at Home Depot for 33-plus years, I say I feel like I grew up there – kind of like a TV sit-com star who starts out as a pint-sized child and grows into an adult by the time the series ends. As a supervisor, I was in my adolescence in the business world but every day I learned the positive and negative lessons that would advance me forward. In today's business vernacular, "leadership by example" is often cited and celebrated. Back in the early days of Home Depot, establishing and elevating the company culture was of utmost importance.

I could go on a little bit of a rant here about work ethic and how businesses function now versus then, but I can tell you this: when a member of Home Depot store management called you to be a cash register reliever when the lines got long, you didn't walk, you *ran*. When a cashier called you for a price-check on something, you hustled to find the answer. I remember when I ran the garden department, a cashier would be on the telephone at her register with a plant in hand, attempting to get the price. I'd be on the line saying, "Okay, describe it to me." You can imagine the responses I'd get sometimes, "Well, it's in a pot. It's green. It's got eight leaves." And I'd literally drop the phone, sprint to the register to see which plant it was, run back, get the price, and run back again...I mean, it was totally inefficient, but it came down to leadership and hustle. I cannot even describe how much the customers loved watching us exhibit that kind of behavior, which helped create the customer expectation of service at Home Depot.

My goal was I didn't want anyone to run faster than me. If we were packing out product, I didn't want anybody to work harder or more efficiently than me because I wanted to show what my standard was and how I would react. I recognized that I was in a fishbowl at every level. People were watching me...and not only to determine the quality of my work ethic or my customer service. They watched what I did, the way I dressed, and how I treated other employees. They noted all my tendencies, actions, and reactions. And because some employees thought I only got promoted because of my dad, I put an intense amount of pressure on myself. Have you ever heard the song or seen the music video for *Pressure* by Billy Joel? That could have been written and produced just for me.

Despite its prevalence in business books, motivational speeches, and business culture, some key leaders tend to discard the concept of leadership by example, especially the higher they go within an organization. Today, *Undercover Boss* is a popular TV show, but Home Depot's founders Bernie Marcus and Arthur Blank never needed a TV show to force them to visit their store environments and interact with their associates. For them, it was an expectation. From the very beginning, Bernie and Arthur, along with the Board of Directors, conducted both planned and stealth visits to keep a barometer on the business.

Throughout their careers and during the company's infancy stages, Bernie and Arthur established a hands-on policy, where they were always out on the sales floor in the stores, working arm-in-arm and leading the way on customer service with the associates. In fact, as an employee, you learned from the get-go that neither one of them had better meet and greet a customer before you did, or else it could turn into an uncomfortable day for you.

Yes, these company founders who held presidential and executive titles said, "We're going to be out there with you in the stores." At first, many people didn't believe it, but it happened often. And one impactful incident stands out in my mind the most.

I was packing out the BBQ grill accessories in the Garden Center – the burners, spatulas, cleaners – everything you'd need for the BBQ grill. I was up on one of our tall, orange ladders (in the old days, they were either nine-step or 13-step) with a counterweight in the bottom and a section of concrete that weighed 300-400 pounds. You moved these ladders all over the stores to get stuff down from the overheads. So, I was standing on the ladder situating boxes when I heard a voice say, "Hey, can I help?" And I turned around and it was Arthur Blank, president of the company. He stood there, dressed in business casual (or maybe a step up from there) holding a carry bag. Setting it down, he asked, "What are you doing?"

"Packing down," I answered.

"Start throwing down, what do we need?"

He'd just arrived at the store. Since you had to enter through the Garden Center because of the way it was routed with the aisles, nobody even knew he was there yet. I threw boxes down to him, got down from the ladder, and for the next half-hour, Arthur and I packed out these BBQ grill accessories and placed them on the shelves.

When we finished, he inspected our work, then asked, "What do you think?"

"I think we're good. Looks great now," I replied.

"Yeah, it does," he agreed. "Keep it going there, I appreciate it." Then he walked away.

Now, a normal person would view this as a positive interaction, right? Well, I was scared to death I was about to get fired, thanks to my introspective – or possibly paranoid – nature. Come to think of it, I probably should have gotten on my meds a whole lot sooner. But before you laugh, keep in mind this was my first real interaction with Arthur and I worried that he thought I was working too slow, so he felt compelled to help me. I mean, here's the freaking President of Home Depot – a man who referred to my father as "Kenny," – and he had to take time out of his day to pack merchandise with a lowly associate. During that visit, Arthur stayed at the store for several hours. After he finally left, I approached my store manager, who instantly sensed something was up by the look on my face.

"What's the matter?" he asked.

"I need to talk to you." He motioned me into the office to speak in private.

"Dardas, what's on your mind?"

"Are you going to fire me?"

"What do you mean, am I going to fire you?"

"Well, did Arthur talk about me?"

"Yeah, he said you were doing a fantastic job."

"What?!" I was shocked because the whole time, I'd assumed he was going to fire me and wondered if I should apply for my old job at Publix.

"Why, what's the matter?" my manager inquired, obviously perplexed by my reaction. When I told him the story, he advised,

"Look, don't be an idiot. Just relax; that's who Arthur is and that's the culture of the company. He never said anything about you working too slow. He just said he stopped, he helped you pack out a little bit and the department looked great."

That was just the way the Home Depot founders operated. They embodied leadership by example through every level and interaction I had with them. In the company's early days, you physically witnessed and experienced it. To me, it's something leaders and managers at all levels must never forget that you're in that fishbowl and your example matters. Whatever you call your teammates – "associates," "employees," etc. – their performance often hinges on management's example and how it impacts them.

This lesson was never lost on me at any rung on the ladder: the attitude "Do as I say, not as I do," does NOT work in business or in life.

Another lesson I learned at the lower levels? When you're in an hourly capacity, especially when you're only responsible for your own performance, you have a higher degree of impact in terms of a direct result. Because *you're* doing it. It's your actions, your behaviors, etc. But as you start to get promoted into management levels, it becomes more of an influence, whereby you accomplish more in collaboration with others than you do on your own. That's true for each level you rise to- all the way to the top office with the wonderful view.

I started to experience it when I ascended from an associate to a department supervisor. As an associate in the Lumber Department, I was responsible for pack-out and orders of products including Building Materials. As a Department Supervisor in Garden, I started to delegate tasks, then follow-up to ensure they were in process or completed. It was a huge realization for me: it's the way you engage your team, communicate, delegate, and follow-up that determines your overall success.

As I climbed the ladder, I learned I couldn't be everywhere all the time. Many people when they get into management – and I've seen this at Home Depot in myself and others – continue to do so much themselves that it holds back the overall optimization of their team and its results. Worse, they can spin themselves into the ground. But I can tell you from my own experience, once you learn how to work through your team in an engaging manner, the results usually take care of themselves. The adage, "If you want a job done right, do it yourself," only works for so long and the higher you advance, the less that becomes a realistic expectation. In the immortal words of Bernie Marcus, to achieve success, "hire the right people, train them, and get the hell out of their way."

Ladders and Learnings

- Whether a member of a team or newly promoted into management, make connecting with your team members the highest priority to foster a spirit of cooperation.
- Regardless of your position or tenure, always be open to constructive feedback to improve your performance and the performance of your team.

Executive Memo – Want a good ROI? Be present with your team whenever and wherever possible and seek constructive feedback from them. Their performance is due in large part to your ability to lead by example in every interaction. Ensure all newly promoted employees focus on connecting with their team *before* they focus on process and deliverables.

2

EFFECTIVE COMMUNICATION: THE BUILDING BLOCK OF STRONG LEADERSHIP

"Forget conventionalisms; forget what the world thinks of you stepping out of your place; think your best thoughts, speak your best words, work your best works, looking to your own conscience for approval."

— SUSAN B. ANTHONY

Back when I was still a garden department supervisor, I learned the hard way how important communication would be for the success of my career. In fact, effective communication is one of the biggest takeaways I held near and dear as I ascended the various levels at Home Depot. Prior to high school, I had zero experience speaking in front of a group. I remember when I was in the fourth or fifth grade, I participated in a school pageant where every class had to get up on stage and do something. For my class, that involved gathering around a Christmas tree and singing the classic carol *Oh Christmas Tree*. Even performing as a member of a group filled me with dread and I scrambled to hide myself in the back, behind everyone else. Oh, by the way, I am tone deaf and cannot sing, so I lip synched like Milli Vanilli. That's how badly I lacked the confidence to stand in front of an audience. It only got worse when I reached my high school years with no experience speaking in front of a group. Before giving a presentation or being the center of attention, I'd have to throw up, due to my nervous stomach.

As I mentioned in Chapter 1, I had no idea as a kid that a future Home Depot manager would help me overcome this fear once and for all. But that's exactly what happened during a mandatory 6 a.m. Sunday meeting at the Fort Lauderdale store. In those days, each Home Depot location held this monthly event; whether you were part-time, full-time, on the schedule that day, or just heading to church, you knew it was in your best interest to attend. The truth is, everybody *wanted* to attend because the meetings were productive and fun. It didn't matter if they were on the clock that day or not. Since this was down in South Florida, people showed up in anything from shorts to sweatpants (depending on the time of year), to dresses and suits, for those going to Sunday services.

Home Depots didn't have auditoriums, just small training rooms. To accommodate the general population of a store back then, which amounted to about 200-300 people, we held these meetings in the lumber department, where we put down board and block. What I mean by that is cinderblocks turned on their side, so they were vertical. Then we laid two-by-two lumber across them, row after row. And this was our seating. We also served breakfast – donuts, bagels, fruit, coffee, juice, etc. Everybody would pile in and fill an entire lumber aisle. Once the attendees were seated, the store manager took his or her place up front to present the content for that day, most often surrounded by the store's assistant managers. After the store meeting, which generally lasted about an hour, you attended your individual department meeting, before ending the morning's agenda with the Home Depot cheer.

Ah, the Home Depot cheer; from the earliest days I can remember, it was an integral part of life for everyone who wore the orange apron. Designed to fire up our associates and involve them in all our meetings, it was quite an honor if your manager asked you to lead the cheer because it meant that he or she trusted you to get the place rockin'. While every cheerleader had the freedom to put their own unique spin and personality into it, generally it went something like this:

"Give me an 'H'!" cheerleader yells.

"H!" the crowd roars.

And so on through all the letters until you spelled "Home Depot."

Sometimes, an enthusiastic cheerleader would bait the crowd with, "I can't hear you!" and they would yell it out again, followed by another "I can't hear you!" and the ensuing cry of "Home Depot!" No matter who led the cheer, there was always an exchange like, "What are we gonna do?" These days, the fiery response to that question is "Kick ass!" Then everyone claps wildly.

As a manager, you had to make sure that whoever you assigned to lead the cheer knew how to spell; we've had situations in the past where the person got so nervous, they spelled it wrong...and kind of ruined the moment. When done right, you usually felt some temporary soreness in your throat from yelling so loud, but whether it was enhanced by classic rock, rap or some other creative flourish – as with our teams in Mexico and Canada – the Home Depot cheer united and motivated associates and management to perform their tasks with passion, energy, and excitement. During my career at Home Depot, I led it several times and took pride in getting everybody involved. However, I also got a little nervous because I didn't want to goof it up. If you effed it up, you'd be the topic of ridicule for the rest of the day.

After the general meeting, we broke into our department meetings in our respective locations, then went back to put our aprons on before returning to the sales floor to greet customers. Prior to opening the doors, the entire staff participated in the Home Depot cheer and regardless of what time the store opened there were always people outside waiting to get in. They peered in the windows to watch us do our thing, but if we knew they were out there we finished up as fast as we could and let them in early. On weekends especially, there was typically a gathering outside because our customers were anxious to get on with their "weekend warrior" projects.

Anyway, one Sunday I got to the meeting and sat close to the front (don't ask what I was thinking, but after this experience, I learned to always sit in the back!). The store manager took his place before our team and greeted us warmly before announcing he really didn't feel like talking that day; however, it was imperative that we discuss customer service, which was always a leading topic. Then, much to my chagrin, he looked right at me and demanded, "Erik, come up here."

Right about then, I thought I was going to have to change my shorts. I mean, I could just feel it in my stomach. With noticeable hesitancy, I stood up and edged towards him slowly, hoping he might change his mind and call on someone else if I took too long to get there. That's when I heard a few people yelling out my name. "For the next ten minutes, I'm going to have Erik tell you why customer service is so important at Home Depot," my manager announced.

Now, I had no indication when I left my house that morning that he was going to do this to me. It was spontaneous, and I was completely unprepared. At first, he held his arm around me, but he soon removed it and kind of stepped off to the side, leaving me alone in the spotlight, so to speak. As I stood there in front of everybody, it felt like my life was flashing before my eyes while I waited for the right words to funnel into my brain. I started out with a couple of "ums" and "ahs" then all the sudden, I remembered a powerful customer experience I had dealt with that week.

So, I said, "Let me start with a story." By the time I got done, the store manager had to give me the big hook and pull me off the stage! I realized that once I started talking about the customer and relaying my experience, I could keep going without fear or hesitation. It held everyone's attention and the store manager even broke in a couple times to validate the things I was saying. By focusing on the value of what I had to share with my team regarding customers and using a real-life story to illustrate my point, I managed to transform a terrifying event into a beneficial learning experience for my audience and me. Thanks to that baptism by fire, I have never looked back when it comes to public speaking...as most of my former co-workers can attest.

Even so, I let my manager (who was a friend of my dad) know in jest exactly how I felt about his actions. I strode up to him and promised, "Someday, I will get even with you for this," with a big grin on my face. He just laughed and walked away, knowing he'd done a good deed. From that moment, I became a better communicator. Throughout my career, if I was giving speeches at Home Depot, or standing on a stage conducting a training class, or out in the field when I was in a position to deal with governments or other large entities, I'd still get a little bit nervous, but that single exercise – and thank goodness he did it that day – helped me change what was probably my weakest point into one of my biggest strengths. Now when I watch other people struggle with public speaking, I see how it could inhibit their careers or hold back their companies.

It doesn't matter what position they hold; I've seen people at various levels – from department manager to company officer – fail at speaking in front of an audience or even communicating one-on-one. When they lacked confidence or held a self-perception that they were no good at it, their negative mindset prevented them from making a quality connection, speaking up to share a great idea or providing worthwhile contributions. I cannot overstate how important communication is to anyone's career.

What did I do beyond my first successful presentation in the lumber department that day?

At every level I achieved, I did my utmost to help my teams feel comfortable speaking in front of a group, voicing their concerns, or sharing a best practice. That's been beneficial throughout my entire tenure at Home Depot. I'll always look upon that incident with gratitude because if it had not happened, I'm not sure that my career would have unfolded as well as it did. It was a terrific learning experience and an example of excellent leadership from my store manager in Fort Lauderdale. By putting me in that (initially) uncomfortable position, he forced me to overcome my fears and helped me develop a vital skill for my climb up the ladder. Not only did I improve my public speaking ability, I discovered how an effective leader can make a positive impact and foster the professional and personal advancement of his people.

I must give credit where it's due: some companies train their employees well in the art of communication. Aside from Home Depot, Amazon, Apple and others are often celebrated in this area because their leaders embrace communication as a strong tenet in professional development. They recognize their immense opportunity to foster this skill in their employees, thanks to surveys where people list their top fears. Believe it or not, public speaking – otherwise known as "Glossophobia," – is a greater fear than dying. According to experts, 75 percent of all humans have a fear of public speaking, and for 19 percent, it's their biggest fear, while death comes in a close second at 16 percent.

It blows my mind that anyone would rather lie in a coffin six feet under than be on their feet and speak to other live, breathing humans. If employees aren't comfortable or competent in listening and speaking (communication is a two-way street, after all), managers and leaders must help them to develop the competency and confidence to listen and share. Home Depot places such a high value on communication skills that they pay for employees to attend Dale Carnegie courses or to become members of their local Toastmasters chapter. Sometimes, these organizations video their presentations for training purposes. While it can be cringeworthy to watch yourself on video, many employees have told me that when they got to the end of their class or progressed through their curriculum and watched themselves again, they noticed their shoulders were broader, their chests puffed out more, and they exuded more confidence. I could see it in their performance and interactions beyond that point. Anyone reading this book who feels they have opportunity in this area should seek out resources/assistance at their school or business – sooner, rather than later. If you're in a leadership position, I encourage you to consider how much you can differentiate yourself from others by embracing this significant opportunity to assist your teams.

However, communication is a double-edged sword.

Up until the day I retired from Home Depot, I had a reputation for being one of the most vocal, direct, honest, passionate individuals in the company. If a difficult topic or dissenting opinion needed to be communicated, I was the one who would do it. Sometimes, I was renowned for it. Other times, it was infamy for me.

There were times when, even with the best of intent, I did it improperly, took it too far, or might not have understood the impact of my communication on others. In fact, one of my last supervisors bestowed a different kind of title on me during a private conversation after watching me interact with someone in the store support center about how incorrect they were about a specific product they were presenting. I remember he called me into his office and announced, "I have a new nickname for you."

"Great," I replied. "Is it good or bad?"

"Uh, depends how you look at it. You are now a glass-breaker." I shuddered a bit as I remembered how I got in trouble as a child for throwing a baseball through a neighbor's garage window. That did not end well.

"What does that mean?"

"In your communication, you knew you were right. You knew you were the one who brought the issue to light, but the way you communicated it alienated the individual who'd brought it, thinking they were doing a good thing. I don't disagree that you didn't do anything wrong, but in terms of understanding your audience, you have to be careful because your intent could be misperceived by those on the receiving end and possibly impact future actions and collaboration."

We discussed it back and forth a bit, but I'll be honest: effective communication was an ongoing challenge for me. Once they cut me loose and I learned how to communicate, I probably did take it too far at times. I truly believe that one of the reasons I didn't become an officer in the company (spoiler alert: I rose to one level beneath it) was because some of my supervisors and resources at the corporate office viewed my passion as immaturity, based on examples like the one above.

It was always my dream to follow in my dad's footsteps at Home Depot by achieving the title of vice-president. On many occasions, the leadership considered me for an officer position. Invariably, however, they'd break the news that they just couldn't put their finger on it, but they felt that the other candidate was more qualified. Up until the day I retired, the vice-president position remained an unachieved goal. Maybe I could have attained it if I'd taken Dad's advice sooner. When I studied the employee they'd selected, I always got the sense that they were more professional than I was and possessed a stability about them in terms of their mannerisms and behavior that I didn't. Although I was 55 years old when I retired, my level of professionalism wasn't proportional to my experience in the industry. I could not elevate myself to the level that others could. And you can tie that back to the communication piece. Recently, I spoke with a colleague named Dan McDevitt, a peer of mine at several levels and a 30-year veteran of Home Depot. During his career, he had worked with and for my father and told me Dad had a kind, gentle soul. Let me be clear: no one would describe me in that manner.

Chapter one began with my dad's advice to me when I started my retail career, "Choose your battles wisely, because you're not going to win all of them. In fact, if you fight ten battles, you're probably going to lose eight or nine. I know you. You will want to fight all ten. But when you fight ten battles, you can't allocate the right resources to win the one that means the most to you." I bring it up again because it was one of the toughest lessons for me to learn. If there's ten things wrong with your company, location, or department, you can't fight all those battles. This applies to communication as well. You've got to decide, what are the one or two battles that are going to make the most positive impact on what you are trying to do? This is where you need to allocate all your resources. Then, and only then, double back on the lesser priorities.

It's safe to say my dad knew me well. Early on, I fought multiple battles when I should have stayed closer to the vest and realized that one or two mattered more than the others. For example, back in the early days, Home Depot did not sell appliances. Many people are unaware of that because now they walk into a Home Depot, see the appliance showrooms, and assume that we've had them from day one. But that's not the case. As the company grew, we added the built-in appliances, a smaller section that goes directly into the kitchen cabinets; however, we still did not have showrooms. Our competitor Lowe's had them in their smaller stores and implemented appliance showrooms before Home Depot did. Today, it is a huge effort to get larger showrooms and more of an appliance presentation into all the Home Depot locations. I remember years ago when we first brought the appliance showrooms in, we immediately started encroaching on Sears with their Kenmore line.

When I was growing up in the 60's and 70's, Sears was the preeminent retailer in almost everything, including appliances. But as Lowe's and Home Depot expanded their appliance showrooms and offerings, they cut into Sears' market share. Now Lowe's and Home Depot sell a very good line of appliances that offer value, along with some higher-end products. But upper-end appliances like Viking, Wolf, Sub-Zero, and Thermador are typically sold by independent distributors.

How does any of this relate to me being a "glass-breaker?"

In northern Virginia, which contains five of the top-10 median income counties in the U.S. – with home values in and around the D.C. area exceeding millions of dollars – I made it my mission to fight for upper-end appliances when I assumed the role of Regional Pro Manager. This demographic includes people from abroad who travel here to work at the embassies for their governments, along with highly paid lobbyists and lawyers, and these folks are not going to put a basic GE appliance in their homes. They have discriminating tastes and demand only the best.

Unfortunately, Home Depot was prohibited from selling upper-end appliances due to vendor buying agreements or the stipulations these upper-end appliance manufacturers imposed on us as far as what we were required to do before we could sell their products.

One of my responsibilities involved dealing with contractors who were building, renovating, and remodeling homes in this affluent area. Every day, it seemed, they told me they would absolutely buy every one of these upper-end appliances from us if we could sell them. Understanding the incredible sales opportunity, I did everything I could to compile proposals and specifics to justify why we needed to change our policy. And every step of the way, I was told, "no" by Home Depot corporate, the merchants for these appliances and their supervisors. However, I refused to let it go because I kept hearing from my contractors that this was a pressing need for Home Depot.

In defiance of my father's advice and my supervisor's negative responses, I continued to irritate people by holding this desire, communicating about it, and pursuing it as an opportunity even though it was a dead-end. I'd been advised multiple times it wasn't meant to be and there was nothing we could do about it, but in my mind, I just could not let go of it because it represented millions and millions of potential dollars for the company.

One of the measurements we use at Home Depot is sales per square foot. That means we must put products in our stores that appeal to most of our customers. Not everybody is going to buy a $5000 – $10,000 refrigerator, and to display those in our stores we'd have to take something else out unless we found another way. Either because of their distributor relationships (where they didn't want to hurt their independent distributor network) or their unreasonable demands to allocate a certain amount of square footage for displays (which, in some cases, we didn't have) we could not accommodate these upper-end vendors. Additionally, Home Depot corporate was concerned about the training programs that would be required for our employees selling these complex products because they would far exceed the training programs already in place with our existing offerings. These were just a few valid factors playing into the decision not to display upper-end appliances in our retail stores.

But my hard-headed take, even though it was wrong and counterproductive, was that the more evidence I provided and the more I kept beating that drum, the greater the chances I'd get my way. And then, the higher-ups in corporate would shower me with praise and adulation for beating the drum so loudly, it finally happened. Yeah... that was a losing battle and a complete waste of time.

The futility of my misguided communication on the issue finally hit me one day when my boss told me he went to the home office and asked what everybody thought about Dardas' proposal on the upper-end appliances, to gauge reaction. Rather than break out in applause and sing hallelujah for having such a forward-thinking employee on the payroll, some rolled their eyes and cringed. That wasn't the perception I needed to have out there. Going back to my dad's advice, in this example I chose the wrong battle and it deflected my energy from other efforts where we could have made a direct impact with the company. To this day, we only have a few upper-end appliance programs in a couple of stores out of all the Home Depot locations across the country. This experience taught me that if you keep fighting a battle you're repeatedly losing, it's probably time to surrender and move on to something that's more deserving of your time. Please, please, do not be like me in this area. With respect to your chosen battles, heed input from your supervisors with comprehension and urgency.

Aside from my innate stubbornness, why was this lesson so difficult for me to absorb? Habit. In the early days of Home Depot, management challenged us to yell, scream, curse and do whatever we had to do to make our voices heard. Therefore, some of us with tenure – me included – had a tougher time letting go of this practice.

After all, we had been trained and built that way from the beginning. We had grown up with this mentality and in many ways, we did not adapt as much as we should have. I guess I was a key example. Of all the things to be good at...way to go me!

"You should worry less about who you might offend and care more about who you might inspire." —Tim Allen

In July 1985, I received a promotion to assistant store manager (ASM) at Fort Lauderdale, a position that required formal training. I was privileged because the salaried management team was comprised of talented individuals including Dan McDevitt, whom I mentioned earlier, an assistant manager at the time and one of my early mentors. Prior to this promotion, as an hourly associate all my training had taken place in the store. But once you became a member of management, much more of your training was held with the higher-ups at the company headquarters. Before we had regional offices, Atlanta was command central. Today the company provides a tremendous amount of centrally coordinated classes again for its employees, which is a very good thing. It ensures clear communication of a common message that does not get broken down or diluted among multiple regions and divisions.

After you walked out of a class or meeting in Atlanta with Bernie Marcus, Arthur Blank, Ken Langone and some of the earlier officers, you could barely sit still on the way home, whether you were sitting on an airplane or in a car. I mean, if one of them had simply stated, "Listen, I need you to go down the street and kill the competitor's store manager," we probably would have done it. It was that intense because their communication made us feel as if we were an integral piece of the puzzle and that our presence and commitment was critical to the company's progress. In the early days our own customers often asked us if we were in a cult, which never failed to make us laugh. They'd complain, "Everybody in this store is always smiling and saying hello. It's downright irritating." However, the positive impact on customers elevated our brand and raised their expectations.

Regardless of your management level, you'd emerge from these meetings so energized, you couldn't wait to get into your store to share what you'd learned. As an ASM, I remember returning from a trip and asking my manager to schedule time for me at the next staff meeting to relate what the home office had shared with me, along with my feelings. It just fired me up. I came back from Atlanta and wanted to work and make an impact right away. I always looked forward to these meetings and when I knew Bernie and Arthur were going to be there, it was simply electric. Attendees would be in tears and you'd feel the hair on the back of your neck standing up because you felt such profound reverence for these two men and the opportunities they offered. For me, it made a powerful statement that the company's original leaders made themselves accessible to *all* associates and managers, not just upper-level management and officers.

Those of us fortunate enough to have interactions with Home Depot's founders during those early days certainly held them in high regard. These incredible men were on a pedestal then, as they are now. A couple of days ago, Bernie Marcus was interviewed about the economy and politics on CNBC and I couldn't wait to hear what he had to say because that's vintage Bernie – outspoken and direct. "Here's what I am, deal with it." In fact, Donald Trump could have been a student of his, owing to their shared practice of telling the unvarnished truth without any concern for who might be offended. For example, Bernie wasn't afraid to speak his mind, and after uttering a politically incorrect phrase or using a profane word, he'd pause for effect, then pretend to dismiss the human resources department with a dramatic gesture and a declaration along the lines of "Pfft! Human resources, what are you going to do, *fire* me?"

But it wasn't always sunshine and lollipops: I can tell you about several moments in my career when Bernie went up one side of me and down the other, but we hugged at the end of it. He could just dissect you, not in a vicious way, but in a teachable way, and you wanted to hug this guy when you were done because you knew he cared that much to take the time to offer such direct, honest feedback. A thought here for all to consider – aside from pure abuse (which is unacceptable), don't be so easily offended. Rather, look for the purpose or lesson your leader is attempting to bestow on you.

Since Bernie was a strong Republican and Arthur a strong Democrat, it was a *freaking* blast when we went to meetings where they both attended and happened to discuss politics. It was hysterical. They tried to stay away from it, but they'd snipe at each other a little bit, leaving the whole crowd enthralled. However, even though they were both passionate about their beliefs, they made it work at Home Depot. They found a way to prevent their political differences from impacting their personal and professional relationship. Unfortunately, that's not what's happening in our culture today; everyone who's at odds with each other over politics could benefit from their example.

As the methodical one, Arthur was known for asking questions during a store visit. Of course, he knew the answers; he wanted to know if *you* knew the answers. Whether it was an out-of-stock, an improperly maintained area or a financial matter, he was looking for your ownership of the situation. And if you tried to "baffle him with bullshit," as the saying goes, you were in for a rude awakening because he'd become more biting in the way he interacted with you. When you were right, he was very good, but when you were wrong or if he suspected you were baffling him with bullshit, it became a rough day for you. Take it from me: never, ever bluff, lie or deflect when interacting with a supervisor at any level. Be honest in your awareness of a situation and always have a course of action for improvement.

On the other hand, Bernie was the cheerleader and the more huggable of the two. Despite their personality distinctions, you still had the same amount of respect and reverence for both. It pained me when the Atlanta Falcons lost to the New England Patriots in Super

Bowl LI in 2017 when the camera panned to the team's owner Arthur Blank on the sidelines. All everybody at Home Depot could talk about was how much they hurt for him because 1. you knew how much he liked to win, and 2. you knew what he had done to help you get into the position you now held at the company, and you wanted the victory so badly for him.

Former Washington Redskins coach Joe Gibbs was the head of NASCAR when Home Depot got involved. This amazing guy would come into our company meetings, take off his Super Bowl rings, and throw them into the crowd, saying, "Hey, just make sure I get them back." You'd have Home Depot employees passing around rings that were worth close to $50,000. Having had several opportunities to talk with Coach Gibbs, I consider myself fortunate. I remember when he told the story of being in the office when the final contracts had been signed for Home Depot to sponsor NASCAR. Since Coach Gibbs was going to have our #20 car, he looked at Bernie and Arthur and inquired, "Alright, I'm on the same team now. What do you want me to do?"

Arthur got inches from his face, looked him right in the eye and replied, "Just go out and f*****g win."

Communication doesn't get much clearer than that!

"Respect is earned. Honesty is appreciated. Trust is gained. Loyalty is returned." —Auliq Ice

Funny, my dad and I are a lot alike when it comes to communication. If you take us to a social gathering where we don't know most of the people, we'll probably grab a beer or a glass of wine and hang out in a corner, even if we're by ourselves. But if you get us in an environment like a Home Depot, we enter a comfort zone that enables us to confidently interact with everyone in the store, from customers to associates. Dad was right about observing and learning from those doing it wrong, because I realized the importance of communication from co-workers and managers who failed themselves and their teams in this regard. When I was a store manager, my employees would visit other Home Depot locations, then return and report, "Hey boss,

I gotta tell ya something. I just went over to such-and-such store and they had no clue about XYZ. You told us all about it. Why don't they know about it?"

It turned out that when some of the managers attended our annual meetings, which featured a packed agenda of important content, policy, strategy, and upcoming changes, they gave their associates the perception that they were all fun and games because they never came back and shared what they'd learned with them. Either they didn't make the effort, or they didn't think it was important. On the other hand, I always came back, put a presentation together and walked my teams through everything. Due to time constraints, my presentations were not as detailed and lengthy, but I shared the vital takeaways with them.

Later, as a district manager (DM), I'd host our own recap about the annual meeting. But since some others did not engage their teams in the same way, I'd hear similar comments about how other stores didn't have the same information. And that strengthened my resolve to the point where I over-communicated at times to ensure my team had a vision of the company or strategy that I could share. Of course, we were prohibited from divulging proprietary information, for example, something about our competition, or upcoming product launch. However, anything I could share I did as soon as possible because I wanted my team to know I didn't just jet off to Hawaii, Puerto Rico, or Las Vegas to lay on the beach, imbibe a few cocktails, gamble, golf, and fish. (What happens in Vegas stays in Vegas...except for valuable meeting content!). I needed them to know that as much as we did enjoy ourselves, we also engaged in constructive dialogue and conversation. I believe my efforts at communication helped with promotions for my employees because I got word to them quickly. While managers should avoid overwhelming or distracting their associates from performing their direct tasks, I always sensed that my people appreciated me coming back from a session and sharing my experiences. It created a larger inclusion and stronger trust between us that proved to be mutually beneficial.

Effective communication involves more than just listening and talking. Throughout my career, whenever coming to a new store or area following a promotion or relocation, I always penned a letter describing in simple terms who I was and what I had done. I didn't brag, I just shared a few facts about me to break the ice and give my team a sense of my personality, accomplishments, and expectations before I got there. Whether I was an assistant store manager, store manager, district manager or anything else, if I felt customer service, for example, was slipping, I would write a letter to my team on the subject. While always positive, these letters kept it real and direct, something along the lines of "Hey, I have a perception or recognition that our customer service levels are suffering." Then, I'd reaffirm what Home Depot was about and what our standards were before asking each one of them to do everything they could to help me to improve customer service. It was a huge topic in many of my introductory letters.

After completing a letter, I placed copies where most people would see them. Depending on the location, team, or situation, I'd have them taped to the time clock or the lockers or leave stacks of them in the break room. Often, we'd tape them to a larger sign in the hallway that led to the employee locker area, or I'd ask my staff to hand them out at store meetings. Whatever the method or location, whether through the written or spoken word, proper communication was a key element for my success, the success of my team, and ultimately, the success of Home Depot. It humanized me as their leader and laid the groundwork for them to feel more comfortable communicating with me in a bottom-up, interactive collaboration. If not for the founders setting the standard for communication right from the beginning, Home Depot would not be the success it is today.

Ladders and Learnings

- Don't be afraid to step out of your comfort zone with respect to communication. It is vital to learn how to speak and listen well. When you push yourself beyond your perceived limits, you build trust with your team and open the door to greater success.

- Remain open to constructive feedback and criticism. Rather than take offense, view it as an opportunity to improve.

Executive Memo

To all leaders, follow the example of Home Depot's founders and help your employees and teams develop better communications skills. It's a worthwhile effort that will yield a significant ROI in the future. If you do not take a bottom-up, collaborative, interactive, and two-way approach to communication with ALL levels in your organization, you are not optimizing your business to its fullest extent.

3

ADJUSTING TO CHANGE

"Everyone thinks of changing the world, but no one thinks of changing himself."

— LEO TOLSTOY

I was an assistant store manager (ASM) at Home Depot for a total of five-and-a-half years in four locations: Fort Lauderdale, Orlando (in two different stores), and Los Angeles. One of the biggest adjustments I had to make after receiving the promotion to ASM was living up to new expectations as a salaried, exempt (ineligible for overtime pay) member of management, versus an hourly, non-exempt (eligible for overtime pay) associate. The ASM role provided the foundation I needed to observe leadership and management tendencies in others and develop them in myself, thanks to greater exposure and experience with my colleagues and superiors, and the fact that a salaried position at Home Depot comes with a serious amount of demands and responsibilities.

First, there's the work ethic and expectation of hours. Because you are salaried, there's no limit to the number of hours you can work – and back in those early days, they expected you to work a minimum of 60 hours over a span of five-and-a-half days. If you had to work 100 hours a week to ensure everything was done right, they expected you to do that. This mentality extended to holidays, nights, and weekends. To illustrate this point, let me share a real-life example of what my work ethic was like – and this isn't me bragging, just relating what I and others in management had to do if we wanted to keep climbing the ladder.

Steve, the store manager of the Orlando location I worked at went on vacation, leaving me in charge of the entire operation. Unfortunately for me, that was the same week I had to do several merchandising resets, where we changed product categories and the way we displayed them inside of my departments. To accomplish everything on my to-do list, I worked 40 hours straight. I went in one morning at 4 a.m., fulfilled my responsibilities of running the building, then worked overnight on the resets. Truth be told, I took a two-hour break somewhere in there to go home, shower, and eat, but it was almost a 40-hour shift over two days. Because that's what I had to do to get my job done, along with the additional duties I took on in my manager's absence. In the early days, your boss never asked if you could you handle more responsibility while he was gone – it was simply expected. And my store manager in Orlando certainly had no qualms allowing me to do that. Once again, I feel the need to speak to the quality of the team that surrounds you. I was only able to accomplish what I needed because of great peers like Sean Sites, who worked with me at that store and was with the company for 34 years. The retail environment is a small world – Sean and I were ASMs, then SMs, then DMs and finally, Regional Managers together – from Florida up to the Mid-Atlantic Region. Never underestimate how important your teammates are to your success and you to theirs.

Of course, it took me seven days to recover and get my sleep patterns back on track. But you know, that's the nature of retail...and this is what the public does not understand, especially with significant retail periods like the Holiday Season. Take the Black Friday after Thanksgiving, for example. For those of you who don't know, many companies rely on the Christmas Season to maintain the health of their bottom line for the entire fiscal year, which means the holiday shopping rush can either make or break them. Black Friday derives its name from the color black, representing profitability. You're probably familiar with the terms, "in the black," used to describe a profitable financial condition, and "in the red," used to describe debt and decline within an organization. To stay in the black, Home Depot and all retail businesses kill themselves with countless work hours and double-and-triple shifts to get their holiday product staged effectively for the onslaught of customers that they know is coming. These days, some retailers open at five or six o'clock on Thanksgiving night, but the Friday after Thanksgiving is the real big day, hence the name "Black Friday Weekend."

For the retail employee, it involves a crazy amount of time. While other people are at home planning their traditional holiday menu or traveling to visit loved ones, the retail worker toils at his or her job. And they do not, I repeat, do not – get enough credit for what they do around any of these holidays to prepare themselves and present their businesses to the public. Only those who have worked within retail have a true sense of pride and a fundamental appreciation for the effort and attention to detail that is required to pull it off. You can visit any Home Depot the Friday morning after Thanksgiving at 6 a.m., and while you're standing in line to purchase your artificial Christmas tree, six-foot ladder, 99-cent poinsettia, Wet Vac, and all the things we put on promotion, our associates and managers are stationed at the entrance while people are waiting for us to open the store, serving hot coffee, cider, and donuts. This doesn't happen at many other retail businesses, but Home Depot associates truly get into the spirit of the season.

I have a large chip on my shoulder for the retail worker. There are amazing folks in the retail industry who truly love people, enjoy their jobs, and put the extra effort into making their customers happy. In most instances, these seemingly small gestures distinguish some companies from others – that overall experience of what you get versus just going into a place that isn't offering anything extra. It's synonymous now with the perception of what's going on at shopping malls, according to recent articles where the experts predict gloom and doom and their eventual demise. In any business, a status-quo operation is an enemy to expansion and success.

In response to this, some of the malls (and more are getting on this game-plan now) are forging more of an experience where it's not just about shopping – whether it involves restaurants, activities, or unique events. These days, everybody in retail is competing with the mammoth enterprise that is Amazon and their eCommerce platform, realizing that to succeed you've got to be different. You can't only provide standard shopping because anybody can do that; it all comes back to the overall experience.

At Home Depot, we used words like "theater" and "sizzle." One of my vice-presidents (VPs) at the time, Paul Raines, nicknamed my team "Rolling Thunder," no disrespect intended to the actual Rolling Thunder, the military motorcycle organization. If something was on special or a promotion, my team built huge, towering displays and created big, dramatic signage, events, and demonstrations to highlight it. We didn't just hope a customer would walk in and notice it; we did what was necessary to ensure they did. And the only way we achieved it was through people...going back to the dedication, collaboration, and work ethic of the retail employee.

As I mentioned, one of my favorite aspects of being an ASM at Home Depot was the training classes I attended in Atlanta, where I was exposed to most of the leaders in the company. Back then, we were small enough that Bernie and Arthur always came into the meetings to spend time with us. They knew our names and our locations. It was awe-inspiring to someone like me, who was just starting out, to be able to interact with these gentlemen at that level, knowing what they had been through. Much to their credit, Bernie, Arthur and their entire team made themselves accessible. You could call or write them anytime. Back then, of course, you couldn't email, but you knew you could call them. And I did on a couple of occasions, to voice my opinion. At meetings, you weren't afraid to approach them, speak to them, ask them a question, or offer a recommendation.

My belief is that's where some companies fail – because leaders don't make that kind of effort until it's almost too late. If you segregate yourself, you won't see reality. Bernie and Arthur would always conduct scheduled events where you knew in advance that they were coming to visit your location, giving you time to prepare. Companies refer to it differently, some call it the "dog and pony show," but whatever you named it, you nearly killed yourself and your team to make your store look perfect because the pressure was on. Knowing you had plenty of time to prepare for a scheduled walk, management had expectations of near perfection for in-stocks, maintenance, cleanliness, and operational standards.

But unannounced walks when Bernie and Arthur just showed up out of the nowhere to obtain a sense of what was really going on in their stores were the best. During their tenure, they did a combination of scheduled and surprise visits. And if you were a member of the Board of Directors for Home Depot, you had a mandate to visit a certain amount of Home Depot sites over the course of a year to get a full understanding of what was happening in the retail stores, or as we called them, the "boxes." Then you reported your findings back to Bernie, Arthur, and the other members of the Board. As a store manager, assistant store manager, or associate, on any given day you didn't know if somebody from the home office was going to pay your store a visit. While the verbiage was, "Always be ready for the customer," in a real sense, we readied ourselves for corporate leadership too, which benefitted the customer.

When you are a salaried member of management, you are all-in.

The "pucker factor" was off the charts: if they showed up unannounced and the visit went badly, which, let's be real, sometimes they did. Even if it was your day off, or if you were attending a meeting with other managers, you dropped everything to get to your store after somebody – whether a district manager or store manager – got to a phone to call you in a peer-organized network of communication.

There isn't anybody at Home Depot who didn't have a walk where they wanted to go outside and scream towards the heavens, thinking they were about to get fired because a walk/visit went badly. This is where the store management network came into play. If the higher-ups showed up in one store, we respected our peers in the other stores enough to call them (secretly, of course...we didn't want Bernie and Arthur to know, though these intelligent men were wise to our shenanigans) to tell them we had company, to give them a chance to do some last-minute, whatever-they-could prepping. Or to be on alert because when the executives hit an area, they didn't just stop at a single store; they would get into as many of the stores as they could from an efficiency standpoint.

Back in the early days, the visits were much more frequent because we were smaller. Even in the book, *Built from Scratch*, I believe Bernie and Arthur said at one point what became disappointing to them the most was that they knew they weren't going to be able to get to every store like they used to. To be that presence, that mentor, and to be that accessible to the people. Because it truly was special when these guys showed up. The prevailing attitude was that they truly cared for and respected us; therefore, we responded in kind, respecting them to an extremely high degree. It was almost as if the President of the United States was coming. Employees and their families would come into the store on their day off just to shake their hand and say, "Thank you for the job opportunity," or "Thanks for what you're doing. My life had no direction, but you guys built this thing called Home Depot, and now I got something." Employees would break down in tears of gratitude to them for what they did. And this occurred at every level throughout my time with the company. (Hmm... maybe we were a cult?)

Other employees brought them gifts. Family members would come in and say, "I can't thank you enough for what you did for my family because my husband, my wife, or my kid was struggling, but now that they have Home Depot, things are so much better." It really stemmed from how Arthur and Bernie started the company; they embraced every single person as a human, not a number, and as an integral piece of what was going to optimize Home Depot. We were happy, and we demonstrated that state-of-mind in everything we did. This is a strong point for anyone in a leadership position: treat others as you would expect to be treated. Just like the Pied Piper, you will create an army of followers.

Don't get me wrong, it wasn't like they just let everybody skate, either. They pushed us hard. They would put you on the spot with passion and sometimes profanity, to make their point. They would tell you that you could not go home until the job was done. In extreme situations, I can remember people being told to take off the apron and leave, IF they could not take it. It was not easy work, but you didn't even question it; you just did it. And there was such loyalty, but I don't think was blind loyalty. As much as you were working hard, you knew Bernie and Arthur weren't abusing you, that they were doing it for the right reasons, and they were trying to make us all better. Those who didn't operate in that manner really stood out and ultimately left Home Depot because – as the phrase went – "they couldn't hang."

My phrase and philosophy?

"Not everybody deserves to wear the orange," referring to the apron we wear. Because if they came in and couldn't execute their tasks well or provide excellent customer service, we did not want them around because they diminished everyone else's accomplishments and results. I don't want to give the sense that it was easy at Home Depot simply because we had exceptional leaders. When they got done walking you, whether your department or store was perfect or not, you'd sit there and think, "WOW! Have I been doing anything?" Because there was still so much opportunity to improve the business, they would not let you get complacent...at least until 1999 (more on that later). That's how they led you, by never being happy with the results and advising you that there was always more to accomplish. While they celebrated the positives and the successes, they always spent far more time on the remaining opportunities.

CALIFORNIA DAZE

Shortly after my promotion to ASM at the Fort Lauderdale store, I transferred up to the Orlando area, to the Altamonte Springs location. It was a wonderful and brief experience. I got engaged while working there, following a rapid romance where we dated for six months. When an opportunity to move to California to open a new store just outside of L.A. presented itself, my fiancée and I decided to take it.

It was an adjustment in many ways, starting with the fact that it was my first time putting up a new store. Back then, the salaried management team reported to the store two weeks ahead of the hourly supervisors. If you can, imagine a Home Depot with all the steel that holds the products in the store; well, the salaried manager team had the responsibility of physically measuring the store, utilizing blueprints and putting the steel up, including all the inner-shelf supports and starter shelves. Back then, it was tradition that with each new store that came after the last, the team in charge tried to set a record for how quickly they got the job done.

A typical Home Depot store is 100,000 – 120,000 square feet, excluding outside garden. As truckloads of steel came in, we had a team that pulled the steel off the truck, a team that measured the floor, and a team that put it up after they brought it in. In California, we completed this task in about four days. It got to the point where the work was so tough that when you went home at night, you could not feel your hands. Because you had to lift all these beams off the pallet and put them on the shelf, you were gripping and working for 18-20 hours. I remember we popped pain medication from our first-aid kits called Pain-Aid every four hours, chased by as much Mountain Dew as we could chug down, just to get through this process. We got addicted to the Pain-Aid, which not only relieved pain but contained a ridiculous amount of caffeine in the pre-energy drink era. Even so, you almost couldn't drive home when your work was done for the day because you couldn't grip the steering wheel.

But you never worried about that because your whole goal was to set the record for how fast you could set up the new store. You had an innate sense of teamwork; that you were accomplishing something amazing together. It became part of our DNA. You were aiming to set the record, and you couldn't do it if any one person was not pulling their weight. So yeah, we did kick each other's butts, but it was all in a fun spirit of unity and competition.

Once we got the steel assembled, hundreds of vendors came into the store to load their products on the shelves, build their displays, and put up the signs. Between the Home Depot team and the vendor community, we had about seven to 12 weeks to get the store ready to open to the public. Everything was going well. As the administrative assistant manager (AM) for this new L.A. store, I handled all the hiring – the bookkeeping department, cashiers, and special service people – in addition managing to the store personnel's training. I had oversight of the receiving department bringing all the freight and initial product into the store. Basically, anything that was operational fell under my jurisdiction.

From the get-go, it had always been my standard to hire the most qualified people I could find. That included front-end personnel like cashiers, return desk associates, and the special services desk. During my time in California, contractors would come in, ask for me and shake my hand. I'd say, "I'm sorry, what did I do?"

"Well, you hired all these people, right?"

"Yes."

"Keep it up."

Of course, my only goal was to hire the best people I could find but this was California and as it turns out, the Beach Boys were right about "California girls." Some of my pro customers even went so far as to send flowers or bring gifts into the store or ask some of my female front-end employees out on a date. However, I made it a point to inform my associates that if it ever got out of hand or if they ever felt unsafe or uncomfortable to tell me right away.

And yes, there were a few occasions when I had to put my arm around a pro customer and say "Hey, let's take a walk outside," or "Listen, I know what you're doing, but here's the deal." When warranted, I took a protective stand. I refused to let any customer abuse my staff, whether it involved throwing objects, threatening bodily harm, or harassing them sexually. To this day, Home Depot takes an extremely hard line with that kind of behavior. In fact, management personnel that do not handle sexual harassment issues in a timely and appropriate fashion face consequences – all the way up to and including termination.

While it presented a challenge during my brief time in California, it also happened at other stores because that's human nature. Anyone who works in retail understands the inevitability of having to deal with difficult customers on occasion, but Home Depot associates knew that management had their back. They would not allow them to be abused or harassed, simply because some "customers" feel like they're entitled or better than our employees.

YES, THIS IS ABSOLUTELY A TRUE STORY

When I was an AM in Fort Lauderdale, one day I got called up to the service desk at the front of the store to handle an unusual request (to say the least). Of course, I ran up there as fast as I could and when I arrived, the associate announced, "Hey, that customer wants to talk to you."

"Okay, great. Do you know what it's about?"

"Nope. He just said he specifically had to speak to you." With that, she pointed at the guy, who stood off to the side of the desk. I walked over and held out my hand.

"Hey, sir. I'm Erik. How can I help you?"

"I know who you are," he announced. Other than the name on my apron, I never figured out how he knew my name.

"O-okay," I answered. "What can I do for you today?"

He pointed to an extremely attractive woman standing next to him. By now, there were other customers gathered around because every time a manager gets called to the front, everybody's going to watch in anticipation of what's about to transpire, assuming it's going to be a complaint or some other negative issue.

"This is my wife," he told me.

"Hello, how are you?" I held out my hand.

"I would like for you to do me a favor," he went on, with no attempt to lower his voice.

"What is that?" I asked.

"I am not able to satisfy my wife." Yup, just like that he blurted it out. If you could have only seen the look on my face. I was completely flabbergasted.

"Sir, how, how is it that *I* can help you?"

"My wife pointed you out to me. We would like to talk to you about how you can satisfy her sexual needs." *Whoa. This was not what I expected.*

There I stood, a new AM, trying to wrap my brain around what was unfolding. Quite honestly, this woman was a knockout, married to a man who was obviously a little bit older. And I was like, *"Sir."* As I looked around, I could see people staring at us and I wondered if I was on *Candid Camera* or something (for my younger readers who have no clue, the old TV show *Candid Camera* was a precursor to smartphone videos and social media).

"Sir, I gotta be honest with you." At this point, I was fighting to keep my voice low, despite the rush of adrenaline through my body. My heart was pounding; never had I dealt with anything like this before. It was just not normal...and NO, this had not been covered in the training manual. "We have a high standard on customer service, but it doesn't go *that* far," I responded. In my mind, I heard Bernie's famous words about customer service, encouraging us "to make love to the customer." Of course, he meant it in a figurative sense, not a literal one, but it underscored the irony of my current situation.

"Well then, you're insulting me and my wife. What, she's not attractive enough for you?"

That's when I took a stronger tone. "No, please do not be insulted. Please understand that I *cannot* do this. It would cost me my job. My goodness, I can only imagine what it would take for you to ask this of me, to even make me this offer. I'll do everything I can for you inside the building while you're a customer of Home Depot. If you're going to get insulted, that's up to you. But, I cannot and will not do what you're asking. Now I'm going to walk away."

It took about 30 seconds for the story to get around the store that some guy wanted me to go home with him and take care of his wife because he wasn't up to the task (no pun intended). That's just one example of a customer taking their demands to an unacceptable level and my employees never letting me hear the end of it.

WORLD EVENTS SHAPE OUR PERSPECTIVE

January 28, 1986. Returning home from the dry cleaner on my day off, I made the turn onto the street where my apartment complex was located. My car radio was blaring, which was normal for me. For some reason, a feeling came over me as I approached the red traffic light. I stopped, looked up through the sunroof, and noticed what looked like a y-shaped mix of light as bright as the sun, connected to thick contrails of black and grey smoke. It seemed as if it was almost directly above me. At first, I did not recognize what is was, but as I entered the apartment, curiosity got the best of me and I turned on the television right away. And then, I knew. The news was on all the major channels – the Space Shuttle Challenger had blown up, 73 seconds into its tenth flight, killing the seven courageous souls on board.

For what seemed like an eternity, I sat there stunned; the more I listened to the news narrative, the number I became over this national tragedy. My wife always tells me I tend to absorb others' emotions in situations like these, so as you can imagine I was devastated. Having attended many launches and landings at the Kennedy Space Center, I had always been in awe of our capabilities and the potential of the space program. Unknown to me at the time, there was a personal connection to the Challenger tragedy: my brother, Dave, who was in the Navy on Submarine Duty, was on one of the subs tasked with identification and retrieval of the remains. That day absolutely sucked. This was not an event anyone would forget anytime soon, impacting everyone's moods, behaviors, and psyches. When something of this magnitude takes place, it spreads itself into work.

As a member of a team or management, the dynamic changes measurably, necessitating communication, enhanced teamwork, teambuilding and presence. Part of a manager or leader's roles and responsibilities is being a counselor when needed. The Challenger disaster was not directly related to work, yet indirectly its effects on your people become your concern. You are expected to be their source for empathy, reasoning, and outlook – in total, a shoulder to cry on. It is an overwhelming responsibility as, in some cases, you must mask your own feelings because you understand that their needs must take precedence over yours. They must know that everything will be okay, that work is a "safe place" for them, and that they can count on you. In the aftermath of such an event, employees' responsibilities and tasks become therapeutic and take on increased intensity for them, because they are tangible. Customer impacts in this area are just as critical, since their comfort-level in your environment determines their satisfaction and continued shopping. Think of the customer who also feels the impact of the tragedy. They also need a distraction as they attempt to balance their mindset, and they are counting on you to provide that. It is in times like these that the perceptions of your customers are cemented.

"True humility is not thinking less of yourself it is thinking of yourself less." —C.S. Lewis

Whenever Home Depot opens a store, we maintain a significant security presence, which means there's only one way in and one way out. Everyone, regardless of their title, must sign in and sign out. To ensure proper protocol, we stationed some of our employees right by one of the doors, either at a desk or some other kind of set-up. I was up front in that area one day when a woman walked in. My folks said hello and asked if she could please sign in for us. "Nah, I don't need to sign in," she replied. That got my attention and I waited to see what was going to happen. Sure enough, she tried to walk in without signing in, so I approached her, not understanding her intent. We had no idea if she was a competitor or a local government official from the zoning department.

"Ma'am, you need to understand, we have policy and procedure," I began. "First, who are you and why are you here?"

"Don't you know who I am?"

"Ma'am, I apologize, but I would not ask you if I knew who you were."

"I'm the district manager's wife," she informed me.

"Oh, I'm very happy to meet you," I answered. "If you could sign in for me, I'd appreciate it." I identified myself as a member of the management team.

Her husband was in the store at the time and she had come by to see him. She said something else to me, involving mild profanity and a venomous attitude, to which I replied with a certain amount of my own attitude, "Ma'am, let me explain something. My father's a DM in the company as well. I know and understand respect, but we have policies and procedures for a reason. I'm sure you understand that."

I thought of my mom, who never acted that way, no matter what level my dad attained at the company. It was the exact opposite: Mom treated everyone with respect. By contrast, this woman standing before me was miffed to no end. She said something to her husband, who mentioned it to me afterward. It wasn't awful; it was simply stated with a slight tone that signaled "Don't ever challenge my wife again," which caused me to lose a measure of respect for him. It wouldn't be the last time I'd lose respect for someone in a leadership position. I have never been a fan of the "Do as I say, not as I do" mentality, nor should any of you.

Now, this DM was a legend in his own mind. He always wore Polo pastels with the collars turned up, and both he and his wife exuded a "holier-than-thou" attitude. It wasn't worth escalating the situation, but again, it was one of those things that made me think, "Wow, maybe it's different out here in L.A. I just gotta get back to Orlando." In my young mind, my California store experience did not live up to expectations, due to a confluence of events like this...and the one I describe below.

"Sometimes things can be right under your nose, the only problem is, sometimes your eyes are above it." — Author Unknown

Another major event that takes place with a new Home Depot store opening involves the transportation of anywhere from six- to- 10 million dollars' worth of merchandise by truckload over a span of a few weeks. It's a ton of product that comes in fast and furious, so you must coordinate everything with the vendors and the staff to keep everybody on a time schedule. In L.A., we were doing well; we were right on pace but every night we had to reconcile the petty cash and training cash for the cashiers with the bookkeeping department. About three- to- four weeks in, we started to notice that we were missing money every day. We couldn't reconcile bookkeeping and never figured it out while I was out there.

In the end, I only stayed in L.A. for about four months. I called my district manager Robert Gilbreth in Orlando and begged him to get me back to Florida because the pressure of being engaged while opening a new store and living in that environment was just too much. Southern California is everything they say it is. As a single (albeit engaged) man, there were a lot of distractions on a personal basis and on a professional basis. Thankfully, my DM agreed to my request, but when I arrived in Orlando, I found out that the Regional Loss Prevention Manager, who often visited the L.A. store just to check on our progress, had been stealing money from bookkeeping for a personal situation at home. It was no wonder why we could never reconcile the money. During that time, my store manager and staff had started to look at me like, "*Why the hell can't you get this fixed?*" We had everybody who was anybody, including this regional manager – the guilty party – looking for an answer.

After I left California, an investigation also revealed a sex-and-drugs scam in the store with the associates, where two of the ASMs and the SM were found guilty. Because they caught some of them on film, they were fired on the spot. But all of this happened unknowingly, right under my nose at the L.A. location, adding to the undercurrent of the culture and making me realize I had to get myself out of there. The sad part was, I loved California...the scenery, the weather...it was an incredible place from that standpoint. Keep in mind, this was in the 80s when Valley Girl talk was popular, and it was way rad to live on the West Coast – like *way rad* to live on the West Coast. Despite what happened, I enjoyed working with some great people, sharing some fun times, and launching an excellent store. On a personal note, I had to make another adjustment. Due to the immense pressure on both of us, my fiancée and I broke up while we were still in L.A. We tried to reconcile when we came back to Orlando, but it didn't last long, and she moved back to her hometown of Winter Park with her parents.

Perhaps in a sign from above confirming the wisdom of my decision, three-and-a-half weeks after I transferred back to Orlando, an earthquake struck, and the L.A. store suffered considerable damage. So, it was fortuitous my DM let me leave. My California experience had its highs and lows, but it was one of the first big moves I made with Home Depot where the company paid for my relocation. However, I had to finance my own way back to Florida since it was my request. I flew two great friends, Jeff and Kari, from Florida to California to drive back with me, and we drove straight through – pedal to the metal, east on I-10, even after I got a speeding ticket in L.A. on the way out. We drove all the way from L.A. to Orlando without stopping because I just wanted to get back as soon as humanly possible. I remember the palpable sense of relief I experienced as we crossed the California border into Arizona, and again when we crossed the state line into Florida. We made it back in a little over a day.

Reflecting on the experience, I thought moving out there was something I wanted to do at the time, but maybe I wasn't quite ready to make the adjustment. The personal turmoil and the professional upheaval got to me. I questioned Home Depot because the negative events that had taken place in the store involved leadership, and I had never been exposed to something of that magnitude before.

Once I arrived in Central Florida, they gave me merchandising departments as a merchandising assistant manager at the East Colonial store, a new location for me. Despite the change in my title, I never lost sight of the fact that it was all about customer service. I remember the day when I went into the store for the first time for an appointment with the store manager and didn't have my apron on. He, of course, knew to expect me at our scheduled time of 10 a.m. But as I walked through the store and arrived at Plumbing and Electrical, which were going to be my departments, I noticed that the associates were absolutely overwhelmed. With ten customers to every associate, they were getting overwhelmed and frustrated because in these departments, there's the highest degree of the "Please show me how to do this project" mentality, due to the technical aspects of the categories of product.

Pro customers also shop in these departments, but when you work in Plumbing and Electrical, you must know your stuff because you field a lot of questions about what to use and how to use it. So, at about ten minutes to ten, I started helping customers even though I didn't have my apron on. I took them to places, helped them find things, tried to answer their questions, and/or married them up with associates in the aisles – none of whom even knew who I was yet. All the associates knew was that some guy without an apron was assisting customers. Before I knew it, it was 11 a.m. and I was still helping them out. In passing, as I worked side-by-side with the associates, I assured them, "Don't worry, I'm your new AM."

By now, other associates from other departments had come over to see what was going on. And I still hadn't laid eyes on any other member of management in the store. In fact, when I finally made it back to the office, the store manager was still sitting at his desk. He'd never left. At Home Depot, what we call "power hours" take place from 10 a.m. to 2 p.m. every day. During the weekdays and occasionally on the weekends, it's our busiest customer rush. When I walked in, the store manager looked up at me and said something like, "Where the hell have you been?" During the highest customer traffic time periods, all managers and associates were to be in the aisles, assisting all possible shoppers. I wondered to myself, *"Why were YOU not on the sales floor, leading the charge and setting the standard?"* If he had been, he would have seen that I was there.

"Well, from the moment I got here at 10 minutes to 10, I've been out helping customers. I couldn't get back here, or communicate because we were overwhelmed on the sales floor," I explained. The whole time he had been sitting on his derriere doing paperwork, not out in the trenches with his people, when it truly mattered.

After that exchange, we had our short meeting, where he laid out his expectations. He was one of those guys, I mean I hate to make fun of him, but his pants were always three inches too short. However, when it came to financials, operations, and numbers he was one of the smartest managers I'd ever come across. Unfortunately, from a people standpoint, he didn't have a clue. Once we finished, I put my apron on and went back out to my departments, where all the associates came up to give me high-fives, put their arms around me, and thank me for what I did. It made an indelible impression that I felt it was a higher priority to be out there with them helping them take care of customers than it was to hang out in the back office with the store manager. Kate would have been proud.

From the get-go, it became one of those legendary stories about me and created instant respect among my peers and subordinates. As I communicated with my people, they expressed their perceptions of how poorly they viewed the store manager and his personal brand as it related to customer service and people skills. I ended up getting promoted out of the East Colonial store to a store manager position in Daytona (more on that later), but every time I got promoted, one of the first things I did at my going away party was to thank my employees for making me look good. That went both ways because they knew they could count on me to be out there when they needed me. I'd made that adjustment years before in Fort Lauderdale, when I first became a department supervisor and Kate let me have it for not being there for my team. I took that lesson with me, especially now as a salaried member of management. It reinforced the importance of something you thought of as basic, and how an hourly associate perceived your actions.

After that incident, every time I talked about customer service, there wasn't anyone who didn't remember what I did. My conscious decision to stop and help that day gave me more validity when speaking to the topic, versus the store manager who sat in his office all day. Eventually, due to his lack of skills and results, he was released from the company.

LIFE IN THE FISHBOWL

When you're in management, everything you say and do is under scrutiny. It's like being in a fishbowl, where you can make either a positive or a negative impression. Being a store manager is kind of like being the biggest fish in the bowl: you have an opportunity to impact every person in your environment. Yes, Home Depot provides a standard operating policy, rules and regulations, but the store manager puts their thumbprint on that store, based on their personality, behavior, ethics, enthusiasm, and their reaction to a crisis. The store really does follow the manager's lead and I can tell you, through the course of my tenure with Home Depot, the majority have been terrific. However, we've had our share of poor performers that should have never been SM's in the first place. Sometimes, management must make selections based on criteria and the information you have in front of you.

The retail industry has a high turnover rate – which includes hourly associates and salaried managers – of close to over 60 percent on an annual basis. In fact, in 2018 turnover caused 230 million days of lost productivity, representing $19 billion dollars in cost. Not surprisingly, people accept positions thinking they're ready for them when they're not; then, when they get there, they realize it's not all it's cracked up to be. I was guilty of this myself. As I reached a higher level within the organization, I thought it was going to be easier, but the reality was, it was more complex. At every rung you climb, there are more things to worry about; the higher you go, the more expansive your responsibilities. Yeah, as you achieve another milestone the compensation, benefits, and things you become eligible for are wonderful, but believe me, you earn them. Or at least, you should. In a meritocracy, the best performers receive the larger share of every-thing related to compensation and benefits. And to its credit, Home Depot was (and continues to be) a meritocracy. Because in business and in life, there should be no "participation" trophies.

In the process, I discovered I loved merchandising much more than operations. I enjoyed working with products, selling products, and helping customers on the floor. When you're the operational assistant manager, you tend to handle mostly paperwork and behind-the-scenes things. Whatever your responsibilities, a salaried manager has the power to motivate or disenfranchise you, depending upon the type of leadership they demonstrate. At the East Colonial store, for example, another AM named Neil and I were working overnights to do a bunch of resets. One morning, he and I walked up the main aisle at about 5:30 after having what we thought was a productive night. We weren't done by any stretch of the imagination, but we felt we were on schedule and the team had kicked butt that day.

Then the store manager came walking down from the other end of the aisle with a pocket protector with 12 pencils and pens and a cigarette hanging out of his mouth (back in those days, you could still smoke inside buildings). As he approached us, he didn't even say "Good morning." Instead, he asked, "What the fuck did you guys get done last night!?" in a combative tone. Neil and I immediately turned to look at each other. I gotta give my peer credit; he looked the store manager in the eye and remarked, "You are such an asshole." In an example of how people leave their manager or leader, not the company, Neil eventually left Home Depot to pursue something on his own.

But in that moment, he had the cajones to say what we were both thinking when I did not, and we just walked away in utter disdain. You may be wondering if there were recriminations and the answer is no; that was the way this store manager spoke to people. Yes, he was smart on the numbers and hosted meetings at his house where he'd take the team through the stats and financials. You'd learn a tremendous amount, but it got to the point where you couldn't wait to get out of there because his personality would begin to show. You hated working when this guy was around. I remember we'd try to get him out of the store, saying, "Why don't you go home? Why don't you take the day off?"

Nobody wanted to be around him unless you felt he could teach you something you wanted to learn. With his authoritative view of leadership, he never understood the negative impact of his words and actions, nor did he even care or bother to ask when someone like my buddy referred to him as an "asshole." He never came back with the simple question, "Well, why do you think that?" or sought any input to clarify where he stood or what the perception of him was in the store. In his own way (and completely unknown to him), this guy taught me the importance of understanding how you are being perceived.

Please allow me to highlight two more behaviors you do NOT want to emulate. The first is "The A** Kisser or "Brown-Noser." Around this time, I learned about the damage this practice inflicts on your brand and others' perceptions of you. It's inevitable that in every profession there are individuals who believe they must constantly fawn over higher-ups. Deep inside, they lack self-esteem and confidence in their own abilities, and they justify their fawning behaviors as a method of enhancing their role or career. I am quite positive that everyone reading this has already thought of someone with whom they work who fits the description of the "A** Kisser" or "Brown-Noser." As such, you recognize how they are perceived by their peer group and by most of the hierarchy above them. You know the type: when the person to whom the fawning is directed stops walking, the A** Kisser will almost bump into their backside. They are also "yes" people who agree almost instantly with any thought or idea from their supervisor. They offer to do anything and everything, short of assisting in the bathroom, to impress – organizing the office, washing the car, providing meals, offering to transport, dropping the dry-cleaning, taking care of the pet, laughing at all jokes even when they're not funny, and having no self-respect or self-awareness about the behavior that everyone around them observes and decries.

As a leader at any level of management, you should not condone this behavior, nor maintain any member of your staff who exhibits this behavior on your team. Why? Your brand and perception and theirs will suffer injury that may or may not be repairable. In the fishbowl, your acceptance of behaviors will be taken as gospel and set a precedent. Your leadership's acceptable standards should be based in ethics, behavior, performance and results. The above individual, if tolerated, undermines any standard you have set. Keeping this individual on your team will ensure you are one step away from optimum success. Please, do not be this type of individual, or tolerate one (or more) on your team. If what I have described is you, or if you value this type of individual on your team, please look in the mirror as soon as possible and re-evaluate. Everyone appreciates when people do things for them; however, when it becomes a disruptive force, all your conscientious work and effort could go for naught.

The second behavior? The dreaded Gossipmonger. I have disdain for individuals who feel the need to intrude into everyone else's lives, with no concern for their victim's well-being or their own perception or brand. This is yet another type of individual that a leader cannot tolerate because he or she diminishes their overall team's productivity, morale, and results. If not stopped immediately, this individual's behavior could result in lost staffing, diminished customer perceptions, and even the loss of their supervisor's job, if they are the target of the false accusations. If you tolerate or even participate, you are condoning, and your supervisor may not appreciate that. My hope is that most of you reading this are like me in this regard – always the last one to know. Too busy doing my job, I did not care who might be sleeping with who, who did not like who, what they may have seen them doing out in public, or who got into trouble for doing whatever. People who engage in this behavior are cancers that slowly eat away at the health of your area and even the company.

Due to my familial circumstances, at times I was the primary target for misguided efforts in this area. At one point, I became aware of things some employees said about my family, while they were "on the clock," on the sales floor, and in front of customers. Being a professional, I set a precedent for accountability and brought all six individuals under my oversight into the office at one time. I looked each one of them in the eye and asked if they in fact had participated in the gossip. At first, they denied it, but their tunes changed instantly when I presented them with evidence from my investigation. Then, they apologized and claimed it was all a joke. I responded with conviction, stated my intolerance of their behavior, and warned them that their involvement in any further incidences would cost them their jobs, **period.** The better news, as human nature would have it, was that they shared the situation with many others and no further infractions occurred.

"The outer conditions of a person's life will always be found to be harmoniously related to his inner state... Men do not attract that which they want, but that which they are." —James Allen

While I was still an assistant store manager at East Colonial, a store manager position became available at our Daytona Beach location. At the time, Home Depot had a report called "The Hit List," which indicated an employee's performance and stature in terms of getting to the next level. Among other factors, it listed your name and ranked you according to management's perception of your readiness for a promotion, e.g. in three months, six months, or one year. I felt supremely confident I was ready; I wanted that store with every fiber of my being. Who wouldn't want to work in a store by the beach, near the NASCAR speedway in a town that was famous for annual events like Spring Break and Bike Week?

However, one of the critical mistakes I made at Home Depot was that when I got a new position, I started focusing on achieving the next level, instead of on what I needed to do in my current capacity. It's kind of like a football team that looks beyond the 0-12 team that's next on their schedule and gets their butts kicked because they were focused on playing their rival team down the road, instead preparing for the game that was right in front of them.

The district manager at the time, a man named Robert Gilbreth, who was also a peer and a friend of my dad's, selected somebody else for the position. From the second I heard that the other gentleman got it, I was pissed off. I was furious. I mean, there's probably not a strong enough word to describe my emotions. I might have thrown a couple things; I might have punched a couple file cabinets. I wanted that store, I thought I was ready, and I put immense pressure on myself because I wanted to get to that position quickly. Taking it personally, I felt like a failure.

For the next two weeks, I wasn't myself at work, either with my people, my responsibilities, or any other tasks requiring my attention. It became apparent to my store manager that I was almost giving up. I felt like if I did what I thought was the absolute best to get it and still failed, then what else in the world did I need to do?

Two weeks went by and I was in the store one day when Robert came in unannounced. Walking right up to me, he said, "You. Me. In the office, now." This was about the third time I thought I was going to get fired (I'll discuss the third instance in greater detail soon, I promise). We got into the office and sat down.

"What is wrong with you?" he asked, not mincing words.

"I'm upset. I'm pissed off I didn't get the job. I know I'm better than him. I know I can do a better job," I answered. After we chatted for a little bit, he said, "Well, let me ask you a question. How good of a store manager do you think you'd have been, or you'll be, if this is the way you're going to react every time a major decision does not go your way?"

Stunned by the question, I kind of just sat there for a second. "Probably not a very good one," I admitted. That's when it finally clicked in my head. The beauty of what Robert had done was, he got me through that conversation by asking me questions and getting me talking to almost rationalize the situation.

"I'm here because I heard you have your egotistical head up your ass. Your performance is failing, and people are starting to talk. You're too good to let this happen. Understand something: when I and others feel you're ready to be a store manager, you will be one. You won't even see it coming. All the sudden, we're going to come to you and ask if you want a spot. For now, your focus is to pull your head out of your ass and start to perform like a store manager."

Reminiscent of my conversation with Kate back when I was a garden department supervisor, and in direct opposition to the store manager's approach to leadership, I left that meeting and went out to talk to my people. "Describe me over the last couple of weeks," I requested. I'll be honest, some if it was hard to hear. The responses ran the gamut from "I hated your guts," to "You were a real ass," to "I didn't want to be around you." Everybody recognized my less-than-stellar behavior and gave me an opportunity to fix it. I always valued people's input and constructive criticism. It's a credit to my many years playing sports and being coached, in addition to my early jobs where my supervisors helped to grow my skills and performance.

Whether you respond with specific communication, action or

follow-up, you have zero integrity if you ask for and receive constructive criticism, then neglect to do anything about it. In business, if you put a wall between you and your colleagues and coworkers, it's much harder to tear it down. You'll never get the interaction, honesty, and quality communication you're hoping for. Guess what *will* happen? The next time you ask for it, they'll say, "No, I got nothin'." Just like customers when you fix a problem, your coworkers' perceptions of you are elevated when they can be honest and direct with you AND you take the appropriate action. Everybody expects you to be on your game when everything's going well, but when the *you know what* hits the fan or an opportunity arises, if you handle it the right way, you'll gain their respect when they watch you make the effort.

Believe it or not, many of the processes Home Depot engages in today came from ideas associates suggested in the stores. In *Built from Scratch*, there are examples of things we do as a company now because an hourly associate once said, "I'm going to try something," and it turned out to be terrific. The original founders and current officers of Home Depot did not come up with all our great ideas by themselves. A good portion of the things that are presently sustaining the company originated from associates and store leaders who asked the simple questions, "What if?" and "Could we try this?" As they traveled the country, Bernie and Arthur stimulated that creativity and dialogue when they conducted their official meetings in the stores, where they allowed their audience of associates and managers to vent, scream, suggest, recommend, and share. It was always like that. And now, current leadership has embraced the same mentality as part of our culture, which is one of the key factors behind Home Depot's longevity, continuity, and success.

I remember some meetings where people stood on top of tables cursing, spitting, and gesturing with their arms and hands because they were so upset, while Bernie and Arthur listened, took notes, and let it happen. In most cases, they took immediate action in response to their employees' feedback, utilizing their team and their resources to fix some of these issues. It was incredibly empowering for attendees at these meetings to know they worked for leaders who were engaged, accessible, open to suggestions, and willing to accept their feedback as valid. Through their words and actions, Home Depot leaders relied on the inverted pyramid model to optimize the company's operations and success. In this inverted pyramid, the associates and managers in the stores are at the top, and the President and the CEO are at the bottom – unlike most companies where the President and CEO are at the top and their associates and managers at the bottom. Bernie and Arthur lived and breathed the inverted pyramid philosophy: they didn't hold these store meetings to check a box, they genuinely wanted to listen and act upon what they heard, gauge their employees' emotional state, and do everything in their power to improve the situation. Do all companies encourage their people to convey their thoughts with this kind of passion and directness? I can't say for sure, but I doubt it.

THE GLASS IS HALF-FULL

Toward the end of my time at East Colonial, Larry Mercer, then our Area Vice President and one of the first store managers in Home Depot history, took over an available office space we had in the back. A resident of Orlando, he ended up rising higher than the VP level. But I always remember him being a great mentor and a fantastic human being. The East Colonial location was convenient for Larry to do some work and get out of the house. When he came through the store, he was charismatic; you could tell he cared about people because he always stopped to say hello to everybody.

Since Larry and my dad had a close working relationship, I had a bit of an advantage. Larry always found me to inquire about what was going on, giving me the opportunity to communicate information directly to him. However, I had to do it in the right way because I was talking to a person three paygrades higher than me. To avoid the perception of bypassing my store manager or district manager, I exercised caution. It became a lesson for me in understanding hierarchy and knowing how to deal with people at various levels: who to talk to about what, and when and where to do it. Thankfully, Larry and I enjoyed a solid relationship for a long time.

As the Area VP, Larry worked according to a standard: he had to walk and spend a day with all candidates under consideration for a promotion to store manager. He wanted to sanction the DM's selection by spending time with all candidates. With about three of us in contention – me and two other AMs including another one from East Colonial – we all met with Larry at a Home Depot store early one morning. When he arrived, he explained how he wanted the day to go and his agenda involved visiting a couple Home Depots. After you spent some time in the first location, you went to lunch before stopping by another store. Once you wrapped up, you had to wait for Larry's summary regarding your performance, numbers, and perceptions, along with his thoughts about the day's activities.

I remember in a telling moment, walking up to a product presentation and Larry asking me to critique it before asking what I would do to make it even better. This was his M.O. with every candidate under consideration. I noticed that the other two candidates did okay but were mainly negative with their feedback. They spent more time critiquing as opposed to making suggestions for improvement. Because of how I'd been trained and spent my time, when it was my turn, I spoke more about how I could make it better and the things I would do with the help of my team. When Larry sanctioned me for the promotion, I discovered that was a key factor that tipped the scales in my favor and gave him confidence in my ability to handle the role.

"Dardas' glass was half-full. Everybody else's was half-empty," he explained. Aware of what new store managers were getting themselves into, Larry wanted people with their glass half-full to join his team. A positive attitude was a prerequisite if they were going to accomplish everything demanded of them in that role.

Robert Gilbreth's prescient words about my promotion to store manager coming as a surprise rang true when I did that promotional walk with Larry in Orlando. At the time, I also challenged him about my dad, wanting assurance that he didn't keep me just because I was a legacy employee, but because he recognized my potential. He replied that he wanted me on his team. That became even more apparent when I got my shot at running the Daytona Beach location because our relationship blossomed right after. As I moved forward in my career, all these adjustments and impacts on others continued to build and set me up for the next rung on the ladder.

I'll never forget that day with Larry. The thing I'll say about him is, he told it like it is, as was the case with a specific interaction I had with the woman he was married to at the time. Remember now, this took place long before cell phones came along (again, to my younger readers- I know it's hard, but do your best to imagine life without them). One day, I'm in the store and the place is complete chaos. I'm running around like a chicken without a head, there were long lines at the registers...it's just a hectic, busy day. And I get a phone call. When I answer, the woman on the line says, "Hey Erik, how are you doing today?" It was Larry's wife, calling on her revolutionary new cordless phone, which was about two inches thick, 12 inches long, and came with its own carry bag. Picture, if you can, carrying and talking into, something the size of a brick.

"I'm doing fine. What can I do for you?"

"I'm parked out in the parking lot and it's full of empty shopping buggies. You need to get somebody out here right away."

"Okay," I answered. "It's crazy in here too. I'll get right on it."

"Well, do I need to call Larry?" She apparently felt I was apprehensive or hesitant about honoring her request.

"No, I'll get some people right on it."

I gathered 10 people in the store and got them out there, which diminished our functionality inside of the building. Here's another situation where, maybe her intent was good, but the way she handled it was wrong. We all dreaded her phone calls or when she would shop in the store because you were always afraid it was going to go sideways...and maybe something was going to get said that you would have to answer for.

Fast forward to the day we did the promotion walk with Larry. Everybody planned to take their own car, but Larry said to me, "Hey, on the way to lunch why don't you ride with me? We're all going to end up back here anyway."

And I thought, *Oh no! Is this where he tells me I'm not going to get it?* About eight weeks before, Larry had some remodeling done at his house using all Kohler products. When his wife came into the store, I was the one assigned to take care of her and manage the process. That entailed arranging the special orders, shipping everything in, making sure everything was right and so on. Thank goodness, we managed to execute it all to her satisfaction.

As we drove in the car, Larry asked, "How's your dad? How's everything?" After I responded to that question, he went on. "Listen, I owe you a very big thank you."

"What for Larry?"

"For dealing with my wife. Trust me, I know how hard it is. I know it's not easy, but you've always handled it extremely well."

"Larry, listen, I'm treating her just like I would any other customer." It was funny because he didn't curse a lot, so when he did it got your attention.

"Cut the s**t. You and I both know. I just wanted to thank you. I appreciate what you do." That little exchange between him and I in the car meant a lot to me and provided a sharp contrast to the previous DM situation I'd dealt with in California. In that moment, Larry exemplified superior people skills and demonstrated how to communicate properly, even under difficult or awkward circumstances.

One of the many benefits of having him at the store was that we could associate with Larry. Every year around Christmas, he hosted a potluck dinner with the management team. Everybody brought a dish to the party and went to the back, where he would hang out with us for a few hours, just chatting about stuff. It was kind of the start of something at Home Depot we ended up calling a Town Hall meeting, where you gather a group of associates and make them feel comfortable to get a barometer on what was going on with morale, and what changes had to be made. Larry would just open everybody up, take notes, and write everything down. To me, it was a symbol of what Home Depot stood for – the VP taking his own time over Christmas (nobody told him to, he did it on his own) and showcasing to me how you could rise to that level yet make yourself accessible to learn things you would not learn otherwise. If you just sat in your office at the company headquarters somewhere crunching the numbers, you couldn't get an accurate gauge, only a partial picture. In his work, Larry often cited two phrases when offering guidance to others: "If you are not making mistakes, you are not trying," and, one of my favorites, "Do it, dump it, or delegate it." He explained to me he never got into any trouble for throwing out a piece of paper because, "if it was that important, they will send it again."

Indicative of the caliber of leadership at Home Depot at every level during this era, Larry followed closely in Bernie and Arthur's footsteps – from the moment he joined the company looking and acting like Grizzly Adams (overweight with an oversized beard) up until the time he walked out an extremely successful executive. During his tenure, he transformed into the man I know and admire, the guy who became fit, shaved his beard, and rose to the second-highest position in the company right behind the founders. No one Larry ever spent time with had a bad word to say about him. He left a tremendous legacy because of the way he treated people, something I always tried to emulate.

Ladders and Learnings

- Make sure your self-perception aligns with your manager's perception of you and your performance.
- Embrace your company's and/or management's decisions, whether they are in your favor or not as a catalyst to keep growing and moving forward. Remember, optimism attracts, and pessimism detracts.

- Always remember to be part of the solution, NOT the problem.

Executive Memo

This is the first time, but not the last time I'll give you a warning: you never want to be perceived as an office manager. I cannot overstate the importance of being present with your teams in their environment, not in your "safe space." If anyone can walk into your office and see the outline of your butt in the office chair, you'll know you have an opportunity for improvement.

4

MANAGING BY EXCEPTION, LEADING BY EXAMPLE

"The deeds you do may be the only sermon some persons will hear today."

— SAINT FRANCIS OF ASSISI

In March 1991, I finally earned a promotion to store manager for Home Depot's Daytona Beach location. I trained for the position in Fort Lauderdale with then Store Manager, Paul West, another mentor of mine and all-around great guy, who has 37 years with Home Depot...and counting. These days, he works as a Divisional Merchandising Manager at the corporate office. It felt like a tremendous achievement, taking about seven years to attain the SM level. This new position came with a salary of just under $45,000, which represented a seven-percent increase from my previous role as ASM. That might seem like a robust increase in pay, but it pales in comparison to the responsibilities and expectations I was about to undertake. In the beginning, I felt good about my preparations for my new position and walked around with my chest puffed out. But as it got closer to my first day as store manager, I kept experiencing those

"God, please be with me" moments of apprehension and awe as I started to comprehend the magnitude of my responsibility.

Back then, I was living just outside of Orlando, a one-hour commute to the Daytona store. As I cruised across the I-4 highway the morning of my debut, dressed in new jeans and a shirt with my inexpensive briefcase in tow (could not afford a TUMI™ at that time), I felt confident and ready. Until I pulled into the parking lot and it hit me: there is no grace period at Home Depot. Once you accept a role, everything having to do with that store and building is your responsibility. For store managers at Home Depot, there is no "In Training" badge. You are the captain of the ship and it becomes a 24/7 responsibility. You start to realize the enormity of the weight on your shoulders.

As an assistant store manager, you had a store manager above you to partner with and bounce ideas off. You were not totally responsible because the buck stopped with the person one level higher. With my promotion to Daytona Store Manager, every single decision, aspect, and result now rested squarely on my shoulders. It reminded me that at each rung of the ladder, the level above seems to be easier until you get there. When you do, it's like, "Lord help me, what did I get myself into?"

Although it may feel and look easier when you're on the outside looking in, you don't get a true sense of those extra responsibilities until you take them on yourself. Every aspect – a customer service complaint, or an associate wanting to talk to you the moment you walk into the building because the previous store manager never gave them a raise or issued them a terrible performance review...the list of grievances and problems goes on and on. And at that level, you must represent yourself and your company's standards with professionalism, confidence and humility.

My staff in Daytona knew of me, but because I'd worked over in Orlando, none of them had met me in person. Although 29 years-old at the time, I looked young for my age (thanks to family genetics), so when I first walked into the store, a couple of associates assumed I was a customer and asked if they could help me. When I introduced myself, the reaction on their faces was one of disbelief. "You're our new store manager? There's no way."

Associates and customers always assumed I was playing dress-up; I could just see it in the way they looked me up and down, checking out my attire. Many customers would look me right in the face, and go, "No way, really, come on, where is THE Store Manager?" For me, it had its positives and negatives, but let me tell you, after the first few times, it got annoying when I had to pull my driver's license out of my wallet, just to prove my age to customers. Of course, many people told me I should appreciate the fact that I had a youthful face, but it became a point of challenge because there were associates and managers in that building who were older than me. I had to earn their respect through my behaviors and the way I worked with them. Daytona was a great mix of demographics and ages. We had a lot of young folks and part-timers, whether college kids, people working two jobs, or those for whom it was their first entry into the workforce. There were also some veterans and older folks in key positions, to whom I referred as my "mature citizens."

Another reason I was excited to take the Daytona store? It sat right next to the Daytona Speedway. You could go on the roof through the hatch, hear the cars, and see activity coming around the corners of the racetrack. Right next to the track was the airport, where notable people like the President (watching Air Force 1 land and takeoff is truly special), and others would fly in, to attend the races. Daily, we could watch the planes banking as they descended. Although the store was a little bit inland and not right on the beach, I had many reasons to like it, despite my commute from Orlando, where I'd just built a home.

Like many others before me, Daytona was where I learned how to be a store manager since it acted as a training location for those just stepping onto that rung of the Home Depot ladder. Considered a *country club* store with a great clientele, but a lesser volume of foot-steps on a weekly basis than our inner-city stories, the Daytona customer base included many snowbirds and Canadians. In a lower-traffic store, it's easier to maintain appearances and keep everything clean because it doesn't get shopped as much. Daytona tended to be one of the best-looking stores in the district and I learned early that I had to maintain that standard, per Robert Gilbreth, who was still my district manager (DM).

District managers could spend an hour with you or stay 10 -to- 12 hours if they wanted to, on visits or store walks. Robert liked to visit Daytona on a Friday, and as I recall our first few visits were excellent...that is, until the day he called me to the office over the PA system. When I arrived, he lit me up over the terrible condition of the store and its maintenance problems, along with the customer service issues he'd witnessed. "I want you to understand something," he declared. "I like coming to Daytona Beach on a Friday because I know it will end my week well and give me momentum into the weekend. I like going home in a good mood, so that's why I always come here because the store always looks good and is functioning well. But today, it wasn't there."

Initially I told him I'd already walked the building and observed some of the same things. Because store managers usually closed on Friday nights, I was scheduled to close that evening. Informing him I was due back on Saturday, I promised to recover the building and ensure that when he came back for his next visit, he would see a noticeable change. And he did, because I followed through on that promise.

Robert's challenge reminded me once more that I wasn't just responsible for one or a few departments; the scale in which I was operating had become infinitely larger. But you can't do it yourself. Each level you attain, your position becomes more influential versus directly actionable. That's hard for many people to process and move forward, and it often leads to their downfall. They continue to do too much on their own, thinking it's the best way to accomplish their goals. But living by the old maxim, *if you want a job done right, do it yourself* only handicaps your team by failing to include and teach them. In the end, it will stymie the accomplishments and progress.

When you're in charge of the whole shebang, you must optimize every individual's talents to the highest degree. As a store manager, don't let your mouth write checks you can't cash. What comes out of your mouth becomes something people take word-for-word, and as I've learned from experience, there is no leeway. I got caught in that a couple times, whether it involved an associate with a pay increase or a customer with a problem. Repeating this mistake in the Philly store would put my career in jeopardy, as you will discover in more detail.

The store manager role is perceived as one of the best positions at Home Depot. To use another analogy, it's like being the mayor of your own little city, where, every now and then, the governor of the state will visit with you to interact on various issues. The personality, execution, behaviors, and mentality of that building all reflect the store manager. If customer service remains prominent on a store manager's radar screen, and he or she not only preaches it but leads by example, the store will be an excellent customer service location. Conversely, if the store manager fails at customer service and leading by example, the store will develop a reputation for bad service. It's a daunting responsibility. Going back to the fishbowl metaphor, as the lead fish in the bowl, you must excel at everything you do and represent everything you want your store to be. The pressure gets so intense that sometimes you can go overboard.

"A genuine leader is not a searcher for consensus, but a molder of consensus." —Dr. Martin Luther King, Jr.

Shortly after taking the store, I started receiving customer service complaints. One day, I sat in my office with my assistant store managers brainstorming the best approach to resolving the issue. My assistant managers felt I needed to get emotional with the entire staff about customer service, since I was the new SM. Due to my own passionate, emotional nature, their suggestion appealed to me, and I decided to create a visual. Turning to Charlie, one of my assistant managers, I said, "I want you to get me every job application that's been submitted to us over the last six months." In the pre-internet era, it was all paperwork; it wasn't like you could just submit online or at a computer kiosk. We used long-form job applications.

The day of the meeting, we placed two office supply boxes filled with hundreds and hundreds of submitted job applications behind me. As I addressed the gathering of about 150-175 people, I started to get into the topic of customer service, relaying to the associates what I'd heard and what customers had presented to me. With our staunch competitor Lowe's located just a few miles away, I made it even more compelling that we were receiving complaints from customers like, "Oh, I guess you just want me to give my business to Lowe's."

I became very passionate, to the point where I warned, "Listen, if any single person here doesn't want to be part of my team or work for Home Depot, or wear the orange apron anymore, I have people who are ready and willing to replace you." With that, we dumped the job applications on the floor.

No, it was not my finest moment.

In fact, it was one of my worst moments because some employees broke down in tears, feeling like I'd threatened their job, which, let's face it, I did. In my zeal for the overarching dramatization to get them to understand policy and expectations, I inadvertently put a wall up with some associates. Others rightly felt they were not a part of the problem. One of the store's supervisors, Jeff Patterson, courageously stood up and yelled, "This is bulls**t!" He was expressing frustration for having to listen to the message and more importantly, how I had delivered it. I acknowledged his input, citing his emotion as the solution to align our efforts with company expectations. Not too long ago, I visited the store and Jeff, who has now worked thirty-three years with the company. We had a good laugh reminiscing about that meeting. Time does heal all wounds. However, back in the day, I had to roll up my sleeves and repair an incredible amount of damage after that store meeting.

True, customer service improved because my management team

and I were out in the store inspecting, but I had to rebuild relationships. I hosted multiple one-on-one conversations with associates about how they felt about that meeting, how they fit in, and how we could make improvements as a team. My lesson? Don't broad-brush a subject with a large audience. In my private meetings with associates, those who already did their jobs well implored me, "Hey, whoever's not performing, get rid of them because we don't want them around either."

It's easier to manage by exception. In this example, based on my observation, I should have recognized in a positive form or fashion, those employees who were exceeding expectations. In the end, the associates told me they respected my passion and understood where I was coming from, but that I hadn't delivered the message in the right way. That was a good lesson for me in self-management, when many were looking to me for guidance. Manage by exception, not in total, and be careful not to generalize topics that were best dealt with in a surgical manner. Address the real offenders, expectations, and results.

We took an ultra-positive approach with the next meeting: we served better food, gave out more customer service awards, and celebrated achievements. From that day on, we avoided negative talk about customer service and instead read praise letters from customers and rewarded good associates. To drive the point home, we made it a big deal and singled out those exemplary associates for recognition. From the experience, I learned that one of greatest things you can do as a leader is praise in public and hold accountable in private.

This authentic fear of dealing with employees individually in private, closed-door meetings delays the solution to the problem at hand and hurts morale. If there are folks in your building who are not performing to expectations, the rest of your employees know it. The longer they witness that non-productive behavior, the more negatively it impacts their motivation to go the extra mile. As a manager, you earn respect not only by rewarding stellar performance but by addressing unacceptable performance as quickly as possible. This practice demonstrates respect and concern for members of your team who are doing it well and allows employees who are not fulfilling their tasks to the best of their ability to make improvements.

In those pre-computerized days, we handwrote the schedules. Often, members of my staff would come to me and say, "Boss, please, I do not want to close the building with this guy."

"Why?"

"Because he doesn't do anything. I get frustrated that I have to do everything and he's standing around."

You begin to realize where and how pieces fit together, and what is important. In a business entity, personnel and morale are one of the top priorities because they can either make you or break you. My focus in Daytona was to build up the morale by helping all team members understand the importance of carrying their weight.

IT'S NOT ABOUT YOU

You cannot impose expectations for every individual who works with or for you as if they *were* you. Because I had been an associate, a department supervisor, and an assistant manager, I started judging my team on what I would have done and how I performed in each of those roles. That is not always fair, because not everybody is you. Not everyone responds in the same way you do.

Whatever you do, avoid the verbiage, "Here's what I would have done." Instead, focus on that individual and how you can maximize their talents and optimize their opportunities. Many leaders think of opportunities as weaknesses, but I always looked at them as a vehicle for improvement. Early on, I learned to talk *less* and listen *more* in my conversations with associates. I've seen managers at all levels who love to hear themselves talk. When they were done, they thought they had checked the box and done something wonderful. Sadly, they had not improved the situation one iota because they didn't listen to what was being said.

One of the other things I did as a store manager was make myself accessible. Once again, I credit my former coworker Kate from my days as garden department supervisor for teaching me the importance of spending time out on the floor with my team. When I achieved my promotion to store manager, I continued this practice as much as I possibly could – no easy task in the days before smartphones, which allow you to move freely around the store and still make or take important calls. Back then, Home Depot had hundreds of push-button phones to access the PA system, take customer calls, etc. As a manager, when a pressing matter dictated that you pick up the receiver to talk to someone on the other end of the line, you had to stay in the area where the phone was located, or transfer the call to another extension and run to that phone to continue. We did not need Fitbits back then, as we passed 10,000 steps with ease, every single day.

Good managers always find a way to be with their team where they are functioning, even if only for five minutes here and ten minutes there. While there, you must be a bit different. Yeah, you could be all business and lead by example, but that was also the time when you could make an impact on your associates, whether you gave them a pat on the back for something you saw them doing, asked them how they were feeling because they'd been out sick three days before, or inquired about their mom because you knew she'd had surgery the previous week. If you're not out on the sales floor, you're not going to hear this stuff. You're not going to know what's going on in your employee's lives to foster a relationship with them on a human level. Being accessible is one way to do it.

My other method for developing mutual respect between my staff and me was my open-door policy. This is nothing new; everybody pays lip service to this concept, including top leaders in variety of industries and corporations, but only those who truly walk the talk, regardless of their business or industry, will be successful. Why? Maintaining an open-door policy gives them a pulse on what's going on and how people feel.

Here's another area where I credit my dad, who formed an employee committee of the most vocal people when he was a SM. He did this because he knew they were in tune with everything going on in the store and would not hesitate to share what was on their minds. Pretty smart, right? Then, all he had to do was listen, take notes and react. Whenever an associate called, approached, or asked me, "Hey, can I talk to you about something?" I'd first respond with, "Hey is this a 9-1-1 or can we schedule something?" If it was a 9-1-1, I'd say, "Come on. Do we need to go back into the office? Do you want to just go outside and talk? What do you want to do?"

At every rung of the ladder, I prided myself on the fact that my associates knew I had empathy for them because I had been one of them. I never lost the understanding of what it was like to be an hourly employee. Since I had that background and experience, I could tell them, "Hey, I was there. I've been in your shoes." Early in my career, I discovered that the way you engage with people can get to the meat of the matter faster, for everyone's benefit. You'll never get to the bottom line unless you open them up somehow. With every advancement up the ladder, I developed these practices until they became ingrained in my mind. And it wasn't only important for me to be strong in these skills-sets, but my teams too. No matter my role or location, I taught every team I worked with to engage with others in this way.

While I am on this topic, I want share something that bothers me: I do not understand why everyone uses the term "I understand" with individuals when they truly do *not* understand. They utilize the term attempting to make the other individual understand that they understand, hoping it yields an overall better understanding.

Did you get all that? I typed it and I don't get it.

Let me put it another way: when interacting with any individual, regardless of matter, IF you cannot, with legitimacy, understand what the other individual is sharing do not say "I understand." You might think you are showing empathy, but instead, you are being disingenuous and possibly damaging your integrity. For example, if you have never been a part-time associate, you cannot, for all intents and purposes, claim understanding when a part-time associate communicates a relatable situation. In a worst-case example, if your parents are still alive, you cannot tell someone who has lost a parent that you understand their grief. It just does not work.

Instead, you can and should acknowledge the communication by thanking them and demonstrating that you heard what they said. Here is a great little phrase that will take any conversation to the next level: "Tell me more." Too many managers and leaders are quick to hijack a conversation in their zeal to resolve an issue as quickly as possible. Men are terrible at this, whether at work or at home, because for them it is all about the bottom line. To this day, I still make a concerted effort to allow Pam to finish her thoughts before I jump in. In addition, avoid closed-ended questions. They may be the easiest to utilize, but they often stymy a conversation and inhibit the real content or basis for the interaction. Stay away from questions that could end with a "yes" or "no" answer. Try these words instead to truly engage with another person: who, what, where, when, why and how. You will be amazed how differently the conversation will go.

This can work at home and at work, as I learned from my own experience. For example, when I got home from work, I would ask Jackie if she had a good day at school. She would respond yes, she had. I would reply, "Good honey." And that would be it, until our next conversation. One day, I managed to get home at a decent time, ahead of her arrival from school. I'd been feeling distant from her and wanted to engage at a higher level. When she arrived, the conversation started the same as always. Then, I asked her to sit at the kitchen table with me while Pam watched and listened. Thinking something was wrong, Jackie felt apprehensive. I asked her to tell me more. She asked about what. I asked her to elaborate on her school day, proceeding in an engaging manner, using all the right words. Then, I listened and responded. A half-hour later, we had finished one of the best conversations I could remember. The difference in this exchange between us blew her away, and I felt better and closer to her. Plus, I had learned things that I did not know up that point in time. Now I truly believe that quality interactions lead to exceptional results. The best way to impact all humans, personally and professionally, is with interactive communication.

In fact, one of the accomplishments in my career I'm most proud of is the amount of people I promoted after they'd worked with me – some of whom rose higher in the company than I did. I'll always consider that part of my legacy as I relocated nine times all over the country and influenced a broad spectrum of individuals at various levels. One of my bosses once joked that instead of the six degrees of Kevin Bacon, it should be the six degrees of Erik Dardas at Home Depot, which I took as a high compliment. At present, one of my former team members, promoted after working for me as a store manager, is now the president of one of the three Home Depot United States divisions.

Aside from a pay increase, the store manager role comes with many benefits. When you're hourly, you're eligible for certain things, but as you work your way up, especially when you become salaried, those benefits increase. The company's annual meeting is one of the perks. Although it now takes place in March, in the early days of Home Depot, annual meetings were held in August or September to coincide with the company's birthday. Store manager and higher-up positions attended. Every year we establish a sales plan for the entire company. If we hit a certain amount of revenue above and beyond the plan, it was a celebration meeting, where everyone could bring their significant other. Thanks to Home Depot, I've been to Hawaii, Puerto Rico, and Las Vegas. In 1996, I met the performance standards and was awarded a trip to the summer Olympics in Atlanta, where we were a corporate sponsor. Having the privilege of attending these functions in wonderful settings truly was a blessing. We took pride in getting there, as we knew we had earned the ticket to the show.

The Hawaii trips of the past, which included an all-together session with husbands and wives, gave me insights into Bernie and Arthur. As a surprise one year, we received a small, Lucite award with mini Home Depot aprons encased within it, and words of gratitude for all we did engraved on the accompanying plaque. Bernie and Arthur stood on the stage and called out each name individually. You walked up, accepted your statue, and moved through a receiving line like a wedding. As I strolled by Bernie, statue in hand, he grabbed me and pulled me into a bear hug. Obviously, because of my dad's elevated position within the company, he was more familiar with me. I'll never forget that moment, because Bernie greeted everybody with enthusiasm. It felt so good when I came out of that hug – a feeling I'll always remember. By the way, I still have the award.

Just as with the "dog-and-pony shows" in the field, Bernie and Arthur were also accessible at these annual meetings. They even hosted separate events with the significant others of the store managers, much like the Town Hall meetings in the stores, where they could freely ask questions and make comments. They understood the commitment that came with a management level position: the hours, the funky schedule, the stress. Invariably, somebody's husband or wife would say something so completely off the wall and ridiculous it made their spouse look bad. Most often, the complaint revolved around the work-life balance and the long hours store managers were required to work. Because nothing remained a secret and everything leaked out of these gatherings, it was embarrassing for the store manager whose spouse made work hours an issue. Regardless, Bernie and Arthur showed much support, and people appreciated them taking the time to host them while they were in paradise.

For the past seven years, Home Depot's annual meeting has been held at Mandalay Bay. Compared to other areas, Vegas is inexpensive and features large enough venues – which is probably why Lowe's stays at the same hotel the week ahead of us. As they are leaving Las Vegas, we are all arriving, much to the delight of the hotel staff, since our bar tabs are higher and Home Depot people tip better. No matter what it was, we had to do it better in our ongoing rivalry with our toughest and most despised competitor, something I'll delve into in greater detail in an upcoming chapter on competition.

However, as I mentioned before, these meetings were not all fun and games. Yes, we had a little bit of free time, but mostly they entailed an abundance of communication about company strategy and guidance, and presentations by various directors of functions like operations, IT, human resources, etc. Sometimes they'd broadcast new things that were coming. Everybody looked forward to that. In 1999, the year that marked Home Depot's 20th Anniversary, the annual meeting was held in its home base of Atlanta. When we flew in, it was obvious how much the city of Atlanta and the state of Georgia loved Home Depot: the city had basically *become* Home Depot, with our banners on every light post. USA Today published an exclusive special edition on Home Depot, Coca-Cola did a run of small Coke bottles with the Home Depot and Coke logos, and we received watches etched with the Home Depot logo and the words "20th Anniversary," along with shirts, pins, and other Home Depot gear.

Bernie and Arthur even brought in the rock group, The Eagles – minus Don Henley since he and Glen Frey were feuding at the time. When Frey walked out on stage he remarked, "Wow, you guys must've had one *helluva* year," insinuating how amazing it was that Home Depot could afford to schedule them to play at the meeting. In addition to the Eagles, this annual meeting's entertainment line-up featured comedian Rita Rudner, who cracked on Bernie and Arthur a little bit – much to the crowd's amusement – and Broadway dancers. In short, the home office spared no expense in celebrating the 20th Anniversary milestone with all its achievements, but as you'll read, complacency set in soon after.

"From everyone to whom much has been given, much will be required; and from the one to whom much has been entrusted, even more will be demanded." —Luke, 12:48

At the beginning of this chapter, I mentioned that my store manager promotion came with a salary of just under $45,000 –

$44,500 to be exact. But as you climb higher in the company, your bonus percentage eligibility increases. As a store manager, you could get 50 percent of your salary as a bonus, versus 25 percent as an ASM, depending on how well your store performed. For me, knowing I could receive $22,250 in one check at the end of the year was a big deal...and no, Washington D.C. politicians, I didn't consider my bonus to be "crumbs." My team and I killed ourselves to earn our eligibility bonuses in full. Once you earned your first bonus at Home Depot, it became like a drug – every year you had to have it. Motivated and driven to earn it? You betcha!

Store managers could also earn more stock options, which gave them a larger ownership in the company. Your obligations and expectations expanded, but you were rewarded for it. By salary alone, we didn't make as much as our counterparts in other businesses, but with the bonus and stock as a total package, we were very well taken care of. Since the bonus was a direct result of our own performance, it felt even better to receive it. Home Depot's bonus policy went against today's prevalent entitlement mentality. Instead of the company announcing, "Hey, you're going to get this much in your pay because of tenure, or just because," you had to earn that sucker. As an assistant store manager and store manager, you drove that accomplishment in the right way – with your team – beginning with customer service and overall operational controls within your store. You did everything you could to make your store as profitable as possible, so you and your assistant store managers could bonus. At that time, hourlies were not eligible for sales bonuses, which meant your goal and challenge was to help them understand all that was available to them at higher levels, providing motivation to achieve that next promotion. Everyone is entitled to the same opportunity, but it is what they do with it that separates them from the rest – it must be earned.

Certain leaders fail to recognize the importance of their interactions on lower-level employees in helping them with their career paths. Reflecting on what I've discussed in the communications chapter, if something was on my mind, I'd pen a letter to my associates and team and make copies. Sometimes, I'd tape one to their paychecks, other times to their lockers. I used a variety of methods. To demonstrate the impact this made on another individual, I'll share a real-life story. Six years ago, at the annual meeting in Vegas, I ran into a young lady named Felicia Lynam. Felicia had been a department manager in the Panama City Florida store when I was a district manager for that area. In that role, I continued my practice of writing letters to my teams; little did I realize that decades later, I'd have a conversation about them I'd never forget.

Felicia, who was with her store manager, Tim Pardue (now a director at the corporate office), said, "Hey, Erik, I want to show you something." With that, she reached into her purse and pulled out a letter I had written approximately 10 years earlier. Unknown to me at the time, she'd saved them all and carried some in her purse. Whether they deal with me or a specific topic, she rereads them often for guidance and renewed perspective.

It just blew me away. You do things in the here and now to address what you think is important, but realize it's also an investment, just like buying 1,000 shares of stock. If you look at everything you do in that regard – coaching, training, communication, behavior or all you do on behalf of your team – it could potentially carry that kind of weight, positive or negative. I'm proud of that fact that Felicia saved every one of my letters and that they have helped her advance her own career at Home Depot. Oh, by the way, she had earned the right to be there through her promotion to store manager and her exceptional performance in the role.

Again, from a leadership perspective, connecting professionally with everyone in your sphere of influence, will differ from person-to-person in terms of the method and amount of time invested. You learn some lessons the hard way. Years later when I became a district manager, I developed a professional relationship with a woman who was the administrative assistant for a store manager. An attractive, talented employee, she helped me organize and communicate district and community events, and store and district meetings. I utilized her skills and talents to help the stores and me – only to suffer false perceptions of a romantic involvement from other team members.

Why did it bother me so much?

There will always be employees who are envious because you didn't work with them to the same degree. Those employees need to look in the mirror, first, for self-reflection before allowing the big, green monster to rear its ugly head. On another occasion, I did not select a female candidate who was a department supervisor for an assistant store manager position. I declined to promote this candidate, as she was not quite ready. She wrote a nasty letter to the home office, making false accusations about me. Although communication had taken place, informing her why we had made the decision, she chose to vent in an inappropriate manner. Thanks to incidents like these, you see how relationships intertwine and what you can and cannot do. No matter how hard you try, the harsh reality is, you are not going to make everybody happy, so always choose the absolute best candidate for a position or role.

WORK AND LOVE IN DAYTONA BEACH

My promotion to store manager of the Daytona Home Depot also impacted my personal life in the most wonderful way possible because it was where I first met Pam Lucas, the computer room supervisor and the woman who would become my wife. Truth be told, this isn't one of those love at first sight stories. She thought I was good-looking, with a nice tush, but thanks to my early behavior and attitude, felt I was impeding her role. An extremely talented lady who just happened to be extremely attractive, with a great figure and huge, blue eyes, Pam was a mainstay for the store. She executed on several levels and roles, providing vital support for the overall operations. Her office was directly across from mine; I could look through my door into her window and see her surrounded by gigantic office printers and computers that seemed to dwarf her...this was, after all, the 90s.

WHY DID SHE HATE MY GUTS?

Aside from being full of myself as a new SM, when I first got there, I challenged Pam to make sure that she and her co-worker in the computer room were trained to be cash register relievers. Per Home Depot policy, we trained everyone in the store to do this, so they could respond when the lines got too long. But it wasn't what I said; it was the arrogant way I said it. "Listen, when I call you up there, I want you guys running. We're going to need everybody's help," I informed her. She just stared at me with a defiant look on her face that said, "What! Are you kidding me?" We butted heads over my order, due to the sheer amount of responsibilities she had, along with my other demands for reports and paperwork. In response to her resistance, I asserted my authority as the store manager, and that was the way it was going to be. I handled it wrong. I should have taken the time to explain my position more, then listen to her side. Believe it or not, from that inauspicious beginning, our relationship grew and deepened over time as I became more professional in my interactions.

Over time, we developed romantic feelings for each other. When I decided to take a vacation in Colorado, I asked Pam to join me and she accepted. In those days, you had to fill out a manual form for your vacation request, which the supervisor would sign off on. Since I was the store manager, I had to submit mine to Robert Gilbreth. Operating under the illusion that Robert didn't have a clue about Pam and me, we flew to Colorado and enjoyed a wonderful vacation that included accommodations at a lodge and a champagne hot-air balloon flight. When we returned, I got a phone call from Robert at the store.

"Hey, how was your vacation?" he asked.

"Man, I had a great vacation. I'm glad to be back," I enthused.

"Who'd you take with you?"

"What?"

"Who did you take with you?"

"Oh, I guess you know."

"Yeah, but I want to hear you say it."

"Okay, Pam Lucas went with me."

And he kind of hesitated for a second before adding, "You know we're not going to be able to tolerate that, right? We're going have to do something."

"Okay, what would that be?"

"Well, I have a store over in Orlando we're getting ready to do a large remodel. I want you to take that store. That way, we won't have a conflict if you and Pam want to continue your relationship."

"Absolutely, I will take that store," I affirmed without hesitation. It was a better option than being terminated.

My budding relationship with Pam led to my transfer to Orlando, which was closer to home. The Southland Boulevard location was a smaller store, so, per the blueprints, we knocked down one of the side walls and added 30,000 square feet onto that side. During this remodel, I had to acclimate to a new team; fortunately, I knew some of them because I'd worked as an assistant manager in that area before. We had to move every piece of merchandise in the store to a new area, but it was a lot of fun to make an older store look brand-new again.

About three weeks after we completed the remodel, Home Depot hosted a meeting for the entire company in Orlando. One fateful day as I participated in the annual meeting, I got word that Bernie and Arthur wanted to bring the Board of Directors to walk the remodel that night (gulp!). Problem was, I couldn't leave to go to the store; they wouldn't let me. At my first opportunity, I called the store and put my assistant store managers on speaker phone to tell them what was going on. Yes, the store looked phenomenal. It was brand-new and ready, but I wanted to keep it clean and make sure it was up to the standards demanded by company officers. Once I told them what we needed to do, the assistant store managers rallied the team.

When the meeting finally ended at 5 p.m., I drove like Tony Stewart back to the store. Lucky for me, I didn't kill anybody or get a ticket. I arrived to discover my team had done an outstanding job: every part of the store looked perfect. By then it was 6 p.m. and I knew Bernie, Arthur and the Board of Directors – which included presidents and CEOs of other companies – would arrive in an hour. On one hand, it represented an incredible opportunity for exposure, but on the other, it was somewhat terrifying. My adrenaline was pumping, my heart was pounding, and I just wanted them to get there so we could showcase my team and our overall results. I was chomping at the bit. But as I said, the team had rallied the entire store. We were perfect, we were there, and everyone was wearing their orange aprons. Then I had an idea. "Hey, when they get here, let's do the Home Depot cheer at the front door." I was going to lead it and positioned my team so I could see the letters – I DID NOT want to mess up this once-in-a-career experience. Very few leaders at Home Depot had the privilege of hosting a group of this magnitude – not too shabby for a Midwest kid who once couldn't speak in front of a crowd without throwing up!

About 30 minutes before the officers' arrival, a small crowd developed outside the entrance – family members of employees who wanted to meet Bernie and Arthur to thank them for the opportunity to be part of Home Depot. It was completely unplanned. When Bernie and Arthur showed up with the Board, this assembled crowd welcomed them with hugs, handshakes, and smiles. As I witnessed the scene, I realized the impact an organization has on everyone, not just employees...and not just me. People had tears in their eyes as they relayed stories like, "We were unemployed and couldn't even put food on the table until Home Depot came along."

Once the executives made it through the doors and we did the cheer (correctly), I led them on the walk. They asked questions and expressed genuine interest in hearing my team's thoughts. Up to that point, it was probably the highlight of my career. I felt proud because I'd not only represented the company well, but the Dardas family too. Everybody knew my dad. Now, here was his kid, who just supervised a remodel, walking this high-level group through his store. Not only was it a cool experience, it just might have been the incident that saved my posterior down the road. (I promise, I'm getting to that; bear with me).

After about an hour and-forty-five minutes, they left. Once you had shaken each person's hand on the way out and watched them walk to their vehicles, the first thing you did was take a deep breath because you lived through it. Your legs felt as if you'd just run the Boston Marathon – you thought you might physically collapse from profound relief. In a real sense, it was anti-climactic when it was finally over because you almost felt numb. In that moment, however, I felt nothing but pride, my future goal of becoming a vice-president and an officer for Home Depot foremost on my mind. I drew in another deep breath, turned around, and saw nearly 30 associates standing there, all inquiring about how it went. They wanted that affirmation because they were also invested in the outcome, having executed to the highest degree possible to accomplish the remodel.

So, I gathered myself up quickly and thought, "Hey, this isn't about you. This is about the team." Then I got everybody together, associates, assistant managers, and all store personnel. After briefly recapping the event and praising them for their exceptional efforts, I advised, "Don't bring any food tomorrow, because I'm buying breakfast, lunch, and dinner for everybody in the building."

Throughout my career, I often told my associates, "I am so privileged to work with people who make me look good. I got to lead the walk, but if every one of you could have been there with us, I would have had you there because you did all the work. They (Bernie, Arthur, the Board of Directors) love this place. They *absolutely* love this place."

After I affirmed their accomplishments, I took it a step further. As a company, we hang big signs at the end of our aisles that we referred to as RBFS: *Really Big F***ing Signs* (*I think you can figure it out*). I wrote a letter on one of those signs and posted it in the break room, to thank everybody because not every member of the staff was there for the walk. Some people had the day off, though some who were not scheduled to work came in. What is the lesson here? Leaders must have a sense of team versus an individual – as a manager and leader of your business, that's where you need to live.

A DOSE OF COLD WATER

The next day, following the success of the remodel, we had a meeting in a hotel auditorium for the entire day. Everybody was there with their coffee and getting settled, then Bernie, Arthur and the Home Depot officers came out on stage to take their seats. During this session, Bernie took multiple questions from the audience, kind of like the big Town Hall meetings, where everyone provided questions or topics they wanted to discuss. With Arthur and the rest of the executive team sitting on the stage, Bernie would get to all of them. This time, however, things went a little differently.

"I want to get to your stuff," Bernie announced, "but first, let me have the entire Orlando team of store managers and district managers stand up." We all stood up with the success of the walk-through fresh in our minds, believing he was about to commend us for a job well done, while we received a roaring round of applause and basked in Bernie's adulation. It was going to be a memorable moment...or so we thought. Instead, Bernie told us how effing unhappy he was with the entire team. We were stunned, but he didn't let it ride. "Let me tell you why," he quickly added. "Over the last two days, do you realize what your comp increase in sales was?" Comp increase is a year-over-year measurement of the same day, the same week, the same month. He'd asked our financial people to give him the comps in the Orlando area, versus the rest of the company, for the weeks before his visit. Our numbers were off-the-charts good. So, you might ask, "Why was he so unhappy?" Here's why – and everyone in retail will appreciate this because it speaks to the dog-and-pony shows and your day-by-day attitude. "I hate you guys today. I absolutely hate you. You want to know why?" Bernie went on.

Our comps were 30% year-over-year, which is an insane number in the retail industry (it's usually in the single digits or low double-digits). "You want to know why you got that number these past couple days. Why do you think?" He paused for effect. "Because you got ready for *me*. You spent all your time, you worked day and night, you killed yourselves to get ready for me. Did I buy anything when I was here? No. So, why don't you get ready for the customers every day like you get ready for me, and our numbers would be even better? This tells me what your effort could be and where it might not be on a day-to-day basis. Now, sit your asses down!"

Stunned, we thought the world was coming to an end. It was just hard to breathe as we all looked at each other like, *what the hell just happened?* We make our stores look perfect when we know Bernie and Arthur, the Board of Directors, and/or any officer is stopping by. You really put on the show, and they discount those visits because they know you prepped. You killed your people for those visits, but you got more kudos if they showed up unannounced and your store looked great, because they knew with scheduled visits, you had time to make everything perfect.

Many associates complained when an officer was coming to town because they knew the urgency was going to pick up and we would put the pedal to the metal on overtime, hours worked, etc. It was a crazy time. As with owning a boat, there are two great days: the day you buy, and the day you sell. You love the fact that you're getting a visit, but the second greatest day is the moment they walk out of your store and drive away in their SUVs because everybody knows it's over; you can breathe and get back to your normal operations again.

Because of their message and intensity, you had more respect for Bernie and Arthur, who cared deeply for their employees. And it wasn't just lip service. They even paid for people to go to the doctor or dentist if they couldn't afford it on their own. In terms of their commitment to a healthy lifestyle, they were ahead of their time. I remember one annual meeting where Bernie got very emotional about everyone's health. He had noticed that many of us had gained weight and some of us were obese. Out of concern for our overall health and well-being, he implored us to lose weight if necessary, exercise, get enough rest, and maintain healthy eating and drinking habits. Bernie engaged in a dialogue about how he wanted every person in the room to live a long and prosperous life, where we could enjoy all the fruits of our labor. It's just another example of how he delivered a message as if he was your dad or your grandfather putting his arm around you and saying, "Listen, here's some tough love." You felt as if he truly cared for you on a human level, not just as an employee of Home Depot.

MOVING ON UP, TO THE GREAT WHITE NORTH

When I worked in Orlando as a store manager, my dad was vice-president of the Northeast Division, based out of New Jersey, with Larry Mercer as the President. Back then, Home Depot had 19 divisions, versus three today. Dad and the other officers came into town for their own meeting. Dad invited me to join them for dinner at Rosie O'Grady's on Church Street Station in Orlando, a cool, hipster area. I felt Intimidated because the whole group of officers would be there, but since my father offered to let me sit with him, I agreed to it. Although it was open to the public, the Home Depot people sat in one section of the restaurant.

All the sudden, I saw a couple dinner rolls fly across the room. You can imagine what happened next: one landed on our table. I looked at Dad and asked, "What is going on?" He replied, "Throw it back." There they were, the Home Depot officer group...and dinner rolls were flying in public. Not like John Belushi in *Animal House*, but a little crazy. I knew many of them because of my dad and my interactions with them. Having played baseball, I could throw a wicked dinner roll. It got out of hand a bit before it finally calmed down.

"How does this happen Dad?" I asked, somewhat shocked at the entire scene.

"Stress impacts people in unique ways. This was just a way to blow off some steam. We didn't get kicked out," he replied, as if that made it all okay. He was right: despite my fears, they did not order us to leave the premises, probably because they knew how large the bar tab would be. I mention this incident because it helped me to realize that stress does not only affect employees at lower levels. It inhabits every level. That evening at Rosy O'Grady's I had been a witness (and a participant) to a scene that personified the human element within an organization, no matter the stature.

Soon after, my dad was asked to open the Midwest division, which included Ohio, Indiana, Illinois and Michigan. It was a natural fit since our family is from Michigan, and he agreed to the relocation. Vern Joslyn, the man who replaced my father in the Northeast division, called me right away. "Now that your dad is gone, I want your butt up here."

"Where do you want me?"

It turned out, Home Depot was opening a brand-new store in Gaithersburg Maryland from the ground-up, the first to feature a two-story parking deck. By then, I'd used the store manager bonus I'd earned that year to purchase Pam her engagement ring. Right after I'd received it, I went to a jewelry store and picked out the one we'd both selected. When I accepted the relocation, Pam and I opted to get married right before we moved. Since I had a high amount of respect for her parents, Barb and Jack, I wanted them to know I wanted to do things the right way. We got married the week before we moved up to Gaithersburg to begin our new adventure, without the time to take a honeymoon. It was yet another sacrifice that seemed appropriate at the time but remains a regret to this day.

Ladders and Learnings

- Differentiate yourself through your work ethic and behaviors.
- Embrace the company culture.
- For critical issues, respond don't react. Take your time, breathe, think your way through it, then act.

Executive Memo

With respect to serious topics, conversations and results, never broad-brush your employees. Always take a one-on-one approach – whether it's to recognize an individual's accomplishments or hold them accountable for something they failed to do well. If not, you run the risk of alienating your team, diminishing morale, and hurting productivity. Never judge others in your own image. Every member of your team is an individual with their own unique skills-set and experience.

5

FROM NORTHEAST SUBURBIA TO THE INNER-CITY: WHAT HAVE I GOTTEN US INTO?

"Of course, it's hard. It's supposed to be hard. If it were easy, everybody would do it. Hard is what makes it great."

— *A LEAGUE OF THEIR OWN*

M oving to Gaithersburg didn't just involve adjusting to a new, colder climate and living together as husband and wife; about a month-and-a-half after settling into our new home, Pam discovered she was pregnant. We were thrilled by the prospect of becoming parents; little did I know then, but my child would impact me in profound ways throughout the remainder of my time at Home Depot. The Gaithersburg store was located just outside the I-495 Beltway, north of Washington D.C. My district manager assumed it was going to be a lower volume store, but we came out of the gate with high volume – well over seven figures per week – thanks to an excellent team, many of whom reached higher levels and remain Home Depot employees to this day. We had tremendous fun opening this store and still refer to it in legendary terms.

Profanity was part of Home Depot's vernacular, from the very beginning. I always chalked that up to passion, energy and commitment. One of the first things I noticed when I interacted with my management team was a heightened use of profanity. That's when I put a profanity jar in place. When anyone cursed, depending on the word they used, they owed a certain amount of money to the profanity jar. As the store manager of Gaithersburg, I maintained these policies and procedures with the help of the entire store team. We placed all the money we collected (hundreds of dollars per week) into an employee fund to be used for events and Christmas parties. I must admit, I made my fair share of contributions to the cause, as I was not exempt, and always held myself to the same standards as my team.

THE HUMAN TOUCH YIELDS PROFITABLE REWARDS

Every Home Depot features an outdoor garden center. Attached to it is a ramp with a fenced area, in the rear of the store, where you bring in all your shipments. In this location, we held our opening and closing pep rallies. Depending on the weather, everybody would come out and I would lead it. If assistant managers and department managers had something to share, they spoke up too. In the evening, we repeated the drill, made sure the store was clean, and talked about the next day.

Our competitors, mainly Lowe's, had been sneaking around, trying to get into our building. One day at the meeting, I decided to fire everybody up. They could sense my palpable frustration. "I really can't say how I feel about them right now," I explained, "because I'd have to put some money in the profanity jar."

For a moment, no one said a word. Then all the sudden, my employees threw coins and dollar bills on the ground. I looked at them in surprise, but they responded, "Go." They wanted to hear what was in my heart, so for the next ten minutes, I used every profane word under the sun – except a couple, to hammer on Lowe's.

I did not hold anything back. Years of doing battle with them for every customer gave me plenty of ammunition. As I continued my tirade, they kept throwing money on the ground. By the time it was over, we collected $100 for the employee fund and I felt completely drained. I sat down and somebody got me a bottle of water. I had started with Lowe's as a theme, then transitioned into the significance of each employee's role in making our store as successful as possible. In the weeks and months following, the employees talked about it repeatedly – it meant so much to them that I cared enough to share my thoughts in such a raw, authentic way.

When I look back on these moments with my team, I realize the importance of demonstrating your humanity, not behaving like some programmed robot. As a store manager, there were things you could do to personalize your relationships while keeping them professional. Instead, I'd remind my staff, "You're working *with* me. I just have different initials behind my name."

In the early days, each Home Depot store had a petty cash fund you had to reconcile by handwriting vouchers for every penny spent. As the store manager, I had to sign off on it. Earlier, I mentioned our monthly, 6 a.m. store meetings (which now take place every three or six months). I decided to make them fun and positive, because if I didn't, why would someone want to get up at 5 a.m. to be there by 6 a.m.? What would motivate them to show up? While some store managers provided coffee, orange juice and donuts, in Gaithersburg I forged a relationship with the neighboring Red Lobster to offer 30- to - 40 platters of seafood at my meetings. My team feasted on shrimp, chicken, and fish fillets and...oh those cheddar biscuits. Sometimes we had to go back to get more platters.

As my employees talked to their counterparts in other Home Depot locations, our store developed a reputation. Even though my employees loved it, some people viewed my actions in a negative light and perceived me as "buying morale." I'd tell them, "If I control my petty cash fund, beat my bottom line in profit while we're taking care of the customers and I'm out earning what we spend on Red Lobster, how can you complain about showing my appreciation to my team?" Even my district manager would remark, "Are you kidding me? You spend *this* much on Red Lobster?"

"Would you like to look at my profit and loss statement?" I'd reply. Having already seen it, he knew he'd lose the argument because I could always provide proof that it was a worthwhile investment. I never considered my choice to serve Red Lobster seafood platters as "over the top." I wanted my employees to know I'd take care of them as long as they took care of me and the customers. They earned it. I didn't want to take the cheapest way out because I didn't want them to think that's what I thought of their contribution. Did I win everybody to my side? Of course not. But I won over the majority and that can carry the day. The lesson here? As you achieve success, never, ever, leave your associates or employees behind. Always do what you can to reinforce their inclusion into the result. Those associates would have moved mountains for me, just as I would for Bernie and Arthur.

MERRY CHRISTMAS TO ALL AND TO ALL A – OH CRAP! WHAT IS HAPPENING RIGHT NOW!?

The Gaithersburg store held legendary Christmas parties. Whether a Christmas party or some other event, I always found a way to up my game when it came to doing things for my associates. When the holiday season rolled around, my management team and I chose the date together. That year, we opted to take our employees and their significant others on the Spirit of D.C. Charter Boat. To allow everyone to have a drink or two and not worry about driving, I chartered buses to transport them to the dock in D.C. and bring them back to the store. Pam will attest, I literally could not sleep the night before, and the night of one of these events; I would worry about everyone enjoying themselves and making it home safely.

Once at the party, I never could relax. I didn't want anyone to get out of control and if I noticed it happening, I'd take them outside, put my arm around them, tell them how much I needed them, and worked it out that way. But on this night, we had a fabulous time without incident...or so we thought. Later, when our four chartered buses pulled into the Home Depot parking lot, I saw five fire engines, with lights flashing, stationed in front of my store. I stood in the driver's area on the lead bus hanging onto the bar, going, "Oh man, WHAT now?" Everyone got quiet, watching me to see what I was going to do. We were all dressed to the nines – with me in a tux and Pam in a formal gown. We looked dang good, to handle a crisis. Talk about going from one-hundred-miles-per-hour to zero!

I jumped off the bus to deal with the firemen. They had broken in through the doors by our Garden Center after frigid winter temperatures and weather blew apart our sprinkler system, which set off the alarm. Because none of us had cell phones, they couldn't reach us or our designated emergency contact from another store. In the blink of an eye, we transitioned from holiday joy and fun to crisis. "What a way to bring this night to a close," I remember remarking to my team. But the fire department took excellent care of us; they were easy to work with and assisted us through an unsettling situation. It was during times like these – when I witnessed our first responders' efforts and commitments first-hand – that my respect for them grew. I could write another book about our relationship and interactions with all segments of first responders and how they assisted us in countless ways through the years.

THE CITY OF BROTHERLY LOVE

From Gaithersburg, I traveled further north on the I-95 corridor, where they asked me to open a store in Philly – one of the most impactful stores in my Home Depot history. The Philly stores I managed represented my first exposure to a real inner-city environment, beginning with Roosevelt Boulevard, located in a historic area next to a chop shop where stolen cars were chopped into parts, and a vacated power plant that was no longer functioning. It had a tall tower, which is still there today, with large Home Depot letters guiding the public to our store.

Roosevelt Boulevard was a type-5 store, a prototype at the time, much larger than the ones I'd previously opened. It was 135,000 square feet on the inside, compared to what was normally 100,000 - 120,000 square feet. It featured a larger garden center of 35,000 square feet, versus the average store's 20,000 - 25,000 square feet. But the biggest adjustment for me was coming from a high-end suburban area to an urban atmosphere, with a higher level of diversity in the customer and employee bases. Again, With the help of an exceptional team, I opened Roosevelt Boulevard, where I spent almost four years. As was typical for a new store opening, existing members of management transferred in. Yes, there were some new hires, but generally the management team relocated from other Home Depots in and around the area, or other parts of the country. Back in those days, they hung a list of upcoming stores by the time clock or break room to give associates the opportunity to apply at stores close by, or in other parts of the country.

Like the others, the Roosevelt Boulevard Philly store was fun to open. Opening a new store for the number of weeks it took to accomplish was a nice break from normal operations of an existing store. One of the first things I did was inquire about the power plant to members of the city council. They didn't know whether it would be turned into a residential or commercial complex – or how soon, which inspired me to work with them on an idea I had.

"Is the tower going to stay?" I asked.

"Why?"

"We're new to the city. How about if I put the Home Depot letters on the tower?"

We signed an agreement where we put eight-foot orange letters on the tower to help guide people to the store's location. For the grand opening, we gave our associates special collared shirts with the images of the store and the power plant with our letters on it. (secret: I paid for them with the store's petty cash fund. Shh...don't tell anyone.) Nearly 20 years later, some associates still have those shirts because they still feel pride in being part of the team that opened that store. If you happen to find yourself driving up Roosevelt Boulevard from the city, you can still see that tower miles away in the distance.

CUSTOMERS AND CRIME IN THE INNER CITY

There are different areas of an inner-city environment: the standard portion of low-income/affordable housing, the middle class/blue collar area and the built-up, high-end tourist commercial areas. Retail environments in inner-city stores are much more complex than suburban stores. There's much more on everyone's plate. It tests you every day. It takes a special breed to survive and enjoy retail in an inner-city atmosphere because as a said, it is COMPLEX, having to satisfy many competing priorities. On many occasions, I arrived home mentally fatigued to the point where it almost cost me my sanity. These days, I often tell Pam that she ought to be sainted for her understanding and support back then.

As you might expect, there's a different clientele with inner city stores. Not only is it more diverse, it is needy and urgent. When inner-city customers shop at a Home Depot, it's because they *need* something. Sure, there's a need in a suburban store, but there's also a want. For example, in the suburbs people remodel their bathrooms on a whim; in the city, they remodel their bathrooms because they must. If the sink is leaking, or something is broken, that's got to be fixed asap. Of course, there are exceptions, but trust me, it is just *different* in the big cities.

But clientele is not the only stark difference between the inner city and the suburbs. The shoplifting and other incidents we had to deal with were phenomenal and time-consuming. Criminal element notwithstanding, the store was incredibly successful; right out the chute we beat our sales plan mightily and continued to beat it. But responding to incidents of crime inside the store added an unprecedented layer of stress to our jobs. To be clear on this point: there is also a criminal element within the suburban and rural stores, though in most of them it is nowhere near the level of the urban areas. Throughout my career, I worked in Los Angeles, Washington, D.C., Baltimore, and Philadelphia, some of the largest and most challenging environments. At Depot, we always did as much as we could to assist the communities and the people within them.

One of the worst incidents I remember involved the day a mother came in with her six-year-old son and attempted to steal some merchandise. It was the mid-90s and at that time you could still chase and apprehend shoplifters. As events unfolded, a few of my people got to the chase long before I did. When one of my associates tried to grab her from behind and took hold of her shirt, it ripped off. So, she ran topless through the parking lot, jumped into her car, and took off – leaving her young son behind.

After someone brought him to me and identified him, we called the police department. Then, the woman's family called the store, demanding that we return her son to them. "No," I replied. "The police are on the way and they instructed us to hold onto the child until their arrival. She needs to come back to the store and face what she has done." We took excellent care of the little boy; we brought him to the back, where we gave him a drink and some candy. He wasn't upset. It turned out that his mother was a drug addict (cocaine, etc.) with warrants out for her arrest, prompting social services to show up. Drug addiction fueled much of the crime there; people tried to steal full trays of batteries because they used the acid for some preparation for drugs. Thankfully, our Loss Prevention/Security staff held black belts in martial arts. I thanked God often for John Martinez and Ben Komadina, two of our best in this regard, who helped our team and location remain safe and optimize its results. If not for them, our customers, my team and I would have been hurt – or worse – due to the frequency of these scary incidents. The Loss Prevention/Security Teams fall into the Operational Category of all businesses. In some cases, they do not always get the appreciation and respect they deserve.

SHOPLIFTING OR SUICIDE?

One day, as I was in the men's room, doing my business at a wall urinal, a gentleman walked in and entered a stall behind me. I was in the process of washing my hands when I heard a package being ripped open. "Sir, just so you know, I'm the store manager. I have Loss Prevention here and we do not take kindly to shoplifting. We'll be waiting for you outside," I warned him. No response. I exited the men's room but decided to go back in and stand by the door to make sure he couldn't get out without me seeing him. "Sir," I addressed him. Once again, no response.

"Okay sir, you've left me no choice. I'm going to call the police and we'll deal with it that way." I left to tell one of my associates to alert the authorities. But when I returned to the men's room, I was not prepared for the sight that awaited me: blood was flowing out of the bathroom stall and along the wall. "Sir!" I exclaimed, my adrenaline pumping. I wanted to go into the adjacent stall to see what he was doing, but I couldn't because somebody was already in there. I ran back out and called 911. "I'm not sure what's going on, but you need to tell the police to hurry," I advised them. This was an unprecedented event.

When I ran back into the bathroom, the blood looked like a small stream flowing out of that stall and down the wall. I rushed back out to discover the police were 30 seconds away. Then I tore into the bathroom again. "Sir, will you please answer me?" I pleaded. Still no response.

At last, the police arrived and kicked in the door. When they pulled him out, it was evident he had tried to commit suicide by slicing up both of his arms with the safety knife he'd taken off the shelf and trying to ingest rat poison. By the time the paramedics arrived, there was blood everywhere and he was as white as a ghost. "This guy is 30 seconds from dead," one of them informed me. Although they transported him to the hospital in time to save him, when I called to check on him the next day, they told me he had escaped.

In the aftermath of traumatic events like these, I had to calm the store down, including customers who demanded to know what was going on with 12 police officers and three ambulances on the scene. I wanted nothing more than to go off by myself and take a deep breath but had to return the store to its normal operations. When you work in the inner-city, you must not only expect to deal with harrowing, gruesome incidents like this on a regular basis, but somehow get it out of your system and return to business-as-usual as fast as possible. It was insanity. Events like these build up over time as a collective portfolio. I often say, "What has been seen, cannot be unseen." Years later, other managers who had ran that location and I joked that we should write a book about that store and all we had experienced. Who knows, maybe that will be book number two.

Amid the craziness in the inner-city, you also find out how important police and first responders are to you. It is just the nature of the beast due to economics and density of population. At one point, we had a police substation in the parking lot with a phone line and water, which provided a good crime deterrent. The police reacted faster to anything that happened in that location because they knew their buddies and fellow officers could also be in danger because we'd hired police officers, EMTs, and firemen for part-time positions to supplement their income. And they consistently performed at an exemplary level.

FOREIGN WARS LOCAL CONFLICTS

When I got home to Pam and our baby daughter Jackie, the last thing I wanted to do was talk about my day at work. That was my weakness. No matter how much Pam implored me to talk about it, I refused. And it started to eat at my psyche. We used to joke that if you spent a year at an inner-city store, it was like spending three or four years at a suburban store, in terms of the wear-and-tear it inflicts on you. Aside from sales and customer service, countless other things become part of your day.

And no matter how smoothly my day went, I learned to expect the unexpected. One day, I left the store on time to get home at a decent hour and eat dinner with my family for a change. It was a productive day with no major incidents, so when I walked through the doors to the sight of Pam cooking at the stove, I looked forward to a peaceful evening. That's when my phone rang. It was the store.

"What's up? My God, what's wrong?"

"Erik, you gotta get back to the store," my assistant manager announced.

"Why, what's happened?"

"The SWAT teams are surrounding the building."

"What?! SWAT teams? What are you talking about?"

"SWAT is here, they're at every entrance and exit, they're up on the roof, they're searching all the cars in the parking lot."

"Are you freakin' kidding me!?" See if you can get one of them on the phone and tell them I'm the store manager."

They weren't allowing anyone to enter or exit the building. This incident took place when the Baltic conflicts were raging with Serbia and associated countries. *"What does this have to do with the Home Depot in Philadelphia?"* you might ask. Well, the SWAT teams reported that there were groups from some of those countries, here in Philly, that were robbing major retailers to fund their war efforts back home. They'd received intel that there was a car in the parking lot loaded for war, with weapons and tools, to take out our Home Depot. They planned to break into it, to steal the money out of the safe.

In the end, the car was not there, but this group had broken into Target and some other area retailers previously. SWAT cleared the store in about three hours without incident, but it was scary. You begin to wonder just how much more you can take. All you want to do is run a great business. I will always look the employees and managers in that store, at whatever level, with admiration, gratitude and wonder, because, we survived and thrived, together.

GOING FOR THE GOLD

For a time, Home Depot had a program called "Olympic Job Opportunity Program" (OJOP). Olympic and Paralympic athletes could work for us part-time with flexible hours, to give them time to train and attend competitions. The bonus? They received full-time compensation and benefits. Our store was proud to have employed one of the athletes, Bill Carlucci, who won a bronze medal in rowing at the 1996 Olympic Games in Atlanta, for which Home Depot was a major corporate sponsor. In our eyes, he was a rock star: I mean, come on, an *Olympic athlete* on our team. As I remember, Bill worked hard, had a great demeanor, and demonstrated humility because he considered himself one of us.

All told, for the duration of the program, Home Depot had almost 600 athletes in the program, with 145 medalists. According to an April 12, 2000 article by the New York Times, Home Depot, by itself, had more athletes at competitions than some countries such as Ireland and Egypt. Pretty cool, huh?

IN A LIMO WITH THE MOB

One day at the Roosevelt Boulevard store, I got a page to come up to the returns desk, telling me a customer wanted to talk to me. (Spoiler alert: this time it wasn't to proposition me). When I got up there, I noticed a gentleman dressed in a dark suit with dark, slicked-back hair and dark sunglasses.

"Are you Erik, the store manager?"

"Yes, sir, how can I help you?"

"Um, somebody outside would like to talk to you; please come with me."

"I'm sorry?" I looked outside the door and saw a black limo out front with totally pitch-black windows.

"Please, it's fine. Just come with me."

I leaned over to my returns desk person and said, "Get one of the ASM's up here quickly, please."

As we walked up to the limo, he opened the door and said, "Please, have a seat."

"What?" I looked in and saw a gentleman I did not recognize, although he looked to be a member of *La Famiglia*. However, it wasn't one of Philly's notorious mobsters – I know who you're thinking, but no.

"Are you going to keep the door open?" I asked with extreme apprehension.

He replied, "Yeah, we'll keep the door open."

I sat down in the limo.

"You're Erik?"

"Yes, sir. How can I help you? This is making me nervous, to say the least," I explained, with a tenseness to my voice. I had no freakin' clue what he wanted from me, or why I'd even gotten into his car in the first place.

"Well, relax, I wanted to thank you," he continued.

Oh, thank God, he doesn't want to kill me! Was he about to make me an offer I couldn't refuse? "Sir, what for?"

"Well, you hired my nephew."

"I did? What is his name?" He told me, and it was a young kid right out of high school, who worked as a lot man, loading and shagging the carts.

"I gotta tell you how much I appreciate that. I wanted to stop by, lend you my support, and tell you I want you to treat him the way you would anybody else."

"That was my intention. Because I do all the final job interviews and make the job offers. I will treat him like I would any employee."

"Listen, don't be afraid, if you have to, I want you to kick his ass. I want him to be something. He's a young kid with a good head on his shoulders, but I want you to kick his ass if you need to."

"Absolutely, that's my typical style anyway."

He did not smile, as I had intended it as a joke, somewhat more comfortable now.

"By the way, how is the store doing?"

"Great. We're well above sales estimates, making our profits. Given the environment, we still feel good about how everything is going."

"Good. How's the theft?"

"Truth be told, we have our share. You probably know as well as we do what the clientele can be like at times."

"You hired my nephew. You take care of my nephew. I'm gonna

get the word out. I'm gonna do what I can to keep thieves away from the store."

"You can do that?"

"Yeah, I can do that. I'll do what I can. You have a good day." It was kind of like being dismissed. By now there were almost 20 associates watching what was going on from inside the store, peeking out the doors. When I got out, the other guy gave me a head-nod, slid into the driver seat, and took off.

He had told the truth; my employee was his nephew. I let it be, but the good thing was, from that point on, our theft remained under control. The man, whose name I never got because I never asked, must've put the word out. However, just between you and me, I will give all the credit to my team, who developed several processes and controls to minimize theft. But I made sure I treated his nephew as I would any other employee and took care of him as requested. I did not want to find a severed horse head in my bed, know what I am saying? (Cue *The Godfather* theme music).

The mob does wield some influence in Philly, and I remember standing there shaking my head as the limo pulled away. All the associates were like, "Are you okay? What was that all about?"

"I am good," I replied. *If he even begins to think I'm mistreating his nephew, what's he going to do?* It was just another crazy day in the city. But as I was about to find out, I still hadn't hit rock bottom in my Philly experience.

LADDERS and LEARNINGS

- Whether in a retail, office, or other environment, treat your coworkers with respect, regardless of their gender, race, ethnicity, religion, sexual orientation. Remember, you are all there to do a job and you'll never know when you're truly going to need each other.

EXECUTIVE MEMO

Always maintain an attitude that your people work WITH you,

not for you. They understand the real hierarchy and chain-of-command, but this mentality will ensure a higher level of loyalty. Be comfortable in your skin and respect others in their skin. Judge your team by their performance – not their gender, race, ethnicity, religion or sexual orientation, and hold every team member to the same standard.

6

ACTIONS AND CONSEQUENCES

"Adversity introduces a man to himself."

— ALBERT EINSTEIN

Okay, take a couple of deep breaths with me. Here we go. This is the chapter you've been waiting for: the moment I hit rock bottom in my Home Depot career and almost destroyed my life, my family, my livelihood and the family name. In 1997, my ego wrote a check I could not cash, in response to an incident that took place at the Northeast Philly, Roosevelt Boulevard store. To say it significantly shaped my career and tested my strength and resolve would be a dramatic understatement.

These days, drug testing is a ubiquitous practice in the workplace, but in the 90s, companies were still defining their drug testing policies. It was a new, sensitive area. We employed a night crew that operated in what we called "the dark hours," non-customer hours. They packed down freight, put out all product that came in through our receiving department and filled the shelves for the customers the next day.

My crew was comprised of a group of people, led by a young man, in whom I had tremendous faith. His work ethic, results and impact on the team were consistently top-notch. One night, he was involved in a minor accident involving a forklift and damaged product. Per our drug policy, if an incident created an amount of damage over $500 – it required a drug test. Since the accident met the company's criteria, I asked him to take the drug test and awaited the results, which came back positive for marijuana. It was incredibly disappointing because I really liked this kid and he worked his tail off.

I sat him down in the office and broke the upsetting news. "Do you have any explanation?" I asked. Right there, I made THE mistake. I should not even have bothered asking for an explanation; I should have gone with the results of the drug test, which mandated termination. But I did ask him for an explanation and – laughable, as it is – he gave me a story about how he'd been at a party and while he doesn't personally indulge, he was there among many people smoking marijuana and might have ingested some. Kind of like the Bill Clinton, "I didn't inhale," defense. (As comedian Bill Engvall would say, "He-e-e-re's your sign.)

I decided, *myself*, to re-test him. Ideally, what should have happened? Instead of going rogue, I should have taken some deep breaths and realized the decision was over my paygrade and partnered with my district manager for help and guidance. But I didn't. Instead, when the re-test came back negative, I told him, "This one's negative; that's great. Get back to work and let's get after this thing." Have you ever had one of those moments, where you would give almost anything to go back and do over? Well, this was it for me.

To enforce their new drug policy, Home Depot's corporate office created a position with the sole responsibility of overseeing and monitoring drug testing and its impact on the corporation. Soon after this incident took place, I received a call Layne, the woman who'd been hired for the role. "Erik, is this the way it happened?"

"Yes."

"Did you, of your own accord, make the decision to retest him?"

"Yes."

"Okay, I need to let you know, you must terminate him immediately."

We talked a bit more and I said, "I understand. I will do that."

Our phone conversation took place later in the week and since I was going on vacation the following week, I felt no urgency to meet with my employee before I left. I *tabled* it, if you will, on my desk to take care of as soon as I returned to work (please remember, I am falling on my sword here to help you). I did not understand the urgency or the precedent I was complicit in setting for this new policy. After my vacation was over, rested and in a terrific mood, I walked the store early on a Monday morning to re-acclimate myself. That's when I received a phone call from my district manager, John.

"Hey, I need to see you over here right away at the office."

I kind of hesitated, then as a joke, asked, "Should I bring my keys?"

He did not respond.

Right then I knew something was up. "What's going on, John?"

"Did you?" And he went through the scenario again.

"Yes," I admitted.

"Okay, I need you to come over here."

So, I went to his office and sat down with him and our district loss prevention manager. "Here's the deal. The home office feels you did not agree with their decision and did not adhere to what they asked you to do."

"I'm probably guilty of not meeting with the young man before I went on vacation, but I had every intention of doing it," I explained.

"Well, you need to understand something. This is bigger than us now. This is a new and very strict policy. I'm not sure what's going to happen at this point, but an investigation is going to be conducted."

"An investigation? But we just talked about everything that happened."

"You need to understand. This is now in the home office's hands and it's purely up to them."

"What's the worst-case scenario?"

"You could be terminated."

"You've to be kidding me!" My heart pounded in my chest. *Everything I have done, everywhere I have gone to help this company, the results that my teams have produced, and this is where we are at???*

During the investigation, they permitted me to work, which was a blessing. In some of these cases, they'd put people on a leave of absence for the duration up until the decision, but the silver lining for me was that I remained employed with pay because it was not an overall performance issue. I drove home to share the news with Pam, without focus on anything but what and how I was going to tell her that the relocations and sacrifices we had made to that point could all be for naught. As soon as I walked through the door and she saw my face, she knew something very, very bad had happened. After hearing my explanation, without hesitation, she expressed her unwavering support and understanding. Then I had to tell my parents, which terrified me. Even though my father had retired by then, the Dardas family reputation remained foremost on my mind. My brother, David, was a store manager for the company, at that time as well.

Legacy.

Thank God, my parents also supported me without hesitation. "Let this play out and see what happens," my dad advised.

"Well, what do I do?" I asked.

"If you're not out on leave, you've got to be you. You've got to continue, through your performance, to be the way you know how to be a great store manager." Again, prophetic advisement from him.

Over the two-week period of the investigation, I conducted orientation with new associates, ran the store, and taught classes for the district, with my usual enthusiasm and passion. No one, and I mean *no one* in the store, at any level knew that I was under investigation. However, I was beating myself up, without mercy, for putting myself and family in this position. While not knowing what was going on behind the scenes, I tried to handle myself appropriately, and reached out to mentors like Larry Mercer and other company officers.

It was funny (not in ha-ha way) because the phones went silent; due to the investigation, they *could not* and *would not* call me back. Although I felt isolated and alone professionally, in a way it strengthened my resolve even further to show what I was made of.

I started to worry about what would happen to my stock holdings, my 401K, and my family if I got terminated. Back in 1997, my daughter Jackie was only three years old and Pam and I hadn't been married all that long. I thought to myself, *what you did – by failing to do several of the things you should have done – is put your whole life at risk.* At the end of the two weeks, Vern Joslyn, my regional vice-president, and peer of my dad, called me. It bothered me that my district manager had never picked up the phone to talk to me, but I knew he was doing anything he could and nothing he shouldn't, to represent me.

"Alright Erik, here's the deal," Vern began. "Obviously because of who you are and my relationship with your father, you and I are flying down to Atlanta to meet with Arthur Blank in his office to discuss this entire situation."

"So, we have to fly me down to Atlanta to meet with Arthur because of this?"

"Yes."

"Well, do we know what the result is yet?"

"No."

That did not sound encouraging, at all. As I stated in the introduction, going to the home office was a usually good thing. But under these circumstances, it scared the *you know what* out of me because I knew there was a real possibility that I'd be flying home unemployed, with a wife and child to support...all because of one egocentric, bone-headed decision I'd made. If I could have traveled back in time to change the outcome, I would have given my right arm to do it. In fact, believe it or not, I started thinking about working at Lowe's (oh the horror of wearing that stupid red vest!). I arrived at the corporate office and rode the elevator to Arthur's office, which was next to Bernie's, and sat in the waiting area outside. Bernie came out, saw me sitting on the couch, walked right over and asked, "Hey, what are you doing here?"

"Ah, Bernie, I might have just messed up," I confessed. I stood up as I talked to him and he gave me a hug.

"You're going to be okay. You want anything to drink?"

"I'm sorry, what?"

"You want anything to drink?"

"No, no. My throat is so dry I can hardly talk, can't stomach anything right now."

"Alright, have a seat and hopefully we'll talk a little bit later."

As I sat back down, it seemed that Bernie had no idea why I was there, which I found interesting. At last, the door to Arthur's office opened and Vern came out to get me.

"Come on in," he said.

My legs felt numb, as if I had been injected with a pain agent, but I made them move. It was time to "own" my actions. Self-accountability is crucial to the success of your career. When you do something wrong, quit blaming others, look in the mirror, and recognize that there are instances when an apology is not enough. As Teddy Roosevelt said, "Complaining about a problem without proposing a solution is called whining.

It was a typical executive office with a couch, large desk, and a few chairs. Vern walked me in, where another gentleman, Steve, our company human resources officer, was also waiting for me (oh, no- if he was here, I was in deep, deep trouble). I'd already met him once or twice; nevertheless, Vern introduced me to him again. Then came the moment of truth: Arthur came out of the back, approached me, shook my hand, and told me to sit down. I sat on the couch next to Vern; Arthur sat in a chair in front of me about four feet away; and the human resources officer sat in a chair to Arthur's left. Which brings us full circle to the beginning of my book.

"So, Dardas, you think you're bigger than my company?" Arthur asked bluntly. *No hello, no pleasantries. I'm dead.*

Without hesitation I replied, "Arthur, I'm embarrassed to be here, but the only thing I can say is that I would not do anything to intentionally disrupt your company or not adhere to a policy, given all you and Bernie and this company have done for me. But more importantly – and don't take this the wrong way – I would not do anything to intentionally embarrass and downgrade the name of Dardas at the Home Depot. I have been beside myself for two weeks, knowing I was being investigated. But I can tell you, if you ask anybody who knows how I've been performing while this was going on, they would say they thought I was up for a promotion, based on my attitude and behaviors. That's what I tried to do the whole time, continue to perform in my job as if nothing was going on."

Arthur, Steve and Vern listened attentively, then asked more questions about the incident to get a full understanding of what had taken place. After about 20 minutes, Arthur told me to go back out and take a seat while they evaluated everything and made their decision. As instructed, I left the room and sat down in the waiting area, where I prayed harder than I had over the past two weeks and engaged in some serious soul-searching while awaiting my fate. I promised God, right or wrong, that if I got out of this and was given another chance, that I would never forget it. To this day, I make every effort to take time to pray, both for myself and others. If an event like this doesn't change you, then I don't know what would.

When asked, I went back into Arthur's office, where he was standing up.

"Okay, sit down," he said.

Of course, I was thinking the worst. "Listen," he continued. "I have to be honest; I don't want to see your life ruined over this because you've done such an outstanding job for us, but you need to understand, we have to do something to you. Because of your dad and the relationship with Vern, because of our policy, we can't just slap you on the wrist."

"Okay," I replied. "Trust me, I'm going to be happy to continue to work for Home Depot if you give me that privilege."

"I have to go. Vern and Steve will give you our decision."

With that, he left the room and Vern and Steve informed me that I'd been demoted to an assistant manager position again. The deal? If I accomplished all they asked of me as an assistant manager, they would re-promote me within six months. That night, I flew back to Philly knowing I was still employed and salaried, which meant I was still eligible for stock options and bonus, although at lesser increments. I was very, very wounded, but alive to fight another day. Relieved, I vowed to myself that I would not blow this opportunity.

To use a military expression, it was time for me to "Embrace the suck."

I'd later find out what had transpired between Vern and Arthur when I was out of the room. "Do you *really* want Dardas working for Lowe's? With all he knows, what he does, knowledge of where we're going? Do you really want to make a decision that will push him to Lowe's?" Vern asked. Because I wasn't an officer, they couldn't prohibit me from seeking employment with the competition, if terminated. I was pleased that Vern had put it in those terms for Arthur, who was in a tough position because of my father. He knew if my performance suffered afterward, they'd have to drop the hammer on me. But, because of how I handled the situation and performed afterward, it created a success story for the company by demonstrating that somebody could get demoted, repromoted, and then achieve an even higher position. That was the grace of Home Depot – so long as I listened, learned, and performed up to their standards on a consistent basis.

My entire family, of course, was extremely grateful I still had my job. Home Depot transitioned me to assistant manager at the Oxford Valley (suburban Philly) store. Although it was customary for the district manager to break the news to a team whose store manager had been demoted, I asked for permission to announce it to my them myself, because I thought they would take the news better if it came from me. It was an unusual request, but due to everything we'd been through together and our overall team mentality, we knew it was the right way to handle it.

If I didn't do it, I felt there would be a big problem for employee morale. After I informed them about what happened, they were as upset as I was about my demotion, so I asked my district manager to give me a few days to calm everybody down. I'd also found out that many associates were organizing a walk-out to protest the company's decision. While it felt incredible to have such a wonderful relationship and allegiance from my team, I knew I had to be a good soldier at this point and do what was right by the company.

Over the course of a week, I conducted multiple meetings with my staff – some one-on-one, some with ten people at a time – to tell them the best thing they could do was stay in the store and continue to do an excellent job because the biggest testament to help me in terms of getting repromoted was for my replacement to see what a remarkable team we had in place. It was a tough message to deliver, because the whole time all I could think about was having to report to Oxford Valley as an assistant manager. Yet I took full accountability for my actions and did not blame the company. Instead, I focused on soothing everyone's nerves and preparing them for my replacement.

What was my lesson here? Number one, I should have gotten a partner and utilized the chain of command. This is one of the most important lessons people learn when they get into the hierarchy of management. Any time a decision is above your paygrade, you must acknowledge that. In serious situations, it's better to slow down, take a breath, and think it through fully before you act. If there's any doubt, there is no crime in reaching out to a higher-up to ask, "Hey what do you think? What would you do in this situation? What would you like to see me do?"

The next time I spoke to Vern was when he called to ask how I was doing at my new store in my not-so-new role. "I want to be honest with you," he began. "I don't know if anybody mentioned this to you yet, but the best thing you did for yourself and probably the reason you got to keep your job was the way you handled yourself during that two-week investigation. Just so you know, there were people watching you to see what time you got in, what time you left, and to witness your behaviors and what you were doing. They monitored your finances to see if you were going to sell all your stock because that would have signaled a personal resignation. The fact that you didn't touch any of your stock told the company your heart was still at Home Depot. Don't ever forget that. The way you represented yourself and the things you did and did not do were the biggest developers of the perceptions people took away up until that point."

YOU ARE YOUR BRAND

Everybody has their own personal brand, even if they are part of a larger iconic entity like Home Depot. I used to tell my teams that.

"What do you mean?" they'd ask.

"What's the first word that comes to mind when I say 'McDonald's?'"

They'd either say "great French fries" or "greasy food."

"Now from a personal standpoint, if I brought up somebody's name like, (here I'd mention a celebrity, sports star, or some other well-known person), "what's the first word that comes to mind?" Their answers would come just as quickly. "At some point, somebody will bring up *your* name and someone else will have an instantaneous reaction to it," I informed them. Throughout my career, I often asked my teams, "How are you going to develop your personal brand and what is that going to look like?" My personal brand had taken a direct hit because of this situation, but I would turn it into a positive by sharing my experience with many others. I was not shy. I was candid about what happened to me, to help my colleagues avoid a similar fate.

Unknown to me, my demotion most likely prevented me from reaching my goal of becoming an officer in the company. Nobody ever said that, but with the demotion on record, I'm sure it gave everybody pause when considering candidates for officer promotions. All I had to do the moment that drug test came back positive was call my district manager and ask, "Hey, I got this drug test situation, what should I do?" I could have saved my family and everyone else, including me, the aggravation. It hit me like a ton of bricks, but it woke me up, checked my ego, and gave me a newfound humility that I desperately needed.

When I reported for work the following week at the Oxford Valley store, it was difficult to describe my mood as anything other than horrifically bad. Yeah, I was happy to still be with Home Depot, but I was about to walk into a store where every employee knew I'd been demoted. Not much makes me cry (other than the movie *Brian's Song*), but the day I pulled into the parking lot for the first time on a scorching-hot summer morning, I sat there in my car with my Dunkin' Donuts iced coffee loaded up with sugar, staring at the store and crying. I felt wholly defeated that I allowed this to happen to me. I was so driven to get to the next level, do all the right things...and I let myself get into a spot where I made a stupid decision. It hit me all at once in the parking lot. I wasn't sobbing, but steady, uncontrollable tears streamed down my face. But I got myself together as fast as I could because they were having a staff meeting and I did not want to be late...plus, son of a gun, I didn't have any Murine eye drops.

At the meeting, I met my coworkers for the first time, most of whom I didn't know. They knew of me and the reason why I was coming to their store. I shook hands with everybody and introduced myself. To his credit, the store manager welcomed me in his opening remarks as if I was the cavalry coming to save the day and rescue the store. He asked me if I wanted to share any words with the team. I briefly filled them in on what happened and emphasized that I was happy to be there. If anybody wanted to learn how to avoid going through my situation, I'd be glad to talk to them more about it in a general sense. They gave me a nice round of applause and affirmed how glad they were to have me, which made me feel somewhat better.

They assigned me to the flooring, paint, and plumbing departments, where I had good teams, and started to enjoy myself. It was as if I needed this time; it gave me the chance to look deeper within myself. The pressure was off a bit because I was not the store manager. I had more fun as an assistant manager the second time around than I did the first time. I incorporated what I'd learned and done the first time around, along with my experience as a store manager. It was just fun. Maybe, just maybe, all things do happen for a reason.

Unknown to me, my former store on Roosevelt Boulevard did something incredible on my behalf. Some of the employees got together to write a letter to Bernie and Arthur – basically a few paragraphs about me and what I'd done for the store and the employees, along with a mention of my demotion. All of them, including members of management (which could have put them at risk) signed it. Then, one of my department heads in hardware, Joe, framed it and put it under glass after they mailed a copy to the founders at corporate headquarters. One day I got paged in the Oxford Valley store, "Hey, some associates from your old store are here to see you."

When I came out, five of my former Roosevelt Boulevard coworkers presented me with a framed, two-foot by three-foot copy of the letter with everyone's signatures. They had me crying all over again. To this day, I still have it, and everyone who comes over to my house reads it and asks, "What was that all about?"

When I explain it to them, they always react with, "Wow, I'd have kept that letter too!" From the associate side, I was extremely proud. On the roughest of days, if you know your team feels that way about you, it's something you can put in the win column. That goes to my thoughts about business. Regardless of technology, the human element remains the key to an organization's success. If a leader has the support of their team, amazing things happen. If they don't, the damage can be overwhelming.

I was an assistant manager in Oxford Valley for about five months. Then, as promised, they repromoted me to store manager at the South Christopher Columbus store, located in Penn's Landing on the Delaware River, another inner-city environment. This Home Depot featured many of the same elements as the Roosevelt Boulevard store, including clientele, and needed a lot of help. To help you get the full picture, a strip joint was located right across the street (I promise, I never went in there, but there were days when I did bump into some of the dancers at the Dunkin Donuts next door while getting my morning coffee). No, life was never dull at Home Depot.

"Champions are champions, not because they do anything extraordinary, but because they do the ordinary things better than anyone else."—Chuck Noll

My first day as store manager at South Christopher Columbus, I pulled into the parking lot, walked into the store, and noticed small pieces of trash all over the floor as soon as I reached the returns desk. I mean, the place was *filthy*. Without even introducing myself to anybody, I started sweeping. Dressed in business casual attire, *sans* apron, I swept the entire returns desk area. As I did, I noticed associates were starting to watch me with strange expressions on their faces. When I was done, I grabbed a dustpan and dumped it in the trash can. Then I introduced myself to everyone. I set the expectation and the standard. After I greeted the associates, I walked around the store to talk to customers.

Just as I had done in Orlando many years before, when I noticed how overwhelmed the associates were with customers, I rolled up my sleeves and dove right in. When going into any environment – whether for the first time, during the normal shift, or at the end of your career – the way you handle various scenarios contributes to your brand. The Philly employees emulated me, based on what they saw I was willing to do myself. Do not just preach it but walk the talk. From customer service to replacing toilet paper in the bathroom... whatever it was, I was obsessive and compulsive about the details. For example, every Home Depot features an employee break room. I couldn't take it when I walked in to find trash cans overflowing or that someone had left their trash on the table, impacting other associates. I'd always bag the trash, run it back to receiving, and clean the tables. But somewhere along the way, I noticed the associates started doing it more and more. You must find a way to truly understand your team, and what makes them tick. Philly is a strong, blue-collar, working-class town, with an intense amount of pride in what they represent. I was able to earn their respect immediately by showing them I was not afraid to do what I was going to ask of them.

The loyalty I garnered in the short term by showing and including them won them over fast. At one of our early staff meetings, we discussed cross-merchandising. We had these little metal devices we called chip clips, that hooked into our racking and hung straight down. About a month into my assignment, I observed that we weren't keeping up with the chip clips, the metal strips that hang on our steel racking in our store, so I got the staff together to talk about the importance of cross-merchandising. An example of this would be smoke alarms, which require a 9-volt battery. The two items are permanently merchandised in two separate locations in the store, but we would place additional batteries by the smoke alarms, so customers would understand the need, and we would get additional sales.

"Let's hear some thoughts from you. How can we get better at this?" I began. And they sat there for a second, completely quiet.

"What's the matter? Nobody got anything?" I challenged.

"Well, before *you*, we were not used to anybody asking us our opinion." They were dumbfounded.

"What?"

"Yeah, usually we just get told what to do and we just go out there and do it."

"Well that's changing, right here, right now," I announced. "Here's what we're going to do. We're going to take feedback from all of you and put it up for a vote."

"Who gets to pick what we're going to do?" they wanted to know.

"Hey, in my book, democracy rules. So, we'll vote it down until we get to one that everybody likes and thinks we can execute; we'll run with that and see what happens."

For the next two hours, we had a conversation about cross-merchandising, where the team led the discussion and came up with a solution. Lo and behold, over the next few weeks, you could see it getting better. "I don't know how you did it, but you've got the best cross-merchandised store in the entire district," my DM informed me.

I owed it to the power of inclusion. Instead of preaching and dictating, involving my people in the solution created a higher degree of ownership, because they took part in its development. Often, when it's your people's idea, it becomes a higher priority. Their reputation is on the line. It created peer pressure to present the store at the highest level possible. If it didn't, when I came in on Fridays to work the closing shift, it was going to be a long night for everyone – remember, we did not go home till it was right. In fact, managers that closed with me on Friday nights were scheduled "from 1 p.m. till "?", meaning it was up to them what time we went home. I stayed with them until the end.

Wing-stacks were another method of generating sales. We stacked cases of product directly in the aisles, close to a complementary product to encourage customers to purchase everything together. At the very least, we cut the top case open to make the product accessible to customers. When I scheduled myself to close on a given night, I always came in about an hour early. If I noticed empty cardboard boxes, I started case-cutting additional boxes to ensure the availability of products for sale. Associates got used to my schedule: they knew I'd hit the wing stacks on Friday, and it became a game, so that when I came in, I couldn't find a wing stack that needed attention. They'd hit it, knowing they'd have to put up with me doing it, when I arrived. There was good-natured ribbing when I had to do it, but we got it done. And it led to better financials for our store via project-selling.

Based on how I handled the demotion and this new Philly store, multiple visits with officers took place, along with communication that I was back in the good graces of Home Depot. Once again, they were looking at me for a district manager position. I'd gotten promoted to a store manager role; suffered a demotion; achieved a repromotion; and in less than a year-and-a-half I was back to where I should have been. Upon hearing these words, I promised myself was I was not going to blow it because there was no way in hell that I would get another chance. I did it the right way with my people, receiving many positive comments about the store's appearance and performance. Employees were getting promoted now, whereas before, they were not.

Don't get me wrong. At the same time, I also instituted a consistent level of accountability on all expectations. One of my pet peeves is timeliness. In my mind, one minute late is one minute late. There is no gray area there, except for when Pam is getting ready for date night. Leaders who do not hold themselves and others accountable punish those who are abiding by the rules.

DEAD BODIES AND WATER HEATERS

One day I got called to the front (have you noticed that I got called to the front a lot?) because officers and detectives from the Philadelphia Police Department needed to speak to me. Our conversation went something like this:

"Hey, we found a body in the Delaware River (right next to the store) last night and it was in one of your water heater boxes."

"What do you mean it was in one of the water heater boxes?"

"Yeah, your brand of water heater. That's where we found the body."

"Wow, really??? What do you need from me?"

"Well, we need a record from you of every single water heater you've sold, so we can see if there's some way to track this box, possibly by serial numbers."

I responded, "With all due respect, you are out of your frickin' mind. There's no way we can do that. We sell thousands of water heaters every year; there's no way we can track all the boxes. People could've paid with cash...there's just no way we could track that. I would do anything I could to help you, but I just can't do it."

In the end, we laughed about it. *Only in Philly.*

GAME ON...IN HOUSTON

Trivia time: did you know that Major League Baseball, to ensure the pitchers have better control and a firmer grip, rubs each, and every ball with the mud from the Delaware River? Yes, it's true. Aside from that interesting tidbit, it serves as a metaphor for my eight months in that store. I was doing the same for myself and career, enhancing my grip on my emotions and gaining better control on overall performance. My last recommendation regarding Philadelphia: never, and I mean *never* root against ANY Philly team, or make fun of their mascots. Just sayin'.

One Friday, I got in early and walked the store. I hadn't put my apron on yet as I sat in the office. The phone operator paged me repeatedly, but I ignored it the first couple times. I should have known something was up, because under normal circumstances they knew not to even page me; just to take a message, until my scheduled start time. I took that time to get a perspective of what was going on in the building, without the pressure that comes with putting on the apron. Once you donned the orange apron, everybody wanted a piece of you. Funny how many times customers either knew or found out my schedule and would be there waiting for me to talk or complain. If you walk into the building and put your apron on right away and start dealing with things as they hit you, you can't prioritize and optimize your agenda. That's why, on this impactful day, I ignored the page the first couple times before I called the operator.

"Hey, you know my rule. What's going on. Can you take a message? I don't care who it is. I don't care if it's the President of the United States, tell them at one o'clock, I'll be in."

"But Erik – "

"Just do me that favor, please."

"Okay."

Undaunted, the operator called me again. "Erik, John's on the phone. He doesn't care what you need to do; if I need to hunt you down, you need to pick up this phone call." John Mullen was my district manager.

"Allllright," I sighed. I picked up the phone.

126

"What the hell are you doing?" John demanded.

"I'm doing my stuff, why? Anything wrong?"

"Dude, I've been trying to get a hold of you, and you won't answer the damn phone!"

"Sorry, you know my routine."

"Well, sort of."

"Why? What's going on?"

"Barry Silverman is trying to get a hold of you." Barry was the President of, what was then the company's Southwest Division, which encompassed the great state of Texas.

"Barry, why?" I had worked with him previously in the Northeast.

"Dude, do you want to be a DM or not?"

"What?! Of course, I do." *Are you kidding me right now?*

"Then answer the *f*****g* phone. I'm going to call him and tell him you will now start accepting calls," he informed me in a sarcastic tone.

Ten minutes later, another page alerted me that Barry was on the line.

"Erik!" he greeted me. I knew Barry because he had been up in the Northeast Division for a time. "Are you ready to be a District Manager?"

"Yes sir, you know it!"

"How do you feel about Houston?"

"Houston!? I've never even been to Texas, other than to drive through it. Houston, really?"

"Yes, we need you down there badly."

Filled with elation, I went home to talk it over with Pam; with mutual excitement, we agreed to accept the promotion. Even better, Houston had a much lower cost of living and I was getting another raise – woo-hoo! Aside from my wife, I could not wait to tell our parents the wonderful news. It seemed all the heartache and the bumps in the road were becoming distant memories.

In an example of coming full-circle, Tom Taylor was the vice-president of the division. When I first got my promotion to assistant manager in Fort Lauderdale, Tom's father, also named Tom (just an incredible man) was the paint department supervisor. His dad worked for me in Florida, and now I was going to work for Tom in Texas. Ironically, early in his career, Tom had worked for my dad, who played a vital role in his professional advancement. At one point, Tom planned to leave the company to attend college, and my dad was one of the Home Depot people who encouraged him to rethink his position because he had an exceptional opportunity within the company. Taking their advice, he decided against college, became one of the highest-ranking officers at Home Depot, and forged an excellent career. Tom was one of the most passionately regarded individuals Home Depot ever had. After he left the company, he became the CEO of Floor and Décor.

As for me? I was about to discover just how BIG everything was in the Lone Star State.

LADDERS and LEARNINGS

- Everyone at every level must accept responsibility and accountability for their own actions.
- If you take an inappropriate action, look in the mirror and own it. You will always make mistakes, but how you recover from your mistakes determines the quality of your overall brand.

EXECUTIVE MEMO

Walk your talk and live up to the demands you impose on others.

7

LIVIN' LARGE IN THE LONESTAR STATE

"In matters of style, swim with the current. In matters of principle, stand like a rock."

— THOMAS JEFFERSON

I had no idea what to expect about living in Texas. Prior to my relocation, I'd only ever driven through it. An exceptional time in my life for multiple reasons, I experienced tremendous personal and continued professional growth. Texas has a very different mindset from the rest of the country – it is true what you hear, they feel like a country unto themselves. Truly, in The Lone Star State there is an abundance of pride, owing mainly to its history of achieving independence (Remember the Alamo!). Is everything BIGGER in Texas? From hairstyles and homes, to cattle and steaks, to egos and interstates, and everything in between, bless your heart y'all, it is *supersized*. Aside from embarking on a new adventure in a new location, I was excited about working with Barry and Tom. It is always nice to work with familiar faces, especially following a cross-country move.

I'll never forget attending my first staff meeting with the entire division of officers and district managers in Dallas. Every meeting, I'd either drive or fly to Dallas from Houston. When I walked into that first staff meeting, I knew some other folks who were in that office, as they had once been in other parts of the Sun Belt, then relocated west. Everyone was gathered in the main room, where I began to shake hands and say hello. Dressed in what I'll call business casual – my Khakis; $200 dress shoes with wing tips; nice buttoned-down, collared shirt; and Fossil watch – I thought I looked damn good. That is, until I gazed around the room and realized my wardrobe was out-of-place. Everybody, and I mean *everybody*, had cowboy boots on. The men, the ladies. I glanced at them, then back down at my shoes and felt like an oddball. As if my choice of footwear wasn't bad enough, my subtly colored shirt (can't remember if it was white or some other pale, calming shade) stood in stark contrast to the flamboyant, fluorescent shirts everyone else had on. I mean, we're talking bright purple, orange, pink, yellow – every color of the rainbow.

"We have to go shopping," I announced to Pam when I got home.

"What are you talking about?"

"I gotta get some boots, I gotta get some bright-colored shirts."

"You've got to be kidding me."

Let's just say, if our life was the game Monopoly, Pam was the banker. From the time we got married, she has handled our household finances. We had a very animated conversation that night, as a new wardrobe was not in the budget. She eventually saw my point-of-view, empathizing with my need to assimilate. I went out and got some Justin boots, along with a bunch of Tommy Hilfiger shirts, all in very bright colors. It was a strategic move because as soon as I adjusted my wardrobe – boots, shirts, shoes – I began to receive compliments like, "Hey, diggin' the shoes." Aside from everything being bigger in Texas, it also had to be the right label, whether Tommy Hilfiger, Polo, or Calvin Klein. This extended to accessories. Another thing everyone in that room had in common (much to Pam's initial regret) was a Rolex watch. Right away, I announced to my wife that in addition to the shirt and shoes, "I gotta get me a Rolex." It was as if I had to fit in with *The Lifestyles of the Rich and Famous* and I put tons of pressure on Pam to make that happen. I wasn't normally a follower, but I felt that to belong I had to change how I dressed – though it did not include wearing belt buckles the size of hubcaps (believe me, they are out there).

Almost immediately, I began to use the phrase, "Hey, I got here, meaning *Texas*, as fast as I could," with customers, associates, and managers. When meeting people for the first time, I'd get questions like, "Where y'all from boy? Y'all ain't from around here, are ya?" And my truthful response of, "Well, I'm originally from Michigan, then my family moved to Pennsylvania, then Florida..." did not satisfy them. For my Texas colleagues and customers, those states represented a foreign world; I might as well have arrived in a space-ship from Mars. In fact, as an outsider I was held suspect by everyone until they knew I accepted everything that defined being a Texan.

Consequently, it became my priority to fit in. When the next meeting was held, I made sure I looked the part and arrived in Dallas wearing my new boots for the first time, along with a peach-colored shirt that almost required sunglasses to look at. Guess what? I fit right in. Although I felt the pressure to adapt, I also noticed there was more of an affirmation of me being there because I was willing to do that. "Now you know what women feel like every day," Pam informed me, without an ounce of sympathy.

As for my Rolex?

Nope. Did not get it right away, due to our need to save money for our plans to enhance our home. However, on our 10th wedding anniversary, Pam surprised with me one: when I went out to my Jeep Grand Cherokee to get something, there it was, sitting on the driver's side seat. And I flipped out; I couldn't believe I'd finally gotten it. I was stylin'. It made me proud to wear that watch on my wrist – even if it meant Pam would rib me about it often. She is famous for asking,

"Hey, what time is it?" After I look at my Rolex and answer, she replies, "Oh look, it's the same time on my Fossil too!"

"You just don't understand," I'd sigh. By the way, I still have that watch, which I save for special occasions.

My wardrobe was not the only thing that required adaptation to Texas standards; we also had to adjust to the real-estate market and climate, though the former was a pleasant surprise after living in the Northeast. During our time in Philly, we lived in a rental home, but once I attained this promotion it was like, "Wow, I'm a district manager now. Maybe the relocation merry-go-round will stop for a while and we can buy a house.

Pam and I will never forget the day we rode in the car with our realtor through a neighborhood of amazing homes, a Master Plan community just outside of Houston, called Kingwood. It had its own schools, pools, shopping center, movie theater, coffee shops, grocery stores – every amenity you can think of. As we drove around, we looked at each other in surprise. I finally remarked, "You know what, honey, if we continue to work at it, someday we'll be able to afford living in a community like this." The realtor retorted, "What do you mean? You ARE going to own a house in this neighborhood."

And we were incredulous, "What are you talking about?!" These were 3,500 square foot, four-bedroom houses without basements. How could we possibly buy one of them? Well, thanks to the much lower cost of real estate in the area, our realtor was right. Homes in that area were half- to- two-thirds of the price of homes in the north-east. And, yes, we purchased a house in Kingwood, which blew our minds. "We can afford to buy one of these homes!" I remember stating to Pam, "This is the neighborhood that I always dreamed we would be able to live." Life was good.

The weather, on the other hand, was another matter. We moved into our new home in the middle of summer, on a day with a heat index of 120 degrees, at 10 o'clock at night. Are you kidding me!? Like most young families, we had a decent amount of stuff for our movers to carry into the house, but due to the excruciating heat, we thought they might keel over and die. We gave these guys water and kept them fed, all the while thinking, "Heat stroke is imminent." No wonder the houses are so inexpensive; why would anybody want to live down here?" Even by Houston standards, it was one of the hottest, most humid days on record. It was nighttime – and if you took a shower, you were sweating the second you walked out, wondering why you'd even bothered.

JUDGEMENT DAY: SAVING CAREERS OR ENDANGERING MINE?

Due to the sheer size and population of Houston (one of the most populated metropolitan areas in the U.S.) Home Depot divided it into four districts and almost 30 stores. The promotion to district manager presented personnel challenges. When a new person takes over the role, the store managers within the district, seek any information about the incoming DM. As soon as the announcement was made, "Hey Erik Dardas, from up in Pennsylvania, is coming down to Texas to be the new DM," store managers started calling other store managers or people I worked with to find out who I was, how I performed, what my hot buttons were, and what they could expect. If you were coming from outside of Texas, they really questioned it because many of them believed there were employees already in the state who deserved the position. Talk about an intensified fishbowl! Their attitude was, *why did they move this guy all the way from Pennsylvania?*

Here again, I discovered the scope and power of your personal brand. Good, bad or ugly, your perceived brand represents you before your new team even lay eyes on you. At my first meeting with the store managers, my biggest challenge was earning their respect. I walked into the room with my predecessor, as we were fortunate to do a power transition with both of us present. I felt as if I was going through a scanner at the airport. Immediately, everybody looked me over from head to toe, measuring me up. This speaks to the power of first impressions. Like a first date, everyone remembers the first time they met, what they thought and how it went.

I could have walked into the meeting room like I was the king of the world: "Hey, I'm a brand-new district manager for Home Depot. Barry and Tommy wanted to bring me down here, so here is what we are going to do." Instead, I went in with humility and spoke about how happy I was to have received the promotion and how privileged I was to have been given the opportunity. I vowed to never take that for granted and always remember where I came from. "Hey, I've had my share of bad visits with officers. I've made mistakes along the way," I told them. Then, I credited the experience with forming me into the leader I had become and influencing my choice as to how I would represent myself from that point on. As I spoke, I clarified that they would be working WITH me, not FOR me.

It went over well. When you get promoted or transferred to an area, your new boss gives you the intel and their perceptions on all the people under your direct supervision. Going in, I'd been told that probably half of my team needed to be released, due to performance or leadership issues. That put pressure on me as I walked into that room and met those individuals. I hit "play" on a metaphorical recorder about what I'd been told about those people. However, I have always been a believer in judging people for yourself because perceptions are formed by a multitude of factors. I replaced some members of the team but turned around others whom I'd been told weren't worth their salt.

I can describe multiple occasions when I felt that one of my colleagues had made an incorrect assessment of a subordinate. Judging others for yourself can create consternation among your peer group and supervisors when you challenge their perceptions of an individual by choosing to give them a chance. Particularly in my role as a DM, I often resolved, "No, I think I can make something out of this person." Then the challenge would come back, "Well, it's going to be your reputation if you try and fail to save them." In fact, many people asked me, "Who do you think you are, Billy Graham?"

"What are you talking about?"

"You can't save everybody Erik."

"Well, that may be true, but I think I can save *this* one," I'd reply. I always had confidence that I could change somebody if I worked with them. Sometimes I won, sometimes I lost. It was a daunting task, putting myself on the line because of how I felt about an individual and what I believed I could accomplish with them. While I embraced my new role as a DM, I still held a vision of becoming a Regional Vice-President someday. As Home Depot expanded, the company became more bureaucratic; communication between the stores and the offices was one of the most obvious examples of this expansion. Due to the sheer number of stores the company was building, higher level management and corporate offices asked district managers to be the filter for all communication from store personnel. This meant that the DM would consolidate information, then forward it to the appropriate resources. Although the policy was intended to create a higher level of efficiency, it also eliminated connectivity with retail employees.

Since knowing your people is an integral part of the equation, I committed to one-on-one conversations outside of the stores because I wanted my store managers to feel comfortable. During these "get to know you" sessions, I asked questions and listened. I began with, "How do you feel about Home Depot?" "What's going on with your career?" Then I'd follow up, "What do you think the company thinks of you at this point?" I understood how important it was to make that time to discover where their hearts were and how they felt about Home Depot. These sessions also helped me to get a sense of their self-perceptions to determine if they aligned with the company's perceptions of them. While I listened, I took copious notes and mapped out a forward-looking strategy for the mutual benefit of the store manager and the company.

Aside from my self-induced blunders, one of the things that held me back the most was the corporate perception of me as someone who "took the side" of an individual versus the corporation. Sometimes I was proven correct; other times, I had to terminate the employee in question. But I'll gladly wear that as a badge of honor. If there's anything on my figurative tombstone at Home Depot, it's "He truly cared about his people and his customers." Still, I believe it was one of the reasons they hesitated to make me an officer in the company: I never forgot where I came from and probably empathized *too much*.

SLOW DOWN TO SEE MORE, FEEL MORE, AND IDENTIFY

Weekends are like the retail Super Bowl because the customer traffic is much heavier than on weekdays. That's why everyone on the team, whether hourly or salaried, should focus their efforts on customer service. One Saturday, I was having a ball on the sales floor, interacting with customers and associates, when I heard myself being paged over the public address system. When I responded to the call, my RVP, Gary was on the other end of the line. He'd shown up unannounced and wanted to talk to me. Anytime my boss was in the building and it was a surprise visit, my sphincter tightened up a little.

"Where are you?" he asked.

"Over on the garden side," I answered. "Just doing my thing. Why? What's up? Where you at?"

"Take your apron off. I want you to come over to lumber and building materials."

"Are we going to lunch?"

"No. Just come over here."

As requested, I removed my apron and ran over there to discover he didn't have his apron on either. But – you guessed it – he was wearing his boots, his bright-colored shirt, and his Rolex.

"So, what are we doing?" I asked.

"How do you think the customer service is in here today?"

"Overall, I think it's pretty good. I've been in here for a couple hours and everywhere I go, the associates are helping customers.

"What do you think your associates do when they know you're in the building and you're wearing your apron? Do you think their performance is enhanced a bit because you're here?"

"I don't know. I don't think so; I hope they would be doing everything I've asked them to."

"Stop right there. Let's do this: we're going to walk the main aisles of the store, just you and I, aprons off, watching each associate to see if they're greeting and helping customers. I want to see if your perception matches reality.

"Okay, let's go."

By the time we finished, I was mortified. I thought to myself, *"Houston, we have a problem."*

As we walked the store, we stood at the end of aisles, where we couldn't readily be seen, to observe. It was humiliating to watch how many associates failed to greet customers or provide service when the SM or I wasn't around. What was the message from my Regional Vice-President? Sometimes you need to slow down and make clandestine observations to get a sense of reality. By the end, I was HOT – I'm talking ice-melting HOT! – over what I had seen. Prior to this exercise, I'd relayed a perception to my boss, only to have him toss it back in my court and prove the point that I needed to conduct it more often. From then on, whenever I visited a store, I left my apron in the car and did a quick-paced walk through the main aisles and operational areas.

It was time to start wearing a disguise. My challenge? To alter my attire and appearance so store personnel wouldn't recognize me. I'd wear sunglasses and loose clothing, throw some dirt on my face, and put on a ripped tee shirt and backwards baseball cap. It became a game for associates to find me and they remained on alert, knowing I could be in a costume. Nobody recognized me unless they REALLY looked at me. In the end, Home Depot customers benefited because employees gave it their best effort.

It was almost comical, the look of fear on their faces, once they realized they didn't do what they were supposed to do. Each time I conducted this exercise, I shared the results with the store manager and instructed them to reaffirm customer service with all associates. During one walk, I noticed a cashier coming up the light bulb aisle and ignoring every single customer she passed. "Hey, can I ask you something?" I asked her. "I was watching you and noticed you didn't say hello to anybody." With that, she started bawling and I motioned to the store manager. We took her into the office to ask if everything was okay and we discovered she was dealing with some personal problems. Once we determined the underlying cause of her failure to greet customers, we sent her home with pay, so she could resolve her issues. Balance is critical in similar situations, as there may be a valid reason for the improper behavior.

In retail, it's mind-blowing the range of issues and topics you encounter. In your people's eyes, as a district manager you *are* the company – the highest-ranking official in their area. As you climb higher in an organization and you've got the title at the end of your name, people want to talk to you more. The higher you are, the more they want you to do something about their problem or the situation. One thing I always did when talking to an associate was ask, "Do we need to go in the office? Can we talk about this is in the open?" I wanted to ascertain their comfort level, so they could freely relay their situation to me. I'd follow up with, "Would you like the store manager there?" Sometimes the answer was yes, sometimes, no. Regardless, I always clarified by inquiring, "Have you spoken to the store manager about it?"

BIGOTRY AND RACISM IN BEAUMONT

District managers were allocated groupings of stores that are geographically and functionally efficient, but sometimes we had outliers. Situated close to the coast, the Beaumont store was a healthy drive of about 90 minutes for me. It was also close to some areas known to be friendly toward the KKK, one of them being Vidor, Texas. I arrived at the Beaumont store on a day when the store manager wasn't there and the assistant manager covering for him was a black man. As we walked this lower volume store, which was normally clean and well-presented with excellent customer service, we talked strategy.

Then, a Caucasian customer walked through the front door with his son, who looked to be about six or seven years old. As he approached us, he looked at me and said, "Hey, I got a situation with..." I can't remember if it was plumbing or electrical, but both were my AMs area of responsibility. I knew he had an excellent background in them.

"Sir, that's not one of my strong points, but my AM here is very strong in those areas. I'm sure he can help you." The man hesitated a bit as he looked at me. Then he looked at my AM and replied, "Okay, here's what I've got." And as he started talking, his child began yanking on his pants. The man looked down at him and said, "Hey, I'm talking here; what do you need?"

The young boy gazed up at him and asked, "Dad, why are you talking to that ____?" And he used a racial epithet to describe my assistant manager.

I hesitated for just a second (although it seemed longer) before responding. To my AM's credit, he handled it well by not saying anything. Whether it's a black/white or male/female issue, or a customer sexually harassing one of your female employees or harming one of your associates physically, etc. you must act right away. "Sir, you are no longer welcome here," I stated, as I stared him in the eye. I remained discreet and handled it as professionally as possible, so as not to involve other customers. At first, he didn't move, so I continued, "Don't make this worse; understand, that's not what Home Depot believes, and you are no longer welcome here. Have a nice day." Thankfully, he turned around and left. Even before I walked out of the store that day, other associates, thanked me for how I handled it. Afterward, the AM and I sat down in the office to discuss what had taken place because I wanted to make sure he was okay.

He deserved the position, but in the end, it was about how he and others would be supported. Every time I went back after this incident, I would ask, "How's everything going?" I didn't even have to spell it out; they knew what I was asking, and it was important to me that they knew I had their backs.

Because I am a copious note-taker, I wrote down what happened that day and followed up with the SM to make sure he had an awareness of what was going on. So, we had a conversation about what happened. It always takes a team; no individual can fix or sustain anything on their own. When the SM considered it, he realized he'd seen an avoidance of some of his black associates from some white customers and vowed that he would do whatever he could do to protect his employees.

HELP IS READILY AVAILABLE AT HOME DEPOT

Home Depot provides an anonymous help line for associates to call without recrimination. Whenever they have a problem, they can either work within the hierarchy of the stores (levels of management) or call the help line. The corporate office maintains a team that listens to the associates, then filters the information to the appropriate resource or member of management for a review and plan of action. Home Depot believes the help line is a strong advocate for the associates, when they feel they cannot communicate with known resources, or feel uncomfortable doing so. Subjects ranged from scheduling issues to dissatisfaction with performance reviews and wage increases, to management behavior. Upper-level management felt very confident about the company's many offerings of assistance to the associates.

KUDOS TO MY BROTHERS & SISTERS IN ARMS

I can't even count the number of incidents where I've asked a customer to leave the store when they deserved it. As an example, cashiers are the last point of customer communication. They are a captive audience behind the register. Whether customers made inappropriate comments, sent them gifts, or stalked them, it could get crazy. Deep down, most people are good, but you must be aware that there's a crazy fringe element within your customer base. The returns desk is another high-volatility area because often customers come in without a receipt or even try to return stolen items. We teach and train our people how to handle that well, but you never know when somebody is going to get out of control because they got caught attempting to cheat the system. Whenever a customer threw something at a returns desk employee or threatened to wait for them after work and kill them, our people (in most cases) stood tall and reacted professionally. In retail, you deal with all aspects of humanity including the good, bad, criminal, rude, insane...the full gamut. It speaks to the strength of the individuals who work in these fields, day after day, year after year. As a retail worker, even if you love people and can deal with these situations, you'll still need an adult beverage when you get home at night. If you think I'm exaggerating, have you ever wondered why Home Depot's toilet displays are high up in our stores? Because in the past, customers would let their kids use them. Yes, really. Then our employees would have to clean up the stinky mess. It's amazing what we've had to deal with. If only the public knew – oh wait – by now, you're getting it. So, is the retail mantra, "the customer is always right" a sound business philosophy? Read the next chapter to find out.

LADDERS AND LEARNINGS

Take advantage of your company's chain of command and/or open-door policy at the appropriate times, to communicate your concerns, thoughts, and observations. Don't let them stew and don't procrastinate in communicating things that are important to you because that will only hurt moral and decrease productivity.

EXECUTIVE MEMO – Establish a balance of scheduled and surprise observations of your business to keep your finger on the pulse of how it's operating. Establish and maintain a viable chain of command, where associates and managers understand who to go to and when for any concern or issue. Don't undermine the authority of lower-level managers; instead, ensure that they take ownership of the situation. If you're a district manager, avoid becoming the store manager running the building. Identifying situations, behaviors, and results that caused the perceptions to develop will assist in teaching and coaching to facilitate progress.

If you're in management, please take this advice: as you represent your people's feedback, validate what you hear before you act. This will accomplish two important objectives: it will enhance their credibility and maximize the time and efforts of office personnel. Interacting with people on an individual basis will provide a truer sense of your relationship with them, both as an individual and a team member.

8

THE CUSTOMER IS ALWAYS RIGHT...
WAIT, WHAT? NO, THEY ARE NOT!

"It is not the employer who pays the wages. Employers only handle the money. It is the customer who pays the wages."

— HENRY FORD

When I wrote this chapter, I experienced a noticeable uptick in my adrenalin flow and blood pressure. I couldn't wait to share it. Because of how hard retail employees strive to do everything the right way, while overcoming the negative behaviors of some customers, it truly is an emotional topic. From the time we start our careers, our companies indoctrinate us with the mantra, "the customer is always right," but I can tell you from experience, this is simply not true. Customers can be wrong too. But, read on, there is a silver lining. Let's begin with an obvious example of when the customer is *always* wrong: shoplifting. Handcuffs, anyone?

The element of shoplifting remains one the biggest problems in retail. It leads to what the industry refers to as "shrink," the physical tally of lost inventory, which impacts the stores' financials. This creates a loss for employees in terms of bonuses and benefits, and for customers it means price increases. When I worked at the Daytona Beach store, we held a "Wild, Wild West" attitude and approach toward shoplifters. Things were much different from the way they are today. Home Depot had codes you could call out over the PA system to let the population of the store know about a situation. Everyone's heard of the "Code Adam" for a lost child; but in addition to that, companies have different codes to address a multitude of scenarios. Whenever there was a criminal incident and/or shoplifting episode in a Home Depot store, we used a specific code to alert the employees. Upon hearing it over the PA system, they would respond.

Not to brag, but I have always been in decent shape and quick on my feet. One day, the appropriate code was called as a "gentleman" (yep, using the term loosely again) tried to steal a drill kit and made it to the exit door. I can't remember exactly where I was in the building when I heard the alert, but I started sprinting toward the area. I led the charge to get outside the door and if memory serves me well, it was a customer who pointed and exclaimed, "He ran that way."

"That way" was toward a road about 300 yards to the side of the store. I spotted the shoplifter with the drill, who by now was starting to run, realizing he was being followed. There were about five or six associates behind me. As he reached the road, I caught up to him and when the two of us got to the middle of the road, I kicked at his legs and tripped him, leaping on top of him as traffic screeched to a halt. When the other employees got there, we subdued him, then we picked him up and dragged him back to Home Depot while the cars around us honked in celebration. Although he tried to kick his way loose, he couldn't overcome the restraints we placed on him.

The good side to the story? It became another legendary tale in the history of Home Depot: the store manager and team took down a shoplifter on a busy thoroughfare, got back our drill, and prosecuted the guy. Because Home Depot prosecuted every time. The bad side? By the time we chased him down, risked our lives, got him back into the store, filled out the paperwork, and called the police, it was a three-hour ordeal – time that could have been spent better. What else could we have done with those three hours in terms of helping customers and coaching our associates? It took us a while to learn that lesson at Home Depot because everybody wanted a good shoplifting story on their resume.

Regrettable things started to happen, like our associates getting beaten up by the people they tried to apprehend, at times sustaining significant injuries. I have read of other incidents in other retail businesses, where customers died from heart attacks after employees chased and apprehended them. How to handle shoplifters became a dilemma and quagmire for our corporate office: What is the right thing to do? What kind of policy should we craft to deal with the problem? The rules for shoplifting are very different today. In fact, you'll often read stories where employees get fired from companies for chasing somebody down because they thought they were doing the right thing.

However, in those early days we took pride in protecting our assets. While we thought we were doing something good, the truth was, we were putting ourselves in harm's way and spending too much time on it. It's not that we don't deal with shoplifting effectively now; we follow different procedures that focus on how to eliminate the potential for crime, versus dealing with people *after* they grab something and run out of the store. Nowadays, you must have sight of an individual from the moment they take something to the moment you get to them. If you can't maintain that chain of sight 100 percent, they escape the charges...and that sucks! I've always said, "How different this world would be if people channeled their efforts into being a productive associate/citizen/person – instead of figuring out ways to steal – they could accomplish wonderful things for our country and the world. Maybe, curing cancer or ending world hunger?" Just a thought.

The best illustration of my point involves a shoplifting incident where the perpetrators demonstrated innovation and creativity. They developed a machine that could replicate and print Home Depot receipts and kept it in their minivan. This enabled them to print the receipts, then go in and get those products and leave the store because they had a "receipt." If somebody stopped them, they'd flash the phony replica of a valid Home Depot receipt and they were good to go. By the time the company caught them, they had stolen well over one-million dollars' worth of merchandise. With today's advanced technology, soon there won't be any paper receipts. But think about those people who devoted that much time to developing a machine and creating a process to shoplift. It's simply incredible.

Businesses determine the real impact of shoplifting when they take a physical inventory during their fiscal year. Depending on the final shrink numbers, the result can make or break them for the entire year.

RETAIL THERAPY

For any customers reading this book, I thank you from the bottom of my heart: most of you treat our employees with respect and act like civilized human beings in our stores. For those of you who recognize yourselves in some of the customer archetypes I'll discuss here, please understand that this is my therapy chapter. I always said that on my final day at Depot I wanted to engage a disruptive customer and tell them how I really felt about their behavior. Sad to say, it never happened.

Whether they admit it or not, anybody who works with the public has a secret desire for one opportunity to chew out the single customer who richly deserves it, despite all the wonderful customers you deal with. Every day, you encounter the best and worst of human nature. Employees go through orientations, where they watch perfect scenarios featuring well-behaved customers. Then, in a real-world customer interaction, it hits them: this is *nothing* like what's portrayed in the training films. Don't take this the wrong way: I'm not asking my readers to play some violins, cry me a river, or offer me a sympathy hug because you feel sorry for me. Nor is any employee. We are all big girls and boys; we just ask that you remember we are people too.

Again, I go back to my dad. When he encouraged me to start at Home Depot, he knew from my early days as an athlete that I was an energetic, hard worker. Dad knew I had the effort part covered, but in terms of dealing with the public he advised, "You're either gonna love the customers or you're gonna hate the customers. IF you hate the customers, you need to get out. Don't stay. Find something that's more suited to you."

Although I gave it my all every day in my computer job, I hated it because I didn't feel like I had a purpose or was helping anyone. Until I got to Home Depot. From the very first time a customer asked me a question and I could help them, it felt exhilarating. When you can see the look of relief and gratitude on someone's face because you are helping them take care of their life, family, home, or yard, it is a tangible reward.

I cannot count the number of times when customers have come running into the store because their water heater busted and flooded their house. "What do I do first?" "What do I need?" they'd ask, panicked. Being able to assist that customer, even when they came ripping through the parking lot just as I was about to close the store at night – almost begging to get into the store because something horrible happened in their home – meant everything to me. In fact, it was inevitable that these situations occurred mostly at closing time. It's a gratifying moment when you can take care of a customer in a crisis, then send them back to their home or business, problem solved.

Regardless of your business, you are nothing without your customers. However, not all of them are good, and there are several archetypes that are common to all businesses. For the respectful customers who comprise the majority I dealt with over my 33 years with Home Depot, I cannot thank you enough for the wonderful memories. Companies like Home Depot and employees like me do not provide perfect customer service every time. We've had issues – whether we failed to greet customers or had a rough day and took it out on them or did not follow through on our commitments. There's plenty of responsibility to go around on both sides of the equation.

This chapter offers me a chance to discuss some of those customers who were often WRONG.

By the way, I don't appreciate being whistled at or called "Hey, boy," to get my attention. I don't appreciate somebody grabbing at my clothes or talking to me in a condescending manner when I'm speaking to another customer. This happens all too frequently in retail. Whether arrogant, rude, mean or harboring unrealistic expectations of what you can do for them, a negative customer experience leaves an indelible imprint on you. It can ruin your day. I dealt with numerous situations where my employees were so upset over how a customer treated them, they broke down in tears. Or they'd come back to the office and want to throw stuff or quit because of a customer's boorish behavior.

Some of these customers get off on being that way. In today's world of intense, endless conflicts over politics, civil rights, religion, or vaccinations it's more pronounced. All joking aside, I hated it when there was a full moon. Whether you believe in that or not, when the moon was full, the customers were just crazy. I remember other days where I'd walk up to a team member and ask, "Is it just me or is everybody bonkers today?" It happened on a regular basis, which is the biggest reason I keep the retail chip on my shoulder. I know from experience that some customers and members of society look down on retail workers. One of my earliest jobs was washing dishes before becoming a cook at Ponderosa Steak House in western Pennsylvania. There are members of the public who think of retail as a job of last resort for people who are somehow "deficient" in their eyes, e.g. "They couldn't make it through college," or "They have a disability," or "They couldn't go into the military."

If you don't believe me, go on the internet and pull up People of Wal-Mart, a source of delight and ridicule for anyone who enjoys making fun of Wal-Mart's customers and associates. Retail associates and managers get bullied by customers. One could say we get paid to do it and we know what to expect, but no one signs up for abuse when they complete an application. All they want to do is an excellent job, advance their careers, and take care of their families, like any other profession.

THE CUSTOMER ARCHETYPES

I've mentioned that Bernie was famous for telling us to "make love" to the customer. At Home Depot, we serve a combination of pro customers and homeowners, but whether a pro customer or a homeowner, one percent of them fit into the following archetypes (or a combination of two of more).

The Close Talker

Hopefully, everyone has seen the Seinfeld Show, at least on syndication. In 1994, the episode revolved around Judge Reinhold's character, Aaron, who is a habitual offender of this archetype. Be it intimidation or their personal comfort, this customer gets as close as they physically can to you, invading your personal comfort zone. Know any "space invaders?" If so, you know what I am talking about and I am sorry for their presence in your lives. Almost face-to-face, depending on height, it makes for an awkward encounter that is most difficult to amend without hurting their feelings. With every step back you take, they mimic your movements, almost as if it were a dance. It takes a creative mind to deal with this customer and find ways to protect the personal space. Oh, and carrying breath mints? A great idea.

The Touchy-Feely Customer

This archetype is like the one above, but worse. Considering recent attention to the women's movements, along with public sexual harassment discussions (i.e., politicians and celebrities), it is a huge no-no; yet it continues. Both men and women can be offenders in the "touchy-feely" customer archetype – always having to place their hand on your shoulder or the small of your back, holding your hand for far too long, or thinking that the two of you have a "huggable" relationship. The problem here is that employees want to get them what they want as quickly as possible so they can escape, which may inhibit their ability to recognize the customer's total potential of product needs. By their actions, the customer is at fault, although their intent may not always be construed as sexual in nature. Often, this type feels they are just being friendly. In most cases, having another employee there with you alleviates the situation with The Touchy-Feely Customer.

The Flirt

Home Depot has been known to be a "target-rich environment" (to quote a famous line from the iconic 80s film, *Top Gun*) for both sexes. Once, while working on the sales floor, I noticed a couple of men who seemed to be loitering in the department. We had offered to assist them several times, only to be denied. Finally, I went up to them, introduced myself and explained I was in management, then asked what we could do for them. One responded that they wanted to invite me to dinner that evening. Taken aback (I know, here we go again, right?), I said that I appreciated the offer, but could not attend. They pressed a little bit and I stated that was not my cup of tea; however, I appreciated their business. Another time, as I was conducting a walk on the sales floor with a group of associates near the entrance door, a woman came in and walked towards me. I broke away from the group and asked her how I could be of assistance. She reached into her purse, pulled out a small screw, looked at me, and asked in a suggestive manner, "Wanna screw?" I replied, "Is that a statement or a question?" With eyes fixed on me she replied, "That is entirely up to you." I took her to an associate in the Hardware Department, handing her off as quickly as possible.

I am quite positive that many of you reading this can add your personal stories about this type of customer to the discussion. Heck, we could probably start a blog featuring *only* those interactions. Sometimes, it is just so hard to remain professional.

The Mr. or Mrs. Know-It-All

This person walks into a Home Depot and whether they've installed a faucet or not, they are the expert on it. They have come in to impress everybody with their knowledge, though they need help. (If you are a reader who works in a retail business, I hope you find solace that somebody has the guts to call it out). Mr. or Mrs. Know-It-

All aggravates you because they won't listen to you. They feel their way of doing anything is the only correct way, but if that were true, they wouldn't be standing in front of you asking for help! Here's a real-life example: a customer came in and wanted to spend hundreds of dollars to fix something in their home; however, the Home Depot associate showed them how to fix the problem for only a few dollars. Sounds like a good thing, right? Well, this person contacted Bernie to complain, saying that Home Depot would soon be out of business. The customer failed to understand that Bernie wanted us to be a value when it came to customer service...and not just on price point. He wanted his associates to truly get the customer what they needed, which often differed from what the customer thinks they want. I cannot count how many times our associates have saved customers money when they easily could have taken more. When you're dealing with a Mr. or Mrs. Know-It-All, you can't reason with the unreasonable. These folks are not usually our biggest problem. As they continue to approach us with questions and unreasonable demands, they become open to our advice, which builds trust. Over time, The Mr. or Mrs. Know-It-All becomes less of an issue.

The Do-It-All-For-Me

If you go to any Home Depot in the U.S., there's a sign on the front of the building that reads – "Your DO-IT-YOURSELF Warehouse." Yet, customers will come in with the attitude that it's our job to do everything for them. However, this apparent negative can be turned into a positive because it represents a shift in what's going on in the overall demographics of our country, where a large segment of population is aging. There's more "Do it FOR me" than "I CAN do it myself." It presents opportunities for you to provide special services like installation and design. Companies that do this effectively can optimize their business with their mature customers.

We've had customers who needed to buy 200 two-by-fours but at a different length than what we sold. They'd want us to cut them for them, right then, right there. Home Depot and others have radial arm and panel saws to make dimensional cuts for convenience. We do not mind doing a few cuts; however, if you agree to their request, it creates huge problems. Personnel must be pulled off the floor to accomplish the task, leaving inadequate coverage. We always want to provide excellent customer service but not at the expense of all the other customers. It creates duress for everybody. Once I gave a customer a circular saw because they could not wait and didn't have any other way to cut what they needed. We want to help, but sometimes a customer's demand is overbearing. They are in their own world, with little regard for the impact their actions have on others. I know you have experienced someone in the airport who is walking and talking on their phone while dragging their luggage, weaving all over the concourse, then stopping so other people trip over them. When you make eye contact, they look at you as if to say, "What's *your* problem?" It's the same kind of person who drives in the fast lane five miles under the speed limit, a line of cars behind them, then gives you a dirty look when you pass them. That's how it is with these customers. They come in and need 36 locksets all keyed the same... and by the way, they need them in an hour. It's not good to wait until the last minute, but those customers do not understand that. Pam likes to say, "Poor planning on your part does not constitute an emergency on mine." The Do-It-All-For-Me customers take a defensive posture and refuse to accept options and alternatives. It is all about them...and they will test your limits on how to appease them.

The Name-Dropper

"I do know Bernie. I was in a meeting one time and I met Bernie Marcus. Do I need to call Bernie?" Someone posed this question to me one day when I was working with them. This is the customer type I loved to deal with the most. I'd think, *if you want to talk to founders, I can give you their phone number.* It's funny when that is one of the first things out of a customer's mouth. The original Home Depot founders, along with its former and current Presidents and CEOs, are public figures, belong to other organizations, and are deeply involved in the community. So, yes, they meet people within the communities they serve all the time. I bristled a bit, but always did my best for them, like any other customer. If they truly wanted to speak to an officer at the corporate office, we were encouraged to allow that, validating accessibility.

Within the last year of retiring from the company, I worked with a customer – an older gentleman who had been in the business world and owned houses in several different areas. In his retirement, he took on a small, multi-family unit as a project and demanded deep discounts from Home Depot. In addition, he wanted us to provide a concierge service above and beyond the scope of our services – and wasn't going to take any ifs, ands, or buts about it. I became involved because from the first instance he felt he didn't get the respect and service he deserved he would call the president of our division. Rolling downhill, it became my problem. I went to the store to meet with this gentleman – a legend in his own mind – who regaled me with stories of everything he'd accomplished in his life. He in fact, told me he invented the concept of the "staff meeting" for business, as part of his career, which I found comical. He made many claims about how he had done grandiose things and knew how to work the system.

"So, I'm going to tell you now. If you don't do everything I ask you to do, I will be calling your president and CEO. How do you feel about that?"

I replied, "Well, we can go about this a few ways. You can choose to work with me and allow me to help and if you feel that's not good enough, you have every right to call them. But I want you to think about that for a second. If you call them, they are going to call me back and ask what you and I talked about. I'm going to tell them my side of the story and we're going to be right back where we started. In the end, they can't do anything to take care of you, other than to direct me to do what's right under the circumstances. I'm going to do that anyway. That's what they pay me to do. To take care of you the best way possible within the scope of my authority."

Upon my retirement, this gentlemen's project was still in play and went to a peer of mine (lucky guy!). But this customer...if I told him I would call him back at three and then called him at three on the nose, he would pick up and say, "I was worried you weren't going to call me back. I was almost getting ready to call the president." That is frustrating and unnecessary to an employee who is providing excellent service. When a customer continuously hangs a threat over your head, it takes time and effort to deal with. However, it does affect you. Other than employees quitting a leader, they quit the difficult customer types. Associates would come up to me and state, "Erik, I just can't handle it anymore. Orientation is one thing; but when you get out on the floor with these customers man this is more than I signed up for."

It doesn't help that they deal with unreasonable, unruly customers. They may comprise a small portion of the customer population, but they are big blows to absorb. Like the news: there could be one thousand positive stories unfolding, but the media focuses on the one, big negative story to dominate their coverage, leaving you focused only on the bad. Very few people react well to threats. Know this: one very bad customer can ruin the entire day, no matter how many positive interactions take place.

The Litigators

These are the customers who, if they don't threaten to call the Home Depot President and CEO, they threaten to call their lawyer. This type takes the customer service aspect to a whole new level. Home Depot, along with most corporations, maintains a legal staff at the corporate office, in conjunction with local representation. If a customer's lawyer gets involved, it puts a stop to what you can do for them. Whenever a customer threatened to call their attorney, I'd say: "Please understand, if you get your lawyers involved, then I'll contact our legal department and get our lawyers involved. At that point, our relationship ends and theirs begins. I would rather assist you without the need to include others, so we can eliminate any more complexity."

This customer archetype is typically a high-dollar purchaser. An example would be a kitchen installation that had issues. The customer ripped apart their kitchen in expectation of our cabinets being delivered and installed, despite our guidance to not do that (Murphy's Law – if something can go wrong, it will). The cabinets were a week late (which happens from time to time) and the customer went berserk. It was an emotional issue because they couldn't take care of their family. Even though they ignored our recommendations, in their mind, it was ALL our fault. It degenerates into, "I'm going to sue you because I can't cook for my family." "This delay...I took days off, and I'm going to charge you for this. My lawyer is going to sue you." It takes a delicate touch and a firm hand when handling these customers because you cannot make everybody happy all the time. It is humanly impossible. Go for the win but be ready just in case. My advice for the best way to handle this customer type: always do everything you can within your power and document your every word and action.

On the service side, be true to yourself when dealing with customers. Be the best you can be and feel good about what you did. Don't let them defeat you: always remember, you need them, and they need you – that's what I taught my people. People who are miserable love to make others feel the same. My goal was to keep smiling, never raise my voice, and never get angry. The angrier they got, the more I made the effort to stay calm.

The Belligerent Customer

Over the years, belligerent customers have caused true incidents within our stores – much larger than necessary. On occasion, our customer service at Home Depot did not meet our company standards, resulting in angry customers. At times, associates said something wrong to a customer and vice-versa. We've even witnessed the (rare) sight of customers screaming at the top of their lungs, "I want that person fired." Many of these customers fit into multiple archetypes. In any business, you see the true nature of humans, which is often angry and child-like. The best way to handle it is to train your people well, and that training involves many factors, like not taking the bait when the customer invariably makes it personal. That's important because they *want* a reaction out of you. *Just breathe.* When they don't get their desired reaction, they might change tactics, but they may also be just stunned enough to listen! When you don't have to defend yourself, you can hear and understand what they are upset about, acknowledge if they have been wronged, and set about making it right. During my career, regardless of my position, I enjoyed dealing with the belligerent customers. You have a captive audience comprised of other customers and associates who will watch with interest and you walk into that bubble where the air gets thicker and the atmosphere gets quieter. All eyes and ears are on you, and the way you handle the situation showcases your level-headed-ness and calmness everyone present. It is very gratifying when surrounding customers commend your actions with words like, "Wow, you did great. You're a better man than I am. I would have told them to shut up or get out of my store." That always made us feel good. They are always watching (yes, there's the fishbowl again!), which means you have an amazing opportunity to be an ambassador for your business and your service standards. If you want to be a Super Star, be the one who deals with these customer types. Chances like this come along regularly; don't shy away from them, take the lead!

The Defiant Customer

Given the sheer number of customers and transactions in a Home Depot store, there were times when our environment was not as safe as it should have been. The Defiant Customer – the archetype who was either careless by nature or couldn't care less about your safety precautions – was one of the most difficult to deal with. We try to do most of the heavy lifting and require the usage of forklifts and other power equipment during dark hours, which as I've noted are the non-customer hours. At times, we have had to take large machinery or equipment out on the sales floor to help a customer during regular business hours. Our orange ladders bore signs saying, FOR HOME DEPOT PERSONNEL ONLY, yet we would often catch children and adults climbing the ladders. I'll admit, sometimes they did it out of pure frustration because they couldn't find a sales associate and felt as if they must climb the ladder themselves. As Voltaire said, "Common sense is not so common."

It's not easy asking someone to come down from the ladder. Often people overestimate their own abilities and get hurt. You just want to keep everyone safe, but you also prepare yourself, knowing they do NOT want to hear this. That's when they get belligerent; they do not want to be told what to do. It is especially scary when you find children on the ladder. I have witnessed far too many little kids falling from ladders or carts...and with concrete and steel everywhere, it is not a friendly environment for them. You try to instruct them in a calm voice, "Hey kids, I need you to do me a favor. I need you to come down from the ladder because that's only for guys and girls wearing an orange apron," only to hear their indignant parents scold, "How dare you tell my kids what to do!" When that happens, you must respond. This will always feel like a losing situation. When they cooperate, they will be angry and if they don't cooperate, they will be angry. In the end a safe, angry customer is better than an injured one. To all parents with small children: if you are in a business environment and somebody who works in that business makes a safety recommendation for you or your family, do not be defensive. Do not be arrogant. Understand they want to help and want to avoid an injurious situation.

One example stands out in my memory, involving an aisle that went from the front of the store to the back of the store with no interruption. I was on one end, walking toward the other end, when I saw a customer with a shopping cart about 100 feet away. Two small children were standing up in the cart, which was wheeling toward me. Then I noticed the child in the front teetering. Something told me they were going to fall out, and I started running. I did not make it in time: I got within about 25 feet when that child fell head-first onto the concrete. All these years later, it haunts me – that sound! – and makes me second-guess myself. *Should I have started running sooner? Should my employees have talked to those parents?* We have unbreakable rules at Home Depot: no customers on ladders and kids must sit down in carts. At one point, we even provided NASCAR-themed carts to encourage kids to sit. We did that for a reason; there's so much happening at Home Depot. When parents bring their kids with them into your environment, you, as a company representative, are as responsible as their parent for monitoring them.

Yes, we employ barricades across aisles. Do all customers honor them? No, no, *no*. They'll pull them back and walk through. I've had customers walk right underneath a forklift, which had a heavy load in the air, and stand there to look at something on a shelf (as my daughter would say, "Did you get hit with a stupid stick?"). Aside from belligerence, it's almost like tempting fate with a "It can never happen to me" mentality. Search forklift accidents on YouTube if you need further proof – it's ugly stuff.

The Troublemaker

Dictionary.com defines a troublemaker "as a person who causes difficulty, distress, worry for others, especially one who does so habitually as a matter of malice." Whether male or female, The Troublemaker creates a range of challenging issues: yelling; getting in your face; talking over you or your associates; cutting the line; deliberately taking someone else's product or shopping cart; using profanity; throwing product at someone or on the floor; demanding a discount "just because,"; and threatening bodily harm when someone won't give them what they want. Whew! That's an exhaustive list, but I forgot to mention one more thing: The Troublemaker will often try to play employee against employer in their misguided attempt to win. Yeah, some people just like to watch the world burn.

Once, I worked in a store with about eight assistant managers, and not all of us dealt with customers the same way. When faced with a difficult confrontation, our associates gravitated toward calling the manager they knew would take care of the customer, while backing them up. If you are a manager reading this who handles customer complaints, here's some advice: in a face-to-face, three-way interaction featuring you, your associate, and your customer, you must find a balance between supporting the associate, the company, AND the customer.

If you approach the customer in public and say, "Yes, sir, you are right. My associate is wrong. Here's what I'm going to do for you," that harms your associate, whether they were wrong or not. On the flip side, if you approach the customer, knowing the associate had done the right thing, you must support the associate while diffusing the customer. When an employee is wrong, don't admit that in public; that should be done in a private and professional manner, behind closed doors. I've witnessed managers who thought they made themselves looks bigger by throwing their associate under the bus to take care of customer. When you lose the respect of even just one team member, it will impact your customer service in a negative way.

At Home Depot's refunds desk (a highly volatile area, as I've described previously), depending on each employee's status within the company, they are empowered up to a certain dollar amount, with guidelines on appropriate incentives; for example, when to offer a gift card versus crediting the refund amount to whatever credit card the customer used. Once, a customer paid by credit card, and our rule at the time was if you paid by credit card, the refund went back to that credit card. Well, this customer insisted on cash, which was a rather large amount. I went up to desk and listened to his story before pulling my returns desk person off to the side to get their version of what happened. Then, I went back to the customer and notified him, "Okay, sir, I've talked to them. I've listened to you. I have to say, my person is correct in what they stated, per Home Depot policy. I apologize if that doesn't meet your needs, but can we come to a compromise? What else can we do?" Sometimes, it worked. Other times, they demanded the cash and I gave it to them. Still other times, I took a hard line and said, "No, I can't do that." But no matter the decision, I put the onus on me as the manager – not on the associate. I tried to get the associate out of the mix as soon as possible, which they always appreciated. The Troublemaker will always try to divide.

While every situation is different, finding the right resolution depends on asking the right questions: "Why do you need it in cash, versus the credit card?" "What is the reasoning for that?" Sometimes, you'll arrive at a satisfactory bottom-line answer that enables you to give them what they want. Other times, you won't.

I've encountered The Troublemaker in the form of customers who used Home Depot as a bank – whether stealing merchandise or printing fake receipts to shake us down for money, or by using a credit card that they never intended on paying, then getting a cash refund. As always, it's important to get help from your superior as you deal with each situation. If company policy dictates a specific action, there are always exceptions. If it's above your head, you must consult with your boss (if you don't believe me, please re-read Chapter 6). In my own dealings with customers, at times I've had to tell them, "Listen, I'm not going to be able to help you today. But I'm going to reach out to my supervisor, partner with them, and see what we can do. I'm going to get back to you." Then, I would follow-through and respond back to that customer. When you reach the management rung of the ladder, handling all the customer types becomes an art form. This is especially true of The Troublemaker.

The Me First (Even If I'm Not) Customer

This archetype feels that they must always be first. In fact, they'll often ask you, "Do you know who I am?" I've had customers pull on my shirt and inform me, "Hey, I'm going to spend about $10,000 in here today. I need your help," when they can clearly see I'm assisting someone else. This type of customer, for some reason, thinks they are more important than any other customer. Invariably in this situation, I'd respond, "Sir/Ma'am, I'm sorry, but this customer was here first. I will get with you, as soon as I can. The "Me First" customer type expresses their unhappiness visibly in most cases, instead of gracious understanding and respect.

Another former Home Depot employee named Ted shared a customer experience with me that fits the "Me First" archetype. At the time, he worked outside in the garden department in our West

Boca Raton store, and as he describes it, it was a busy day with both gates open. To separate the cashier aisles, they'd placed pallets of mulch down the middle, stacked up high. Ted was speaking with a customer on one side of the cashier's aisle toward the middle of the garden center, when he looked out toward the cashiers and couldn't believe his eyes: a woman was beeping her horn, trying to pull her Mercedes into the garden center. He took off running in her direction, waving his arms and exclaiming, "No, no!" He kept gesturing for the woman to back up, but she had no regard for other customers or the associates as she drove her car against the bags of mulch, tearing them open. Ted finally reached her car, got her situated to where it was safe, and moved the other customers out of the way. When she backed up to where she could open her door, he asked, "Ma'am, what are you doing? Are you okay? You need to go park in the parking lot. It's huge. It's out front, you couldn't have missed it."

She simply handed him a shopping list and ordered, "I only need these few things and I'm in a rush."

The West Boca store was in an area full of country clubs, with trailer park communities on the other end. So, it was big mix of customers from one end of the economic scale to the other. During his time there, Ted had been handed shopping lists before, necessitating him to remind the customer, "This is a warehouse. We have big carts where you can put some mulch and potted plants." Of course, if an elderly customer needed help, he would always offer, "Come on, I'll walk with you," to guide them in the right direction.

In Ted's experience, it seemed as if the County Clubbers most often fit into the "Me First" mentality while the shopper who lived in the trailer parks understood your labor and tried to give you his last buck. He or she was probably smart enough to realize the people working there were also blue collar like them.

The Violent Customer

I've said it before, but it merits repeating: most customers are legitimate, civilized, and appreciative, but this segment bothers me the most. Among the many codes I mentioned at the beginning of the chapter, Home Depot had one to alert the store when somebody witnessed or experienced a physical altercation with a customer. Often, by the time you arrived (for these, you full-out ran) on the scene, the customer would have left. One time, a customer threw a chainsaw at a returns desk associate. He was trying to return it with no ID, no receipt, nothing. When she upheld store policy, he threw it at her, so she called the code and he ran out. By the time we got out to parking lot, he was gone…with any luck, to attend an anger-management class, which would serve this customer type well.

Understand, retail isn't just about you as a customer. When you interact with an employee, you don't know what's going on in their life either. When you follow The Golden Rule and treat others as you would like to be treated, I'm willing to bet that 90 percent of the time, you will get it back in spades. Again, we're not perfect at Home Depot and that's up to us to work on. From the customer viewpoint, when you go into any business, acknowledge that the people working there are not your indentured servants. Yes, they get paid to serve you and owe you good service.

The Pillager

Since we're on the topic of customers not always being right, one of my pet peeves was the customer I call "The Pillager." These customers would come in and just trash our stores. It is an insurmountable task to ensure that the right item is in the right bin every day, which is why Home Depot employs teams to keep up with it. Prime examples are PVC parts, electrical devices, and the nuts and bolts aisle. It was simply amazing to witness customers pull out products, rip packages open, then put products back in the wrong location – with the attitude that Home Depot pays someone to clean it up, so it is fine. They are also the first ones to complain to management that they can never find what they are looking for because everything is in the wrong place. *Go figure!* Sometimes they come in seeking the perfect piece of lumber and I can't fault them for that. However, I *can* fault them for pillaging through the top 100, throwing them on the floor, getting their couple of pieces, and neglecting to put the 100 back. The Pillager simply leaves them on the floor for an associate to deal with. That's the nature of retail. Again, I am not asking for sympathy; just defining the different customer archetypes and venting about how they take commitment and effort, which detracts from time and energy from other legitimate actions.

I can tell you our mission has always been to provide the greatest customer service on the face of the planet. We're not there yet. I don't know if we'll ever get there. Even with specialized teams employed to help us maintain our stores, it's a problem – one we challenge our associates with solving every day. But in the end, you have a limited number of resources. You must optimize those resources to the best of your ability and move forward.

Let me be real: I can't count how many times I've had to grit my teeth dealing with the above customer types. I can guarantee there are file cabinets in every location I've worked with my knuckle marks on them from when I went to the back to "take a breath." I am not kidding. I almost put my hand through a wall on multiple occasions in the aftermath of dealing with one of (or a combination of) these customer archetypes. It was always a game to not let them win.

"Folks, I worked in Philadelphia," I'd inform them. "You are not going to hurt my feelings. You're just not. Curse all you want. I'm going to sit here with a smile on my face and then I'm going to take care of it for you. You don't need to scream. I'm going to help you. If you think you must act this way because of something that happened at another company or business, it doesn't need to happen here."

Every time I visited one of our stores in the D.C. area, I dealt with a specific customer who shopped there every day and always wanted to talk to me. He was a PRO customer who favored this one store and visited each day at about the same time. My first few inter-actions with this guy were very uncomfortable, with him threatening, and complaining, "Oh my God, I can never find anything I want in this store. Do I have to shop at Lowe's?" (by the way, that's another customer archetype I'll get to on the list). Whenever I walked into this store, I searched for him; it could be once a week, once every few weeks, whatever, but when I was there, I'd find him first and say, "Hey, lay it on me. What do you have for me today?"

When he finally smiled, I said, "This is good."

"Why?"

"Well, you're giving me valid information that the store and I need to react to. I'm going to find you every time I am here." Sort of like what my dad said about gathering your most vocal associates together to obtain their feedback, I wanted to talk to these loud, boisterous, complaining customers. Why? Aside from their personality traits and the fact that, at times, I wanted to take them out in the parking lot and give them a real piece of my mind, they gave me valuable information. And, somewhere in the middle lies the truth, the content you want to receive. I've seen too many managers fail to get the data from these types of customers because they spend more time focusing on being offended by them than they do in garnering the information they need from them to improve their business. We've discussed multiple customer archetypes in this chapter, but one trait they all have in common is their ability to tell you how to make your business better.

When you make it a game, it's much more enjoyable. It creates an adrenalin rush and a competition among your employees. The associates at this D.C.-area store started to respond to this guy because when I came in, they wanted me to spend my time with them, not him. He gave us the real, raw information we needed to make positive changes to our business.

The "I'm Going to Lowe's (or insert another competitor's name)" Customer – THIS ONE IS PERSONAL

These days, there's a Lowe's and Home Depot within 10 miles of each other, everywhere, which means your customer has a choice. They can either shop at Home Depot or go to your competitor. You can look at it as "here we go again," or in a spirit of competition (a topic I discuss in detail in an upcoming chapter). Every time a customer remarked, "Well, you're forcing me to go to Lowe's," I would always teach my team to do something not to let that customer go. We would do anything we could to keep them from going there: substitute a product, reduce a price, etc. In certain cases, we had employees go to our competitors to buy a product, then deliver it to the customer. We let them think it came from us, even though it came from our competitor. There is much more to come, regarding Lowe's, our nemesis, in an upcoming chapter.

The "Package Opener/I Only Need a Few of Them" Customer

Another time in the West Boca store, our former associate Ted told me a guy was stealing the little rubber washers that go in the garden hose. At least he had some respect for the store where he was just trying to pull one off from the sealed ends, while Ted just sat there watching and giggling. Keep in mind, the package of ten washers is only 25 cents. Ted let him finish, witnessed him placing the washers in his pocket, then walked over and said, "Sir, please don't tell me you are going to walk out of our store with our merchandise without paying?"

"Excuse me, I only need a couple," he replied indignantly. Then he proceeded to go off on Ted, as if he was in the wrong. The associate walked to the register and asked the cashier to call security. Yes, it was only ten cents' worth of product, but we can't allow theft in our stores. The employee from security was like, "Don't worry, I've got this. I deal with it all the time." She took him in her office, where she made him call his wife to tell her what he did as a punishment. When warranted in these situations, this store would call the police.

You could also call this archetype "The Empty Package Customer," because they only wanted "a something" and they would not pay for a whole package regardless how inexpensive. It's crazy what some customers perceive about retail to rationalize their criminal behavior, "Don't worry, they have a budget for this kind of stuff."

The Clueless Customer

Imagine standing in the middle of the aisle with your orange apron on. A customer walks up to you and the first thing they ask is,

"Hey, do you work here?" It got to the point where I'd look down at my apron with my name on it, then look back at them. "Uh, yes, I work here." Harmless, but funny.

YOUR MISSION, IF YOU CHOOSE TO ACCEPT IT

While the customer is not always right, at the end of the day, the ones described in this chapter can put you over the top: in a figurative sense, with your brand, and in a literal sense, with your results, profits, and metric you use to grade your business. You want to kill them – in a manner of speaking, of course – but you must understand that despite the turmoil they create, they can provide legitimate information and situational awareness you might not have otherwise. If you had a choice to spend time with 10 of your favorite customers or 10 of your most difficult, I challenge you to go into the session with your 10 most difficult customers with a notepad, an open mind, and a willingness to listen without being defensive. I guarantee you'll come out of that meeting with more credible and actionable data and situational awareness than you would if you'd chosen to meet with your favorite 10 customers.

Whatever your business, position yourself where you can watch your customers walk out empty-handed. Why? Two reasons: 1.) You may never see them again. Most unhappy customers do not complain; they just leave and go somewhere else, and 2.) If you ask, they will tell you why they are not buying anything...and that information is critical and urgent because it is impacting more than just one customer. Take a cue from the military and its slang term/philosophy, *Embrace the Suck*. Defined, it means to consciously accept or appreciate something that is extremely unpleasant but unavoidable for forward progression. I believe the term is appropriate for the customer service aspect of business.

Sure, managing these customer archetypes all day, every day in retail gets fatiguing: imagine 33 years of doing it! In season (summertime), the typical Home Depot store averages 15,000 to 45,000 customers per week. To all sales associates: when you deal with these situations, please know that most customers are legitimate. Don't make the masses suffer for the actions of a few. It's easier to punish everybody than it is to deal with the one person at fault.

In business (and all aspects of life), conflict management skills are vital. If you surround yourself with "yes" people, you will only get so far because all they'll do is kiss your butt and fail to offer constructive criticism. Only those willing to tell you the unvarnished truth will help you learn and grow – even if they are a**h***s about it.

Ladders and Learnings

- Regardless of all customers types, your job is to be "Best in Class" when it comes to customer service, representing your personal brand and the brand of your company.
- Be that person who always leads the charge to handle the most difficult customers, understanding the value they have to offer in terms of feedback, perceptions and actionable items.

Executive Memo

Foster an environment that is inclusive of all members, where your organization's expectations of customer service is fully understood. Ensure that every employee and team-member comprehend the value of service to them, both professionally and personally.

9

EQUILIBRIUM

"We have overstretched our personal boundaries and forgotten that true happiness comes from living an authentic life, fueled with a sense of purpose and balance."

— DR. KATHLEEN HALL

E verything is BIGGER in Texas. Since Houston represented my first district manager assignment, I include my passion and intensity in that statement. I was all-in with my new role and my team, acclimating to my environment as fast as I possibly could – and not just in terms of loud shirts, cowboy boots, and a Rolex watch. I'm not joking – I worked a *ton* of hours. I got up at five a.m. every day and arrived home at various times during the night, which made it impossible for Pam to plan dinner since she never knew exactly when I'd walk through the door.

Sociologists will tell you that one of the most important times for a family is when they share a meal at the dinner table. I could go into a store with every intention of leaving at 6 p.m. so I could get home in time to eat with Pam and Jackie, only to have an associate or a customer approach me with a problem or receive an urgent call from the vice-president about a project that required my input. Other times, I delayed myself because I lost all track of time while engaging with the team. Yeah, I was doing my job and impressing everybody with my commitment and diligence. I was going for it with everything I had, making up for lost time.

As for my family, I assumed we were living the dream in our gorgeous house complete with a koi pond, an amazing deck, and a playground for my daughter. I had even installed a zip line for her that extended from behind the garage and through the backyard – every little kid's dream, right? In my convoluted brain, I was doing everything well at work and at home. That is, until the day my five-year-old straightened my keyster out, making me realize that while my professional brand was excellent, my personal brand was lacking.

To this day, I don't understand why homes in Houston had fireplaces. Ours did, standing against the living room wall, looking ornate and welcoming; I don't think we lit that thing once the entire time we lived in Houston. But as the focal point of the room it had a mantle and a lower portion that extended out. After work one evening, I walked in to find Jackie sitting on the lower portion, drawing on a piece of paper. "Hey, let me see your picture," I said, sitting down beside her. Looking at it, I noticed a smaller person and a larger person.

"Who's that?" I asked, pointing to the larger person.

"That's Mommy."

"Okay. Who's this little person?"

"That's me, silly."

"Oh, cool. Where am I?"

"You're at work."

Man down, man down! I felt like I'd just been kicked in the groin with a steel-toed boot. It hit me harder than anything I could remember, possibly even the demotion. It's difficult to calculate the number of events I have missed over the years because of business requirements. Birthdays, holidays and activities took a lower priority. Prior to that incident with Jackie, I demonstrated empathy to my associates and their personal needs but hadn't looked in the mirror and questioned what I was doing for my own family. It was a pivotal moment that made me realize I was going down the wrong path when it came to my family life. I reorganized my calendar to support Pam and Jackie to a higher degree in terms of being there for doctors' visits, recitals, sporting events or other occasions. Whereas before, Pam did all the basic stuff with Jackie on her own. It's no wonder management positions in general have one of the highest divorce rates; for every 100 people in management, 35.75 are divorced. Thirty-six divorces for every 100 managers? That's too high a price to pay for professional success. Like turnover in the business world, this impact to families is momentous. Something had to change.

In terms of supporting my own family, where was I? Nowhere to be found. Sure, I might have attended some events at random, but when I relayed the story to my wife, who wasn't in the room at the time, she gave me a look of resignation that told me it was, in fact, true. My innocent child meant no harm; she simply expressed her reality. That was the first time I doubted if I was wired to be a regional vice-president, willing to take on the obligations that the position mandated. After this interaction, I felt a strong inclination to strike a better work-family balance. We only had one child and wanted to raise her right.

Another time Pam, Jackie and I were riding in our car, with Jackie strapped into her car seat in the back with a play telephone. She was mimicking me talking on the phone to my store managers, using my specific verbiage at the start of the call. Again, I remind you, there were no SMART phones in the 90s. If a district manager wanted to reach their store managers, they used a voicemail system, which could be set up for an individual or a group. Every time I left a voicemail, I'd begin, "Hey store managers, this is Erik." I had no idea how robotic I sounded until I heard Jackie imitating me on her play phone, "Hey store managers, this is Erik," in the sweet voice of a toddler, pretending to leave messages. You can perceive that as cute, which I did at first. Then I thought, "How much have I been doing this around my family and taking time away from them?" It must have been way too much if Jackie could mimic how I conducted the calls. Not the impact I wanted to be imparting onto my daughter.

It created an inward struggle: where did I want my career to go? I was still in love with the company and my job. Every time I put that orange apron on, I felt like Super Man putting on his cape. I still felt that passion, drive and commitment, but WOW, here was my kid, proving my deficiency as a father. As I looked in the mirror, I asked, "What am I doing and what do I want?" That's when I suddenly realized the proper question to ask was, "What do **WE** want?"

A CHIP OFF THE OLD BLOCK

Many years later, when Jackie was in her early teens, she accompanied me to a Home Depot in D.C. We walked in to discover that the store was in total disarray. it was awful. Without any prompting, she looked at me and asked, "Why does the store look like crap today?"

"*Excuse* me? What did you say?" That was my first reaction; I taken aback by her use of the word "crap."

"It looks terrible in here, Dad. Look at the out-of-stocks, the clutter on the floor." *Oh my!*

Jackie took it all in as if she was one of my store managers. To keep her occupied a bit, I said, "How about this?" and explained a worklist to her. For readers who don't know, a worklist is a tool that allows management to assign and delegate tasks. It makes the people who work for them shudder. You make your worklist as you walk – observing, critiquing, and analyzing, writing down your findings. It's one of those good or not-so-good gifts you can give to people when you leave to inform them about needs and objectives. It's also a tool to follow up and confirm all requested actions are happening within the agreed-upon time.

After I described it to Jackie, I asked her to walk the store and make her own personal worklist. Then, I cut her loose. A while later she brought it back to me. I was blown away by the quality and the depth of her analysis, and how she truly looked at the store from the eyes of a shopper. I was so impressed I took her report to my next staff meeting with my store managers. Without telling them who wrote it, I presented it to them and asked them to critique it in terms of the content. Most of the managers felt that whoever compiled it should be complimented and promoted.

"What if I told you that my thirteen-year-old daughter wrote that?" I asked.

"What?" they were shocked.

"Yep. My kid."

Today, at age 25, Jackie is a success in her job, performing in her role with dedication, a strong work ethic, and a willingness to accept additional responsibilities. I like to think that maybe I gave her a solid foundation by the things I did and what she observed, but there was a price to pay. Luckily, I caught it in time to strike that work-family balance...and it all goes back to the eye-opening interaction by the fireplace with my little girl that forced me to check myself.

What is the lesson here? No matter your level within an organization, you are a human being first. You are flawed and you have many of the same issues as others. Early on in my time, I was trying to be "Super District Manager." But I was failing to make the effort to be a good father and husband. Once I acknowledged my mistake, I started asking Pam for as much notice as possible about upcoming doctors' appointments, school events, dances, choir, and sports competitions. If I was in town, I made the commitment to get to all of them and found a way to incorporate them into my work schedule.

I told my team about the fireplace story. I spoke first about what I was going to do for them, wanting them to understand the profound and difficult lesson I learned. Many of them were hard-chargers and would do anything to be successful. I cautioned them "If I find out that you didn't go to a specific family event you should have attended at a minimum we're going to sit down and discuss why." Then, to show how serious I was, I added, "Hey, if you're worried that I'm going to fire you for something, THIS is it. I started tracking everybody's birthdays and made sure that they knew, no matter what day of the week it was, they could take the day off to celebrate with their family members. "I better never find out from your spouse or significant other that you didn't show up for your family because you never bothered to ask for the time."

Of course, I was only kidding about firing them. I wanted to convey the intensity of my emotion on the topic. I talked about how I was going to change, and how I needed their understanding and communication. If they really needed me to be at their store but I couldn't get there at a certain time or had to leave early for an event, I was putting the onus on them to communicate in clear terms with me. They had the responsibility to be precise so that I could understand and adjust Jackie and Pam's appointments if necessary.

Thanks to Jackie, recognizing and implementing a policy to uphold a work-life balance for my team and our family provided a wonderful dynamic for our life. However, in no way did this decrease the obligation to perform to the highest of standards and results.

One of my store managers, Bill, suffered a debilitating back injury that relegated him to a wheelchair not too long before the annual store manager meeting was to take place. Due to his physical condition, he had to remain in a wheelchair and could not fly. Bill was a valuable part of my team and I wanted him to be there. At meetings, you wanted to sit together with your team. One of my goals for my teams, was to instill a sense of pride in the unit. It became important for us to be together at all events. When Bill broke the news to me that there was no way he could go, since he could not travel by plane, I asked, "Well, what if we drove?"

"What do you mean, what if we drove?"

"What if I rent one of those vans that would accommodate your wheelchair and then you, me, and our wives drive together? That way, you can go to the meeting," I offered. We discussed it for a while, but based on his medical condition, his doctor did not approve it.

At the annual meeting, Bernie and Arthur sat on a panel on a stage, talking about how we treat our managers and associates, and how we're all a big family. Then Bernie announced, "I want to read you a letter." As soon as he got a couple of sentences in, I knew it had been written by my store manager. It began, "Hi, my name is Bill. And I want to tell you why I love working for this company." He took Bernie and Arthur through the whole scenario about how I'd offered to drive him to the meeting and went on about how that's the culture of the company and how much he appreciated my efforts. It was one of many, many examples where associates and managers took care of each other, not letting circumstances dictate the outcome. The culture of Home Depot was, and is, a living testament to what makes the company strong, carrying it through the toughest of times.

You realize the importance of the human touch to those who work with you. You recognize that when you do the right thing for others, they will do more than they thought they would because of their loyalty to you as their leader. This is one of the easiest investments to make at any point in your career – paying dividends in incredible ways.

Companies survey their employees to receive feedback on what matters most to them. Every single one I've read – where employees rank the top ten reasons why they feel so strongly about the company and why they want to stay with them – money, wages, and compensation are most often ranked around five or six. One through four are all about the experience; the respect, the appreciation, the ability to succeed, and how they're regarded as a human being, not a number. That was never lost on me when I reviewed these surveys, reinforcing my beliefs and my actions.

A Grandfather's Love for the Orange

Recently, I connected with a guy via Facebook messenger who told me the story of his grandfather, a former Home Depot employee:

"Hello Erik, I'm contacting you now not for businesses purposes, but I saw that you were writing a book about Home Depot and your time there. I personally have an attachment to Home Depot. My grandparents raised me to be a strong kid, a tough son of a gun, but I just wanted to share with you a story.

"My grandfather, who died last year, was a Home Depot employee for about thirteen years, after he retired from AT & T. He loved it and worked there until he couldn't work anymore. In fact, he loved it so much that after five years of working there and taking care of people, he lost his vision and was no longer allowed to drive. But he wouldn't let that stop him. He rode his pedal bike to work every day. I saw him throw on his apron, jump on his bike, and ride the two miles to work. He did that for eight more years, until the age of 82. One day, he was riding his bike back from work and was hit by a car in a hit-and-run that left him helpless until someone found him with eight broken ribs and lacerations everywhere. A year later, he died, from his injuries. Grandpa loved what he did for Home Depot, the people, and the culture. I buried him with his orange apron on almost two years ago. He totally disregarded the doctors, so he could keep working at Home Depot."

I replied, "Wow, I'm humbled by stories that are shared with me, especially yours and your grandfather, whom I am sure was a great man in many ways. Your story brought tears to my eyes, for the love I have for the company is shared by many. I admire you for your love and respect for him."

"He was the best. He really did give his life for the chance to work at Home Depot. Best of luck."

"Hey, thanks for the info. I just shared your story with my wife and mom, and they were blown away. I hope they caught the SOB that did this to him, or at least that karma did the work."

"I hope so too. And hey, if you know of any regional operations jobs for Home Depot, let me know."

Even now, two years into my retirement, I still get goosebumps when I hear stories like these that illustrate Home Depot's commitment to treating its employees as family, and the positive impact it makes on associates when they feel valued and needed. You cannot measure the ROI you receive as a company when its leaders demonstrate personal humility and humanity.

YOUR FUTURE FOR A CORVETTE?

Bernie Marcus had something on his mind as he stood on the stage at our annual meeting one year. He knew our stock had been growing, enhancing our financial portfolios; he also knew some folks were using their stock money to serve their short-sighted personal choices. When he asked us, "How many of you sold Home Depot Stock to buy a Corvette this year?" Close to 50 hands went up.

"I want you to know how stupid you are," he scolded. Hands were lowered very quickly. "Do you realize how much that $50,000 cost you down the road? How much do you think that same amount of stock is going to be worth ten years from now? Fifteen years? I'm telling you here and now, you spent over a million dollars for that Corvette. So, you'd better enjoy it. I hope you do, because down the road, you're going to be missing a million dollars. Now you know where it went. I hope you're happy with yourselves." On many occasions, Bernie had indicated how much he wanted to give his people the same opportunity to achieve financial security, wealth, and prosperity that he and Arthur had been given. No doubt, he felt frustrated by some of his employees' dubious choices. None of us were upset at his message, again, understanding it came from the heart. We knew it was delivered with love.

Today, some politicians and activists make an argument for wealth distribution by pointing out that high-level executives earn on average 273 times the amount of money their employees do – as if that's a problem. Most of them have never worked in a corporate environment. In my opinion, there's no rational way to compare an executive officer's pay to the average associate when you consider the risks a founder takes to start a business. Factor in the tremendous obligations, financial results, and life commitments that ensue once the business succeeds and expands, and you get a fuller understanding of the risk they take on. Daily, the executive must make multiple decisions that impact thousands to millions of people. It's a tremendous responsibility, one that cannot be truly understood unless one has been there. Thomas Jefferson once referred to the office of the President of the United States as "splendid misery."

Relating that to business, everyone believes life is easy at the top. No, it is not – due to the tremendous sacrifices, obligations, risks, and responsibilities.

Bernie went on with the meeting. He knew he had to tell some harsh truths. He was never one to shy away from sharing his thoughts and feelings, and if he had to use a group of people as his vehicle, he did. Truth be told, many people at Home Depot (me included), were not used to having that kind of money. You'll recall I started out as a part-time associate making six dollars per hour. As an assistant manager, I remember purchasing my first house in Orlando. To finance it, I exercised stock options. I made a phone call to our brokerage partner and received a check for $100,000 two days later. There I was, in my 20s and I could get my hands on that kind of money with a simple phone call. It was crazy good, but also crazy bad. Looking back, I would not do it the same way. Other than Bernie's dose of reality on the Corvette, no one mentored us on how to manage finances of that magnitude. We were so young and uneducated in these matters and believed the stock growth would continue unimpeded – our pot of gold at the end of the rainbow.

Many folks sold stock to get their hands on a ton of money, only to be in for a rude awakening when tax time rolled around because we didn't understand the concept of capital gains. A vicious cycle began of having to sell more stock to pay taxes until they finally got themselves out of the mess. Corporations must teach their employees how to handle significant amounts of money. Today, Home Depot does an excellent job of providing resources for employees at all levels, but back then we were on our own (although it was a good problem to have). With his personal leadership style and philosophy, Bernie pushed messages utilizing tough love when warranted. We loved him for it. To this day, he still possesses that fiery passion and rhetoric that nearly drives you to kill for him. It's the same with Arthur. Their leadership philosophy was something to behold...and at its heart was a genuine desire to help others, including their employees and customers, and the communities in which Home Depot had a presence.

THE OLDER I GOT, THE SMARTER MY DAD BECAME

Referring once again to my dad's advice, with respect to human interaction and relationships, I learned as much from the ones doing it wrong as I did from the ones doing it right. Even today, I still get feedback from former coworkers. I'm connected to a former member of my team named Matt on LinkedIn, who used to work for me as an assistant manager (yeah, for an old geezer, I'm pretty good with social media), a guy I hadn't heard from in years. Back in our Home Depot days, we had a conversation:

"Hey, Erik, I'm thinking about selling some stock and I'd like your opinion."

Shoot, I'm not a stockbroker; that's why I have a financial adviser (something I'll discuss more later). Given Bernie and other Home Depot officers' presentations and comments at multiple meetings and gatherings, I kind of questioned my assistant manager about what he planned to do with the money and why. In the end, I recommended that he not sell the stock and consider other options.

Almost 10 years later, he messaged me on LinkedIn that he wanted to talk. When we got on the phone our conversation consisted of him thanking me for talking him out of selling his stock, which had grown at an incredible pace over the span of a decade. "What I have now, versus what I would have had, blows my mind," he told me. "If not for you that day, I would have sold it."

You could do an online search for the number of millionaires Home Depot created through their employee stock program; according to an interview with Ken Langone in 2018, the company boasts 3,000 *multimillionaires*, thanks to its incredible success. Looking back on the incident, I remember thinking, *Oh my! I told him not to sell and if something happens to it, he's going to hate my guts.* But it worked out. You realize your position of influence isn't just professional, it's personal. Your employees watch how you do everything. If you put yourself out there as a flawed human being like everybody else who pays bills like everybody else and puts your pants on one leg at a time like everybody else, it expands your approachability and guarantees that people will come to you for advice and/or guidance.

Often, employees asked me, "Hey, you've been around a long time. How do you manage your 401K?" I was always honest enough to share. One of my flaws is that I share *too much* (just ask Pam, who asked me repeatedly to limit the amount of personal information I divulged). I'd tell my associates how I'd done some stupid things with stock or with the compensation that I'm probably going to regret for the rest of my life, hoping that it would help them understand.

I learned from my mistakes and remained open and honest about them. There aren't many leaders who have the guts to drop their guard and let people know they've screwed up in their lives too. Goodness, I've talked to some holier-than-thou types who think their s**t doesn't stink. They come across to others as inaccessible and untouchable, putting up a wall that separates them from their team members. I witnessed the way others got treated, discovered how I wanted to be treated and how I wanted to treat my coworkers. I put the *Golden Rule* into action in my professional life, not just my personal life. With every step up the ladder in the Home Depot hierarchy, I carried that lesson forward.

LIKE FATHER, LIKE SON

That pivotal moment with Jackie by the fireplace made me look back and compare my life with my dad's. It is crazy similar: neither one of us obtained a college degree and both of us worked multiple jobs until we found "the one." We moved all over the country dragging our families with us. We achieved successful levels, retiring in our 50s. It's not lost on me that my life has mirrored my father's life to a remarkable extent. My parents did the same thing I was guilty of at the time: they were so busy working that they weren't there for us as much as they could've or should've been. It was because they sacrificed and worked hard to provide for the family's material needs and elevate themselves level-by-level in their respective companies. Yeah, I might've started this book by sharing my youthful doubts about ever becoming like my father. As the saying goes, when we're little, we think our parents are the smartest people on the planet until we reach age 12. Then, from 13-20, we think they're completely stupid and when we turn 21, all the sudden we realize, *Hell, they really knew what they were talking about!*

Now that I'm older, I've come to some realizations. Despite a rough transition my senior year of high school, my parents did what they thought was right by keeping the family together. They did the best they could under the circumstances. Fortunately for me, thanks to my daughter, I got the gut-check much earlier than my mom and dad. I feel blessed that it happened when she was only five years-old, so I could react in time.

NOT MY FIRST RODEO

We loved Bernie's road shows. They were a two-day event, rotated through the 19 regions. Comprised of two store visits within the host district on day one, they were followed by a dinner with the entire region's complement of store managers and district managers. While at dinner, Bernie would ask us to provide a list of topics that we wanted to discuss at the general meeting, which lasted all the next day. At the general meeting on day two, Bernie and all attending officers would address the list of topics, and provide thoughts, potential solutions, and next steps. These events offered us unrestricted access to Bernie and the officers, giving us a proactive mechanism in two respects: first, the ability for all attendees to vent frustrations and make recommendations, and second, the officer team attained a barometer of the morale, along with opportunities, that were inhibiting the stores.

While in Houston we hosted one of Bernie's last events. A month-and-a-half in advance, the company announced that the Humble store (one of mine) was selected as one of the two stores Bernie wished to visit. *Game on.* Remember, I had experience with events of this magnitude, vis-à-vis the Orlando remodel visit. To prepare, the store manager Dwight and I sat down and strategized. For 40 days, we killed ourselves to make that store perfect. We did not do it alone. The store's associates were also excited, knowing that Bernie's time with the company was getting short. They were aware that it could be their last opportunity to interact with him, and that drove them to make the store as fantastic as possible, out of respect. Numerous resources were in the store every day by our sides, assisting in all preparations: merchants from the corporate office, vendors, and associates from other stores — everyone wanted to be part of it. When all was said and done, it seemed each employee wanted to put it on their resume.

Thankfully, Dwight was the man for the job. I didn't have to challenge him on the commitment and effort needed to prepare the store. Its importance was unspoken; it was an unstated honor to be selected. Although upset at first, other managers offered to assist. One of the keys to Dwight's success was his competitiveness. We lived in the same Houston subdivision and competed over Christmas decorations on our houses every year. Like little kids, we had to one-up each other. His goal was to outdo the district manager and my attitude was there was no way I'd let a store manager beat me on my home's Christmas display! Our wives hated having to spend more money every year, but Clark Griswold had nothing on us.

To facilitate his visit to Humble, the company requested that we rent SUVs and pick him up at the airport. The Home Depot founders flew on corporate jets into private airports. I was tasked with picking Bernie up and driving him to the store. *No pressure, none at all!* A billionaire, founder of Home Depot and I'm gonna drive him through Houston? My mind swirled with all the "what ifs:" *What if I get in an accident? What if I get a flat tire? What if I get a ticket because of my lead foot?* By the way, in my 33 years with the company, I never had the privilege of flying in any of the company jets. Oh well.

The day of his arrival, I got to the airport an hour early, parking on the tarmac. I had a tough time sleeping the night before, with zero trust that my alarm clock would function properly. When he arrived, I walked to the plane, shook his hand, and we exchanged pleasantries. Getting into the SUV, Bernie and my Division President Barry sat in the back seat, while Bernie's security guard sat up front with me. Seeing the guard added more pressure. They had talents, not discussable in public. We heard rumors from our military associates regarding their skillsets.

As we rode through the Houston area, we drove by a new Lowe's under construction less than a mile down the road from one of my peer's stores. "Hey Erik, what are we doing about that Lowe's?" Bernie asked. "Bernie, that's not one of my stores; that's one of...," and I mentioned the other district manager. "I haven't been included in any strategic plan discussions to react," I replied. I had to be honest. And truth be told, I later found out there was no plan. None, nada, zilch, much to everyone's surprise.

Bernie blew up. "What the *f**k!?* What are we doing? How come I didn't know about this?" After the outburst, we talked it through. He made some notes while Barry's blood pressure was rising off the charts, as he knew he was ultimately responsible. It set Bernie off that we had no strategic plan at that point to do anything against that Lowe's. My thought? it was one of those incidents that made him look in the mirror and wonder why he didn't know about it. Were we becoming so large that he and Arthur could not be involved to the extent they had been accustomed to? It could have possibly contributed to their perceptions that some changes needed to be made. There weren't enough days in the year for Bernie and Arthur to interact in a personal way with each store location to gather intel and plan accordingly. FYI: as soon as we arrived at the Humble Store, I found my peer, who was waiting there and informed him of the conversation on the way from the airport, so he could be ready when Bernie approached him.

We arrived at the store around lunchtime. It was ready, but the whole time, while driving, I was freaking out: "Is the store right?" "Has it been shopped?" But I understood the necessity of having confidence in Dwight and his team. Numerous members of corporate merchandising and operations teams were there, and the visit could not have gone better; the store was perfect. Bernie was thrilled. When they conducted these visits, everyone dressed in business-casual, to include an apron. Perish the thought if while walking the aisles, Bernie beat you to a customer: if he greeted them first, you'd get that wonderful thrashing for which some associates had a *healthy* fear. It amazed all of us that Bernie and Arthur, to the very end of their careers, continued to hold the culture strongly in their hearts. No short-timers disease; none.

When officer walks took place, a customer would inevitably approach the group and ask, "Who's here this time?"

"What do you mean?"

"This store hasn't been this clean in months and everyone is saying hello again," which would cause the store's manager and district manager experience significant discomfort. The officers, however, understood that neither you, nor your team could operate at "Bernie/Arthur Ready Status" all the time. But the stinging input from the customer reminded us that there is never, ever an acceptable reason for a lack of customer service.

During these visits, at some point Bernie would announce that he had to take a bio break. He asked everybody to disburse and help customers. What we came to learn is that he would walk the store, start putting his arm around associates, and say, "Follow me." He took them back to the training room, sat them down, got them a drink and a snack, and spent time with them, alone...no salaried managers allowed. He urged them, "Talk to me. How's the store doing? What's going on? What are we doing stupid? Get it all off your chest." He wanted an unscripted, honest conversation with the associates. It's an excellent leadership example that demonstrates why Home Depot was such a success; what better way to learn what truly was on the minds of the associates, how the store was doing, and what kind of help they needed. Bernie would address the feedback at the next day's general session, challenging the appropriate resources to fix deficiencies. Again, the inverted pyramid demonstrates its dynamism.

At the end of the Humble visit, Bernie took off his apron, signed and dated it, and presented it to Dwight and the store team, telling them how proud he was and how much he appreciated everything they'd done. They framed and hung it in the employee breakroom area, knowing such a gesture from Bernie added to the history of the store. That was a wonderful moment for the team. We rewarded them for their efforts with a ton of food the next day as a thank you. Yes, we ate a lot of food at the Depot (You ever read how many calories Michael Phelps had to eat to maintain his regimen???) The employees also received extra merit badges that they could collect over time to earn more money in their paychecks. All of us rode that high for a long time.

HAPPY CUSTOMERS, HAPPY LIFE

One day we were taking inventory in one of the stores when Home Depot corporate announced a stock split: three for two. At the time, I was back in receiving, where the command center for the inventory crew was located. The announcement came toward the end of the inventory and everyone was exhausted. We just wanted to get the final inventory result, hoping we would be able to celebrate the store's diligent work and go home to rest. I jumped on the PA system and announced the news to the store: "It's because of associates like you that we can continue to produce the results. I'm so proud of you and you should be proud of the company." Oh, by the way, the customers heard the news too, but I did not care – we were pumped!

I heard thunderous cheers from the sales floor. Due to the compensation plan, 401K sharing, and employee stock purchase plans, most of our associates owned stock. It gave them more opportunities they would not have had otherwise. After the cheering subsided, I got a call from an associate, "A customer wants to talk to you." I could hear the customer in the back saying, "It's not a complaint."

"Alright, direct him back toward receiving and I'll buy him a soda."

He walked back to meet us, where there were 30 or 40 Home Depot employees.

"I have to tell ya," he began. "Did you hear that cheering on the floor when you made your announcement?"

"Yes, sir I did," I answered.

"I was one of the loudest ones cheering."

"Thank you, but why?"

"I'm a frickin' stockholder for this company; I don't just shop here; I own a lot of Home Depot stock. I am proud of your associates and your team and what the company is doing. Keep up the excellent work." We were stunned. At the end of a long, grueling day, you didn't think it could get any better. Everyone high-fived the customer or shook his hand. Before he left, I gave him a business card, encouraging him to call for any need.

"Just keep it up, man. Just keep it up," he urged. "You're making me rich!"

I looked at the associates. "Now, tell me. Why would we ever ignore any single customer in our buildings?" Powerful moments like that provided an avenue for me to validate what we were doing as a team.

AN OUTSIDER'S PERSPECTIVE

One day, I received a call from my district manager John, to tell me a visitor wanted to attend the next store meeting. Back then, these meetings were attended by nearly the entire team. Everybody who could possibly go would attend, unless they had a valid reason not to.

The visitor was an executive for a national grocery store chain who'd heard about Home Depot and some of the things we did; he wanted to attend a store meeting to see for himself. We had close to 300 employees, we set it up as usual – with cinder blocks laid out on the floor in rows, with 2 x 6 x 12 boards laid across, along with resin stack chairs. That was our wonderful, comfortable seating. We provided food and a packed agenda of important discussion topics.

Our visitor arrived on time and we sat him in the front row. I advised him I wasn't going to introduce him right away because I wanted him to get an authentic view of what and how we did it. Once everybody arrived and sat down, we started out with a loud, boisterous cheer. Then it was onto our agenda.

Midway through, I introduced him. Everybody applauded and gave him a great welcome, which surprised him a bit. We talked about customer service, results, goals, etc. and rewarded our associates for great service or execution. Managers and department supervisors came up with me to give a short, concise spiel about why they were awarding their person or persons. Afterward, I asked our visitor if he'd like to address my team and share any impressions he might have. It was comical as he got up from his seat and walked towards me. He started shaking his head, with a bemused look on his face and said, "You know what, I just...we can't do this. There is no way I'd be able to get my employees and teams up at 6 a.m. to come to a meeting like this, and be this involved, this vocal, this intense, and this into what you're doing as a company." As he spoke, he kept shaking his head.

This gentleman's business was unionized in several areas within the Midwest and the Northeast. "With union regulations, there's just no way we could do this," he informed us. He could not fathom how he would communicate with his teams to get them up that early on a Sunday to attend a meeting. I took that as a huge compliment on behalf of Home Depot and a credit to our people, who were invested in "the orange mission," if you will. Your people's desire to be part of events, along with their involvement, is a sure sign of a healthy work-place. Morale is sure to be good as well, along with results.

Our visitor walked out of the meeting that day feeling a bit defeated because he just couldn't see the same thing happening in his organization and wished he could do what we did at these monthly events. However, I hope it gave him some inspiration to see what he could do differently. One thing is certain: we impressed him that day and he left our store with more respect for Home Depot and its emphasis on building solid personal and professional relationships as a foundation for success.

WATER BALLOONS ARE IN SEASON

Checking on the weather ahead of a store meeting in Philly, I found it was going to be phenomenal day, with plenty of sunshine and warm temperatures. We agreed to hold the meeting outside, in front of the garden center. We set up the board and block, along with resin stack chairs and 12 of the largest trash cans we sold. The night before, we filled them with water balloons and swore my assistant managers and supervisors to secrecy, wanting to surprise the associates.

These trash cans were strategically spaced, with some up front and others set up around the perimeter of the seating area. We stationed a manager by each one to prevent associates from taking off the lids to reveal what was inside. When they arrived, they were surprised that the meeting was being held outside. We began the meeting, starting the agenda, then I stopped. "You know what? I'm just not feeling it right now. We need do something a bit different." On cue, the managers and supervisors took the lids off and started lofting the water balloons at each other.

Before the managers could toss water balloons into the crowd, I gave the go-ahead for everyone to participate: "It's free territory right now. Pick your target." Before I knew it, we had hundreds of people running for trash cans in a free-for-all. When the balloons were gone and everyone stopped, there wasn't a dry participant to be found. Everyone was soaked. I was one of the prime targets and fending off more volleys than I could count. We were laughing so hard we were crying. There's a time to be serious and professional, but there is also that time to surprise your team and shake things up, for the pure fun of it. Oh, in case you are wondering, no calls to corporate, complaining.

Other stores did pie tosses, where they built contraptions for store managers to stick their head through while everyone threw pies at them. I have countless memories and stories about how we conducted store meetings back then, and I believe it went a long way toward serving our culture. Happy employees are the key ingredient to the recipe of success, no matter the business. Adequate focus in this area will guarantee the results take care of themselves.

LADDERS & LEARNINGS

- Strive to give 110% every day in effort and productivity. Understand that there will be bad days, but if one more thing gets accomplished on those days, it is a step in the right direction.
- Partner with your significant other, with regularity, regarding family/life obligations. Be there for as many as humanly possible.
- Communicate with your supervisor about upcoming personal events in your life, giving him or her proper notice. Don't wait until the day before to ask for the necessary time, which could put your supervisor in an awkward position, making your request impossible to fulfill.

EXECUTIVE MEMO – Foster two-way communication to ensure that your team members understand your commitment to their work-life balance and challenge them to always keep you in the loop. Oh, and practice what you preach.

With my two great bosses and terrific mentors, Tony Drew and Que Vance.

A "Glamour Shot" the company took. Notice the badge on the apron: three years to go at that point. Please excuse the bags under my eyes.

This is what happens when you ignore concerning health symptoms, thinking you are superhuman. I hate those gowns and those are not the kind of bracelets anyone wants!

Small in size, but large in significance. Presented to me by Bernie Marcus in Hawaii at one of our annual meetings.

Pam and I at one of our anniversary dinners. I am a very lucky man!

George Elwell- one of my early hires in Philly, who has gone on to higher success with the company. Just a great young man.

My Outside Sales Team was one of the best ever! Erin Reay, Tiffany Moore, Lily Monroy, Jeanine Beatty, Zsa Zsa King, Crissy DeMarco, Tara MacNamara, Gidget Jones, Kristen Bingham, Bill Krum, Kevin Cain, Harold Morgan, Shane Gagne, Craig Richardson, Mike Pasta, Lilay Gebremeskel, Dan Gartrell and Rodney Korver. Oh, and yours truly

Dan McDevitt, District Manager, Southern Division. 30 years-plus plus with Depot. Check out that apron and name badge!

*I am incredibly proud of my smart, talented, hard-working and
beautiful daughter Jackie.*

*Jim Emge- District Manager and owner of one of the largest
hearts for service to community and others.*

John Martinez, Loss Prevention. A skilled and trusted adviser I could always rely on.

Zsa Zsa King- Pro Account Representative, Northern Virginia. A tremendous example of hard work and success.

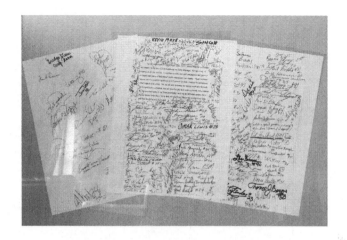

Letter sent to Bernie and Arthur from my store team during my demotion. Loved every one of them for their support.

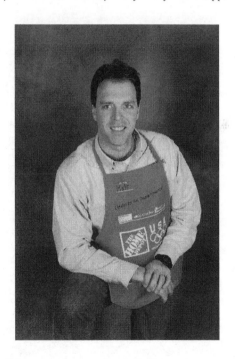

Matt Salerno, another one of my early hires and a success story due to his work ethic and commitment. Thank goodness, he listened to all my financial advice! Matt is now a Senior Project Manager at the Mayo Clinic.

Felicia Lynam, now a store manager for Home Depot in Indiana. While a department manager in Panama City, she'd saved the letters I wrote for my teams when I was a district manager. Proud of her success!

My father Ken (left), sister Jennifer, brother David, Mom Julie, and me. Ss

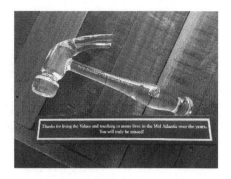

My final award - the totality of it all.

Paul West, Sean Sites and myself. All 33-plus years with the company.

NO PEACEFUL CO-EXISTENCE –
COMPLACENCY AND COMPETITION

"It doesn't matter whether you are a lion or a gazelle...when the sun comes up, you'd better be running."

— SUCCESSORIES

In 1999, Home Depot turned 20 years old. Earlier in the book, I described how the company celebrated this milestone at our annual meeting in Atlanta, complete with a private concert with Glenn Frey and the rock band the Eagles; a comedic performance from the famed Rita Rudner; and an overall Broadway show atmosphere. Attendees arrived at their hotel to discover goodie bags brimming with all kinds of gifts featuring the Home Depot logo – from watches to shirts to backpacks. The founders announced the formation of the Homer Fund for hourly associates in dire need, to deafening applause and a standing ovation. One could have thought we had achieved the pinnacle of success, with nothing left to strive for. There was plenty to celebrate. Going into that pivotal year, Home Depot had continued to secure its reputation as the phenomenon of home improvement, retail, and business. For the first time in our history, our stock rose to over $100 per share and the future looked so bright, we had to wear shades (emblazoned with the company logo, of course).

However, the re-entry into reality soon after the meeting struck a blow that rivaled that of any meteor careening toward earth with supersonic force. Home Depot paid a high price for indulging in endless celebration. Not long after we returned to our stores, we were stunned to learn that our despised competitor Lowe's had surpassed us in many measures of success. Aside from positive media coverage about what they were doing, Lowe's momentum was increasing while ours was decreasing – evidenced by the comp sales numbers. One of Wall Street's highest regarded measurements, comp increase numbers gauge your success in the current fiscal period versus the previous year. Up until 1999, Home Depot had blown Lowe's away in this metric, until numbers came out after our anniversary celebration. They revealed that they had started to close the gap, significantly. Suddenly, without warning, they were better than we thought...how had this happened?

To make matters worse, over time Home Depot stock prices declined from over $100 per share to just $19 per share – *alarming* news for anyone invested in the 401K program and/or one of Home Depot's stock ownership programs. The company offered several options for investing your money, but the stock had been doing so well that many people, including me, invested every penny in it, creating an unbalanced, non-diversified portfolio. At $103 per share, you looked at your account balance, beat your chest and thanked God Almighty; when the stock price dropped to $19, you wanted to jump off the highest building. In the blink of an eye we'd careened from the top of the mountain to the bottom of the ravine.

We all knew It was getting close to the end of the road for Bernie and Arthur, and we were getting our proverbial butts kicked. Coming out of that meeting, we expected everything to just continue as it was, but somewhere amid the euphoria of seeing classic rock legends, imbibing cocktails, and patting ourselves on the back, we'd forgotten that our competitors were still out there, and they were not giving up. They had snuck up on our backsides. If the world is dynamic, business must be too; if you remain static, you will be left behind after the last shred of confetti has been swept.

To its credit, without defensiveness or denial, Home Depot took a hard, inward look at what they needed to do and how to react. It was as if the beast had been awakened; the company's response retained multitudes of excellent employees who would have otherwise left for greener pastures. No excuses were made, nor was there a "woe is me" attitude. The company and everyone in it reached down deep within and forged a path forward. Again, the culture was brought into focus, eight segments strong.

The 8 Core Values of The Home Depot

1. Taking care of our people
2. Giving back to our communities
3. Doing the right thing
4. Excellent customer service
5. Creating shareholder value
6. Building strong relationships
7. Entrepreneurial spirit
8. Respect for all people

Call it Home Depot 2.0, for lack of a better term. The company woke up and our competitors had to take note. The situation spurred many to enhance their performance for the sake of their teams and the company. I have always been a believer of "lead, follow or get out of the way." Whether it pertains to highway driving or positions of management, it is always better to lead. There was no time to whine and sit on our butts, hoping someone else would figure it out. No, we knew exactly what we had to do. Blue became our least favorite color.

IT'S ORANGE CRUSH TIME

Shortly after arriving in Houston, the vice president of merchandising introduced a term that fueled our need to annihilate every competitor: "No Peaceful Coexistence." We created a logo with the international "no" sign and the words "peaceful coexistence" in the red circle with a black slash mark through it. I loved it! It became our rallying cry, revitalizing our division's intensity against Lowe's, to whom it was primarily directed, along with the multitude of independent competitors giving us a run for our money. We owned that phrase. With passion and purpose in what we could do for customers on a case-by-case basis, we brought it to our teams and challenged them with not letting a customer walk out empty-handed. We told them, "You take care of the customer, *period*. If the customer gets to us, they WILL be taken care of."

Home Depot has competed with thousands of companies in the home improvement industry. In addition to Lowe's, we've faced challenges from regional businesses like Menard's and Hechinger's. If you took a day to drive around town, you'd realize that wherever you saw a Home Depot, just blocks or a few streets away you'd find numerous competitors including countertop and cabinet shops, flooring and carpet outlets, tile and appliance retailers, electrical and plumbing supply houses...and the list goes on and on. Although the public views Home Depot as the dominant player, thousands of others are fighting for the same customers.

If customer service is first, what's Home Depot's second biggest passion? Competition. Every employee of the company must take a hard look in the mirror. Your worst competition and your most competitive force is *you*. If you fail, by lack of effort and failure to exhibit the correct behaviors, you create more damage to your overall success than your identifiable, external competitors. Remember, there is always a reason a customer walks out empty-handed. Do not let it be you. The combination of inward reflection and individual effort is a strong philosophy, ingrained upon me by each mentor. When asked about my competitive focus, I responded, "from the moment I wake up, I know I've got to run faster and jump higher than my competitor." Healthy pressure was applied to all of us to be our best and not let the competition win.

To use a sports analogy, if every member of a team fails to execute their position, it doesn't matter how exceptional their leader is. For example, the quarterback many consider the G.O.A.T. (greatest of all time), Tom Brady (remember, I am from Michigan) of the New England Patriots, could not have achieved his remarkable stats and career if not for a strong offensive line that blocks for him and quick receivers who elude their would-be tacklers and catch his passes. An individual can bring a team to a certain point, but it still takes a team to win championships and reach the pinnacle of success in their sport. It can't just be Tom Brady putting on his Super Man cape. His teammates must step up and execute. The same is true of Lebron James in professional basketball. It's not possible to go 48 minutes straight in every single basketball game, even when you're an incredibly talented athlete. You can achieve short-term success, but not long-term, sustainable success.

We always had it in our heads and hearts that we wanted to destroy the competition. It has caused others to mock us over the course of our history, but it is something we have never, and will never apologize for. There should not be any business that takes a submissive stance regarding competition. Your shareholders and associates will not appreciate it. When it came to Lowe's I hated the company – a professional animosity not a personal one – because I knew if we didn't do our job, customers would shop there. I noted earlier that the one thing that upset me was when a Home Depot customer, in response to some interaction that upset or angered them, would not hesitate to announce, "Well, then, I'm just going to f*****g Lowe's!"

You bristled at these words. At times, our people would get defensive, but then it became a challenge. Home Depot conducted countless surveys where questions were posed to a group of people behind a two-way mirror allowing employees to sit behind it and listen to their responses without being seen. A common outcome every session? If they asked 100 customers where they first went for a home improvement need, the majority answered, "Home Depot." If we couldn't satisfy their need for any reason – poor customer service, didn't carry the brand they wanted, or were out of stock– then, they would go to Lowe's or another competitor. Once they left Home Depot, most of them did not come back, having been satisfied somewhere else. To put it in concrete terms, over 90 percent of the U.S. population lives within 25 miles of a Home Depot store. The message was simple: take care of the customers every time. They were ours to keep, if we did our jobs.

Michael Phelps is the greatest swimmer in history. Remember the iconic photos of Phelps swimming in the Olympic finals, fully focused on his goal and looking toward the end of the pool while the competing swimmer in the next lane focused his eyes on Michael? It became an internet meme: "Winners focus on winning. Losers focus on winners." Prior to the swim, his competitor had tried to get in Michael's head with motions and gyrations as they awaited the call to come to the pool. The guy acted like a fool, while Phelps sat in his chair, mindful of remaining present and focused in his own head. Maybe he first saw himself winning in his mind's eye, but either way, his ability to stay calm and collected translated into a gold-medal worthy performance in the water. As they swam, you could see his opponent watching him while Phelps focused straight ahead...and won the race.

This is a powerful observation: keep your eye on the ball, not where it didn't need to be. This philosophy yields powerful results. I challenged my people to do anything they could within reason and informed them about what the expectations were. We didn't want to let anybody walk out empty-handed. Bernie, Arthur, and other officers used to stand at exit doors in stores. If they saw anyone leaving without purchasing something, they would talk to them and ask them why. We measured this, and it turned out that you could turn half of them around and get them something related to their shopping search. The customers would answer, "Well, I didn't get good service," "I didn't feel I was heard, or my questions were answered," or "I couldn't find it." There were a variety of reasons, but the officers of Home Depot led by example and proved you could change the outcome simply by talking to these customers and getting them the proper assistance before they bought it at a competitor. You naturally assumed they were not going home but to another business. Every associate needs to understand their role, with absolute clarity.

Not too long ago, Pam and I shopped at Home Depot, where we talked to a part-time cashier, about 70 years-old, who has worked there for five years. When she asked us how we were doing, we introduced ourselves and initiated a conversation. She talked about how, through her 70 years of life, she'd never worked for a company that took better care of its associates than Home Depot because they truly cared about them. Hearing her heart-felt words filled me with pride. She asked me how it was back in the early days and I replied, "The same as today, except then, we were just learning how to do it right." It was a wonderful interaction, though not unique to Home Depot. I've also talked to Lowe's associates that feel the same way about how they are taken care of. You've got to respect that.

TECHNOLOGY EVOLUTION

Companies that do not prioritize technology damage their business and put their futures at risk. Home Depot was one of those companies, but thankfully, the higher-ups realized what was happening and responded to it by hiring the right personnel to move us forward. It is funny now, but when our new tech officers analyzed our current systems and reported their findings, we were flabbergasted. Two comments stand out: one, that we were one step above a number 2 pencil; and two, that one Apple Store had more bandwidth than a large grouping of our stores. As my retirement approached, I remember how scared everybody was of Amazon – their logistics, media, website, and all it could do – versus what companies like Home Depot could do to compete.

Due to their proactive mindset and adaptation to this new reality, these days Home Depot's websites and logistics systems receive kudos and awards. The company enjoys positive press for their urgent, thorough response to technology, but that only happened because its leadership did not rest on its laurels. Companies and individuals today must follow their example if they want to remain competitive and achieve their goals. According to Moore's Law from 1965, every two years, the number of components on a single computer chip would double, while the cost of the computer would be halved. Over 50 years later, the efficiency gains have proven to be true with the evolution of TVs, laptops, microprocessors, speed, and artificial intelligence (AI). Five years from now, life will resemble the Jetson's cartoon even more. Come on, how many of you thought we would have Roomba robotic vacuums and drones that anyone could purchase? If companies and individuals can't or won't adapt and evolve, they won't make it. Many companies, governments, and individuals are slow to change; that is human nature. In modern society you must embrace change regardless of its inherent difficulties or how much you dislike it.

WHAT WE SEE IN OTHERS IS A REFLECTION OF OURSELVES

At Home Depot, there are some memorable customer stories, shared thousands of times over to illustrate needed improvement. Here is an example: one of our officers was visiting a Home Depot and walked up to a customer in the parking lot who had a handful of four-inch by four-inch ceramic tiles.

"Hey, what's going on today? How was your experience?" the officer asked.

"Terrible," the customer replied. "It sucked."

"Why?"

"Well, I brought these ceramic tiles back." He had about 10 pieces, worth less than a dollar. "Your store wouldn't take them back."

"Why wouldn't they take them back?"

"Well, they are from your competitor. I made a mistake and I didn't buy them here."

The officer replied, "Come with me," and they went back into the store with the product, where he asked the returns desk to credit the customer as if he bought them from us. He apologized and explained to the customer that employees were trying to do the right thing by protecting our assets. We teach our people to put themselves in the customer's position and treat them the way they would want to be treated.

Shortly thereafter, the officer walked the store with the management team and saw this same customer who now had one of our large, rolling orange carts loaded to the gills with more tile and all the accessories needed for a tile job. He spent hundreds of dollars that day. If that officer hadn't been outside in that parking lot and engaged that customer, we would have lost that customer to a competitor, along with the $500-600 in tile sales on his cart. This is an excellent, real-life illustration of knowing what to do with your customers. Most importantly, management must engage every associate at every level to articulate a vision of what a true customer experience looks like. Customers never forget an extraordinary experience. One of the easiest ways to ensure your long-term success? No matter your business, engage them as often as possible. Bernie's famous phrase, "you must make love to the customer," always rings true. Due to misinterpretation, it almost got a few people at Home Depot into big trouble, but we won't go into that.

My dad always said, "I could go into a Home Depot and know in five minutes if it was well run or not." His observation was not only based on what he heard or saw, but what he *felt* in those five minutes. What was the energy level? What were the associates doing? Did the customers seem happy? He called it "the feel." In retail, you get shopped. What that means is the cycle of the store's readiness; the number of customer transactions (imagine having thousands of guests every day in your home!) followed by the store's recovery. Maintenance and product placement must be re-done, and organization is crucial. How management reacts to that cycle and how quickly it is customer (guest)-ready is easily visible. This is a vital point: he who performs effectively and efficiently wins! Moving forward, together, will yield the optimum results. Like Dad, I wanted that "feel." If I had it, then the customers would feel it too. I never forgot the first time I entered the Home Depot; the feel got me then. When I shop businesses today, I look for that feel, which tells me which ones are the best managed.

Trends have shown that females, whether a residential or commercial shopper, make the majority of purchasing decisions. That was not always the case in our industry, which brings me to another crucial lesson: YOU CANNOT STEREOTYPE YOUR CUSTOMERS! About 15 years ago, Pam and I went furniture shopping after one of our moves to furnish the new home. On my days off I dressed in either shorts, tennis shoes, and a baseball cap turned backwards on my head, or sweatpants, a sweatshirt, tennis shoes and maybe the same ball cap. I may or may not have worn my Rolex, but most of the time, I looked like a youngster without a lot of money. During this shopping excursion to a higher end store, we planned to spend seven- to- ten-thousand dollars on furniture. Many people who walk into upscale retail environments receive an urgent and often solicitous greeting. The store employees say hello, ask what you're looking for, and offer a beverage. Such high-end places tend to treat customers well.

When we walked in, no one greeted us, although they did make eye contact. Not one employee offered to help, so we curled off to the left and started browsing. On the other hand, a nicely dressed couple that came in right behind us got a warm greeting and offers of assistance, along with a beverage. Pam and I kind of stopped, recognizing the fact we had been dissed. It hit us that we should have dressed accordingly, but then we thought, "This is us. It should not matter how we are dressed." We walked the entire store. During that time, we passed several employees, none of whom said hello. We decided, based on how we'd been treated, we were not going to buy from that store. We felt insulted by their assumption of who we were and what we could and could not afford. Before we left the building, I approached the saleswoman who'd greeted the other couple. "Hey, my name is Erik," I began. "I am a district manager for Home Depot. My wife and I planned on making large purchases today and I'm assuming you're on commission. In the future, you may not want to ignore somebody based on how they look."

Envision the scene in the movie *Pretty Woman*. In case romantic comedy isn't your preferred genre, let me set up the scene. Julia Roberts plays a young, beautiful woman who turns to prostitution to survive. After she meets a wealthy executive looking for company, she needs some appropriate clothing to attend various functions with him. She was told to go to Rodeo Drive, only to find that the rude and snobby employees won't help her. When she finally does get help, she returns to the store in upscale attire to find the woman who dismissed her. She asks the clerk if she remembers her, but because she is dressed to the nines in designer clothing now, the woman does not. Julia's character explains that she was here yesterday and "you wouldn't wait on me." As she shows off an abundance of shopping bags in her arms, she announces, "Big mistake, big, huge!" before sauntering out the door and leaving the salesperson with her mouth hanging open.

That's how we felt that day in the furniture store. I told the sales-woman, "That couple that you greeted, I think I saw them walk out (which I had). They didn't buy anything, did they?"

"No."

"Well, we were going to buy quite a bit of furniture today, but since you didn't help us, we're not going to spend our money here. We're going elsewhere." She just stood there with her mouth open. (Big mistake, big, huge!) Truth be told, most retail businesses are guilty of stereotyping, but at Home Depot we discovered we couldn't do that if we wanted to succeed. One key example of this principle involves my regional vice-president when he visited one of our stores in D.C. As he approached the entrance, he noticed a woman with cartload of product loading her car in the loading zone. When he asked if he could help, she accepted.

"So, what are you doing with all this stuff?" he asked. She was casually dressed, with a cartload of building materials. Now, if pressed, we could generate some assumptions of who she was and what she was doing, but it turned out she owned a very large property management company that ran a billion-dollar portfolio of properties in the Mid-Atlantic.

"Did anyone greet you in the store today?" my RVP inquired.

"No, not today. I got this on my own." She continued, "I'm in here all the time. I rarely get help. Sometimes when I do get help, I can tell they patronize me because I'm a female."

"Has anybody ever asked you what you do and why you shop with us?"

"Nope. Never had that conversation." Before she left, he got her business card. Afterward, he relayed the entire story to me...and not surprisingly, we had an intense conversation about customer service and how the team could have missed this customer.

How POWERFUL is this story?

Can you fathom the revenue this woman represented with a one-billion-dollar portfolio in Washington D.C.? She shops one day and purchases a buggy of miscellaneous products. She informed my RVP of the millions she spends each year to maintain her properties...and we had no clue. Sometimes we gave her service, sometimes we didn't. When we did, we patronized her. Luckily for us, we had a lot more locations in D.C. than our competitors, so it was the convenience factor that kept her coming back. We had not engaged her. Service is not just a greeting; it is an art form that involves asking questions, listening, and reacting to what is important to your customers. When you truly engage, you create a clientele. Customer cultivation is an impactful term: each subsequent interaction with them should add value to the previous one, creating a loyal customer base.

As a business, you want to hear that your customers do business with you because of the service, your people, products, and reliability. At Home Depot, we were no different regarding those expectations. We did market track surveys, where a third party contacted a large base of our customers and demographic, to ask numerous questions. When asked for the strongest factor as to why they shopped at Home Depot, the highest-ranking answer was convenience of location. *Say, what!?* What happens if a competitor eliminates that advantage by opening a site? When we read these surveys, it upsets us. Yes, we realized we had thousands of stores, especially in highly populated areas, but, if that's your strongest draw, you've got some opportunities for improvement.

The impact of turnover on service cannot be overstated. As companies are continually hiring, the opportunity will always be there for high turnover. When reading business articles from CNBC or Bloomberg, especially in the spring, you will read how companies like Home Depot and Lowe's are hiring new employees in the tens of thousands. What a tremendous occasion to advance your company's agenda. Or, you could ensure your company is doing all it can to provide an incredible work environment, resulting in low turnover, negating the need to hire to such an extent. Just saying.

At Home Depot, we wasted a good amount of time celebrating the negative things we saw in Lowe's. It made us happy when they did not greet customers, when they were out of stock, when their stores were not clean, and more. But then we learned to look for what they were doing right and react to that, enabling us to reach another level of maturity and professionalism. Everyone wants to focus on the negative aspects of themselves and their competitors because that is easy to do. It is more effective and productive to focus on the positive and how to enhance that further.

YOU ARE KIDDING! WHO WENT TO LOWE'S?

Business is fluid. Everything is in a constant state of change, with outcomes ranging from innocuous to momentous. Approximately a year ago, a change occurred that sent shockwaves through the retail industry, if not the entire business world. Marvin Ellison, former Home Depot executive and CEO of J.C. Penney was announced as the new President and CEO of Lowe's, replacing Robert Niblock. Lowe's would now be led and managed by a former Home Depot executive. It was historic. The relationship between the two companies just got a whole lot more interesting. In all honesty, no one at Home Depot ever wanted this to happen. So, why did it?

When Frank Blake announced he was going to retire, the rumor mill kicked into high gear, postulating who would be his successor. Largely, it came down to three individuals: Craig Menear, EVP of Merchandising; Carol Tomei, Chief Financial Officer & Executive Vice President-Corporate Services; or Marvin Ellison, Executive Vice President of U.S. Stores. Once again, the company was going to endure a transition at the highest level. Anxiety for the enormity of the transition was minimal, as most everyone held all three of the rumored candidates in high regard. Craig was awarded the position, rightly so. Representing the best of both worlds, he had been there for the "good old days," with Bernie and Arthur and the resurgence led by Frank.

Not long after Craig took the helm, it was announced that Marvin was leaving Home Depot to become the CEO of the struggling JC Penney Company. Fast-forward two years, to Niblock's departure announcement and the subsequent shockwaves of Marvin's appointment as his replacement. Although I was no longer with the company, it caused concern in my mind. I was happy for Marvin, having much respect for him and all he did at Home Depot. Lowe's now had a leader who truly knew not only the business, but everything Home Depot had been doing and planning for the future. The game had changed! From the get-go, the business community and Wall Street expressed high hopes for Lowe's future, centered around their confidence in Marvin's abilities.

Marvin employs simple thought processes into his management style. While at Home Depot, he enacted the W.I.N. process for each proposed process or function for the stores. If the item under consideration could answer three questions, it could move forward. Was it worthwhile (W), intuitive (I) and necessary (N)? Simple, but very straightforward. During his tenure, he formed numerous professional relationships and created loyal followers, some of whom moved to JC Penney to become officers for him there. Home Depot was not especially concerned with JC Penney's, although they attempted inroads into some of our prolific product categories like appliance, flooring and installation services. Lowe's, however, was very, very different – our archrival, our nemesis, the bane of our professional existence – you get the idea. Now, it was personal. The same officers who followed Marvin to JC Penney's followed him to Lowe's, and it did not stop there. Seemingly, every other week, whether on social media or from one of my former colleagues at Home Depot, I heard of another former officer or mid-level manager (most of whom I knew and had worked with) going to Lowe's. Oh, by the way, some of these individuals swore (quite literally) that they would never, ever work for Lowe's and wear that red vest. Situations and people change.

I regard most of the people Marvin recruited to Lowe's as excellent choices. However, even more important than people, he took Home Depot's culture with him, having lived it for 12 years. In his brief time with Lowe's, it appears he is attempting to run a huge portion of the Home Depot playbook, along with imparting its culture. This may take some time. These actions and beliefs were not created overnight; it took decades to incorporate them as part of the orange DNA. Still, any progress will be wonderful progress for Lowe's. Judging by the media reports, hopes are sky high for Marvin and his new team's effects and results. Social media indicates a strong new enthusiasm from the employee base, centered on an "orange crush" philosophy of hurting Home Depot and capturing market share. Did I mention it was personal?

Just this week, I heard that one of my direct team members in the pro organization had transitioned to Lowe's with a promotion. A talented young man, he will be an asset to Lowe's. Meanwhile, under Craig's leadership, Home Depot will not take this lightly, nor will they take a wait-and-see stance. Proactive strategies and growth mechanisms are well under way. The addition of Marvin to the rivalry will no doubt generate an enhanced adrenaline flow at Home Depot, creating a duel for the ages. Can you guess who will benefit the most? If you said customers, you would be correct. It's a fantastic time to be a home improvement shopper.

LADDERS AND LEARNINGS

- Understand that the customers are the lifeblood of your organization. Each one is vital to your success, whether you are in management or not. You as an individual must lead the charge to serve your customers according to your company's standards, setting an example for the rest of your team.
- If possible, never let any customer exit your business empty-handed.
- Each day that you work, ask yourself how you plan to be better than your counterpart at your competitor up the street and take steps to make that happen.

EXECUTIVE MEMO

It is incumbent upon you to establish a proactive process that focuses on awareness of primary competitors, their successful actions and your subsequent reaction. Enact an empowerment discipline with your team members to improve ownership and provide efficiencies.

11

NATURAL DISASTERS AND HUMAN NATURE

"The successful warrior is the average man with laser-like focus."

— BRUCE LEE

A popular phrase among Home Depot managers who were climbing the ladder went like this, "Just when you get comfortable in a geographic location, be very careful when answering the telephone." As the company underwent its rapid growth phase – in some cases, opening more than 10 stores in a given week – we understood and accepted the likelihood of being asked to relocate to facilitate its expansion. Once you felt confident about your efforts and results, inevitably you'd hear from either your supervisor, or a supervisor of a different geographic area. In Houston, following an enormous amount of diligent and dedicated work from the team in attaining results and standards, we were in an excellent groove. Pam, Jackie, and I lived in a nice house in a lower cost-of-living metropolitan area where my wife and child were very happy. I was still a younger guy with ambition, contemplating the possibility of becoming a VP. Life couldn't get any better, or so we thought.

One day, completely out of the blue, I received a phone call (yes, I answered) from Marc, the Regional Vice-President of Florida, asking, "Are you ready to come back?" One of the company's early territories, Florida was one of the most desirable locations in Home Depot (it still is by the way, with over 150 locations). Within the ranks of Home Depot, everyone knew that if you left The Sunshine State, you'd almost have to kill somebody to get back. Countless people from other parts of the country had a hankering to move there. If you were stupid enough to leave, you could never entertain a realistic expectation of returning because the odds were not in your favor. But there were exceptions.

When Marc reached out to me with the offer, I was ecstatic; in my mind, there was no hesitation about the decision. Immediately, I went home to talk it over with Pam. She felt the same way because it would allow us to return to the state where our parents lived – Pam's on the east coast and mine on the west. The district offered to me was in the Panhandle, extending from Tallahassee into Southern Alabama – eleven stores, east to west (250 miles) on the famed "Redneck Riviera." Time to trade in the Justin's for flip-flops; yippee kay yay – grab the Coppertone!

With multiple positives and few (if any) negatives factoring into our decision, we accepted the offer that same day. No matter where you relocated with Home Depot, you always worried about the geography and finances involved, even though the company took very good care of us. Once again, a relocation coordinator at corporate guided us through the process step-by-step with the realtor, lender and movers. We received all appropriate counsel and finances to efficiently and quickly transition to the new area.

We had made good friends in Houston, but as I said, there's not much to debate when you get an all-expenses-paid chance to go back to Florida. We settled in the beautiful town of Gulf Breeze, just east of Pensacola, which was the mid-point in my district. We could watch the Blue Angels out of Pensacola Naval Air Station and take road trips to Destin, one of the preeminent vacation resort hot spots in Northwest Florida. It was heaven on earth. We were beyond jubilant to live in such a desirable place. At that point we did not understand how severely the weather – specifically hurricanes – would impact our lives. In a sense of foreshadowing, following the hurricane prep meeting in Atlanta a few months before the 2004 season started, Tom Taylor, then an EVP of US Stores, yelled across the room to me, "You need one."

"One what?"

"A hurricane." That's when I knew my team would be dealing with one. Just because he said something, we were jinxed. Little did we know then that four named storms would pummel the state.

Home Depot transferred me to the Panhandle to replace a district manager who was not performing to expectations. He had indirect family relationships within the stores and created an "us vs. them" mentality between his team of stores/personnel and the Home Depot corporate office, which led to his demotion to store manager within my district. Talk about an effect on me: my predecessor still had a familial relationship with store employees and here I was, transferring in to be the supervisor of what was once his district, including this gentleman himself. At first, I thought there wouldn't be any issues (wishful thinking?), but my assessment turned out to be wrong. In fact, years later the RVP who made the decision to relocate me acknowledged his error.

Upon arrival, I held conversations with the RVP and other resources at the Florida office about the perceptions of my new district, which enabled me to go into the new area forewarned. Some of the input I received included, "defensive," "argumentative," "they don't execute," and "they fight everything." They gave me 45 days to make notable progress before the President of the Florida Division would visit. It was widely acknowledged that he avoided my area because he didn't feel welcome. With no collaborative presence, he couldn't stand being there. I could not imagine an area in the company having this dysfunctional relationship with officers and corporate. I worked diligently on changing the mindset and productivity of my team, involving them every step of the way. As the Queen and David Bowie song goes, I was *Under Pressure*.

Early on, I held a staff meeting that included my predecessor and two of his family members who were also store managers. Looking them all in the eye, I announced, "We're not gonna have this. I'm just gonna be honest; we will not survive unless we change." And I let them know, "No offense to my predecessor or the people in the room, but I'm going to tell you what I heard. Right now, I'm going to take it as gospel until I can make my own judgements. You're either going to help me change this or before we walk out of here, you're going to tell me you don't want to be part of this team." It was a productive "Come to Jesus" gathering, where we discussed what we were going to do to help ourselves transform the reputation they had generated. Then, we strategized our approach to changing the mindset of all the store personnel, now understanding that they followed our example in this area. *Everyone* had to change.

My predecessor tried to work with me, but I could only get him so far before having to make a change and assign him to a different position under a different supervisor. By the time the walk took place with Tony, the President of the Florida Division, our stores looked tight on all the standards and expectations we'd imposed, thanks to the associates' response and willingness to get it done. People were wound up; all they needed was guidance and direction. They could feel a different passion and intensity and it lit a fire within them. The President noticed the much-improved condition of the stores and the obvious effort our people were making. He pulled me off to the side and complimented, "I don't know how the hell you did it; I don't know what you did but keep doing it. What else can I do to help you?"

"I'm going to need a few things done within this district that are going to require some capital money."

"Erik, whatever you need. You keep doing this and I'll sign the checks."

Capital money is allocated for physical items in the stores, for example, a new pro desk or shopping carts. Typically, you submitted your capital request at the beginning of every year and then they either approved, denied, or tabled for later consideration. I utilized the process as a risk/reward motivator. I wanted them to understand the difference between thinking you're out there on an island all by yourself, versus being part of a larger corporation. We accomplished things for stores that had previously been frustrated by the lack of consideration from corporate. The change in personality and beliefs was the catalyst for the area to achieve higher levels of performance and results.

I took note of employees who were truly working their butts off, approving merit pay increases, above and beyond their normal performance evaluations. For me, it was all about the meritocracy. Hourly employees were instructed to keep matters regarding their pay to themselves. Despite that counsel, some shared with their peers. Associates who did not receive a merit increase would approach me, asking for one. This represented a terrific opportunity for a discussion, focused on what they felt they had done to warrant the consideration. Most of the time, their answers were the basic expectations of their role, which opened the door for me to collaborate with them on what they felt they could do above and beyond, to earn approval for extra pay. At that time, the DM approved each salary increase. A funny thing happened – associates listened, exerted more effort, and accomplished more. The word got "out on the street" via the associates, causing the requests to diminish significantly. Treating team members with honesty, fairness and consistency will elevate the performance of an entire entity.

AN EARLY LESSON IN LEADERSHIP

From the ages of 10 through 12, I played midget tackle football. I loved the game then, and still do now (why can't Peyton Manning play forever?). If you could have known Bill, my coach at the time, you'd have thought we were a Super Bowl contender in the NFL. Competitive and mean with an intimidating appearance and manner, this dark-haired man stood over six feet tall. He pushed us like the world depended on it. Once, while playing quarterback at a practice I got hurt badly when I took a rough tackle that resulted in a nasty cut that was bleeding pretty good. Coach noticed what had happened and started screaming at me, "Get your ass up, rub some dirt on that, get back in here!" Here I was, a 12 year-old-kid and he lit me up. "Get some dirt on that thing, get in the huddle!"

While his tactics might come across as extreme, Coach helped to establish a solid work ethic in me and the other kids. At the end of the year, he gave a speech about who was going to receive the MVP Trophy for our team at our awards ceremony. I sat there and listened with no recognition factor whatsoever when he talked about the kid who had the drive, wasn't afraid to bleed, and got right back up. He called me up to the stage and presented me with the award. Even at that age, I realized that my coach was somebody who wanted the best out of us; he imparted standards, a code of conduct, and an ethic. He made us better, pushed us when he had to, and was not afraid to take a strong approach. By the way, the term "coach" is defined as someone who provides instruction or advice. Nowhere in that definition does it say they have to be liked.

My award marked a bright spot in a season marred by tragedy. One afternoon during practice, we waited for the rest of our team-mates to arrive, including my best friend, Mark. He was riding in a car with a bunch of other kids, driven by one of the older kids in our neighborhood. The weekend before, I'd stayed at his house and had a ball with his family. On the way, the young driver lost control of the car and Mark was killed when he was ejected from the vehicle. When we got word at practice (which was cancelled), it hit all of us hard. It was surreal because none of us had been exposed to death prior to this incident. But then...the funeral. I remember going to it dressed in a suit, not knowing what to expect. As I approached the family and the closed casket, Mark's mom saw me and started screaming and calling my name. She grabbed me and pulled me toward her and the family, talking about how I was his best friend and recounting the wonderful weekend we all shared. The pain of her loss gutted her, and she clung to me as if her life depended on it. Again, I was 12 years-old – devastated, crying, and shaking like a leaf. When she finally released me, I needed some air. I went outside, where I walked around aimlessly until, out of nowhere, Coach appeared and put his arms around me. "Are you okay? Do you want to talk?" he asked. He did not leave until he was sure I was okay.

That day I saw a different side of his personality, one I never knew existed...an empathetic aspect. I'll always look to him as an early example of what constitutes a good coach or leader: toughness and a willingness to challenge others when appropriate, and empathy and a desire to express compassion at the right times. From that point forward, I saw him in a new light.

NO, NO, NO!!! THIS IS NOT HAPPENING

Tuesday, September 11, 2001. My team and I were having a productive district staff meeting at our Fort Walton Beach Store, when all the sudden, our computer room supervisor Sarah rushed into the room in an agitated state. She interrupted me and insisted I come to the computer room right away. With no idea as to what was happening, I resisted at first. However, her continued urgency compelled me to follow her.

Inside each of our computer rooms, we had small television monitors. As I entered, she pointed to the television, where I saw that one of the World Trade Center Towers was engulfed in fire and smoke, with a gaping hole in it. She informed me that a large airplane had, in fact, struck the tower. As she updated me, the second airplane struck the second tower. I felt an unprecedented shock and a degree of numbness...and at that point we had no clue that the Pentagon would be hit by a third plane or that a fourth would perish in a Pennsylvania field. I returned to the store managers and district staff to explain what was happening with the information I had at that point. The staff meeting was now over. As we watched the training room television, we witnessed the horror of the collapse of the two towers, while confirmation came from the news outlets that the United States was under attack.

I received communication that there was an emergency conference call with the RVP for the DMs. During that call, all information was shared, and we were directed to visit every one of our stores as quickly as possible to be the stabilizing presence for our teams in the middle this horrendous event. On the television, they broadcast satellite images of airplane traffic in the skies, which diminished each second as one plane after another landed at the closest airport, per the mandate. Remember when I shared the Space Shuttle Challenger Disaster in chapter three? In the same way, but on a much larger scale, the world had come to a complete stop in a figurative sense. Adding to our geographic area's dynamic, there were numerous military bases and military personnel and/or their families working in our stores. The efforts, alerts to action, and execution of readiness status overtook the entire region: phones were ringing, and people were running, while the sole job of all managers and leaders was to keep everyone calm.

Everyone who was a small child or older on September 11, 2001 will remember where they were and what they were doing. While speculation continued as to the perpetrators of the attack and their origins, uncertainty reigned. Millions of people were glued to their TVs, hoping for miracles as they learned of the 3,000 lost lives and the extensive damage...then abject sorrow transformed into righteous anger towards those who were guilty of the despicable act.

It took me almost two days, but I got into almost all the stores, where I focused on general demeanor and personal impacts. In the beginning, I did not care what the stores looked like, as this was not the time to appear "businesslike." To the extent that it was possible, every DM channeled their own feelings into a compartment within our minds, to be released later when on our own. Emotion can be a double-edged sword: wonderful or volatile. In times of crisis, everything you have done to build relationships, establish expectations, and encourage communication with your teams will be called upon. You are the stabilizing force.

I will say this. We can agree to disagree, but you will have to change my mind. Patriotism – for the generations who witnessed the heinous acts of 9/11 – was much more intense, passionate and widespread than it is today, which worries me. What happens on the world stage affects a multitude of people, in both personal and professional ways. No, it is not as simple as "some people did something." You must understand the interconnectedness of these events and your role as either an employee or a leader in your company. Your influence must be positive and inclusive.

IT'S RAINES IN FLORIDA, AND IT WAS GOOD

Remember Tom Taylor, the guy who was Vice-President of the Southwest Division when I relocated to Houston? When I first got to the Panhandle, he was in the process of shifting to a home office position as EVP of US Stores. Having been in the Florida district for a bit and based on my ratings within the company, I knew I was on the list for consideration for an RVP position. One day, while at the Tampa Regional Office for a meeting, Tom called me about the open RVP spot for Florida. "You'll never get promoted out of that country club," he began. "Everyone knows and is aware of the area you have in Florida. Their perception is that it's a country club. It's a nice area, it is resort living, it's vacation land, it's beach. It's going to be hard for you to get promoted out of that district. But there's something else."

"What?"

"You know, Erik, I am going to be honest. Your name comes up every time we talk about VP positions. There's just something that doesn't quite get us to the point where we're ready to offer it to you, so we're going to go in a different direction." He didn't tell me anything I didn't already know, since I had not been contacted about interviewing for the open spot.

"Really?" I countered. "It doesn't matter that my team is surpassing our financial goals, the standards have improved dramatically, and the district team is now a quality partner to the offices?"

"Erik, I'm telling ya, nobody's gonna promote you out of there," he repeated. Resigned to the fact that I was not getting the position, I asked, "Okay, so who's coming?" He informed me they were going to select Paul Raines. I started to think an officer position at Home Depot was not in the cards for me. However, I replied, "Listen, at the end of the day you've made your decision. I'll support him, I won't change. There will be no problem. I will support him to the nth degree. We'll be good."

"I appreciate that."

This is another example of how the company was a meritocracy. Paul was younger than me and had been with Home Depot far fewer years than I had been. A native of Costa Rica, he spoke multiple languages. When I first met him, I could tell he was MENSA smart and had a wonderful personality. From the beginning, we clicked in terms of how we felt about each other. I promised him he could count on me as his right-hand person, whatever he needed. We cultivated an excellent professional and personal relationship that counted years later. At the get-go, Paul was a good RVP, but became an exceptional leader during the horrendous hurricane season of 2004 – one of Florida's worst, with four major hurricanes. In terms of natural disasters and crises, Home Depot truly rises to the occasion. We were never better than during the times we're needed most. You've heard all the clichés, but we truly kick into high-gear in high-stress situations: adrenaline flows and commitment and dedication increase. From each associate in the stores to all the personnel at the corporate offices, the company ascends into a devoted force.

The moment a hurricane forms and begins its journey across the Atlantic from Africa, Home Depot's command center tracks it. Preparation begins in terms of necessary product supply, personnel, and all tasks that must be accomplished. Home Depot created such an effective disaster-management process that the federal government has studied it, all the way down to visiting our command center in Atlanta. It has evolved over the years, largely due to lessons learned from previous hurricanes, especially the devastating Andrew in 1992. That storm revealed multiple opportunities for improvement; by the time we got to the 2004 hurricane season we'd put together a much more effective response. Following a hurricane, we imported associates from all over the country via personal vehicles, bus, plane, or train. The purpose was to assist the stores that had been impacted. These associates carried basic supplies, food, and water, often on trailers for the store teams and the communities affected.

The Orlando/Daytona area got hit first at the start of 2004's season. My Panhandle team, comprised of volunteers, and I traveled down to help. We split the team between two stores: Daytona Beach and Port Orange. When we arrived, we sent the original staff and team home to tend to their own houses and families, whom they might not have seen in weeks, due to extra work demands. For many, it was their first opportunity, which is why we tried to get there as quickly as we could. Home Depot is deemed "a necessary resource," by municipalities due to the nature of our business. Local law enforcement agencies issued certificates to Home Depot managers and other primary leaders that entitled us to jump to the head of the line for gas, groceries, and other vital services. They knew we needed those resources to keep our stores open, functioning, and helping residents with their needs.

Unfortunately, it created much animosity, as the public did not understand the municipality's mindset of giving us priority. Imagine waiting in line with hundreds of cars to get gas and when the gas truck finally shows up, here comes Mr. Home Depot with an official certificate that entitles him to cut to the front of the line. Let's just say, the public does not always perceive it as a good thing. In fact, it reached the point where local law enforcement had to escort us. I remember driving my car with 50 gallons of gasoline in containers in the trunk. God forbid, the tail end got hit in an accident; I'd have blown up and gone to the pearly gates (at least I hope), well ahead of schedule. But you did what you had to do to get to the stores. I always joked with Pam that I was worth more dead than alive...much to her chagrin. My attempts to make light of the situation to ease her worry did not work.

In the aftermath of the hurricane, the weather continued to be terrible, with major thunderstorms. As I walked around the Port

Orange store, I wound up in the paint department, where an elderly woman approached and asked, "Do you guys have any tarps left?"

"Yes, ma'am I believe we have some. What size would you be looking for?"

"I don't know yet, but I probably have to cover my whole trailer."

"Well, how bad is it?"

She told me that when she sat in her trailer, the water level was approaching knee height.

I thought, *what?* Can you imagine your grandmother living in water past their knees, all alone, with no one to help her?

"Your roof is leaking, but you're living in this trailer?"

"I have nowhere else to go."

"What are you going to do with this tarp when you get it home?"

"I'm probably going to wait for my neighbor to help me." She had no idea when that would be.

"You've got to be kidding me," I responded. "You're going to go home to a mobile home trailer with all that water? No, here's what we're going to do instead."

With that, I grabbed a cart and called one of my assistant managers to gather the rest of the assistant managers, excluding one to remain in the store. Together, we loaded her cart with tarps, nails, bungy cords...everything we thought we'd need, without any thought of asking her to pay for these items. Then I walked up to her and announced, "We're going to follow you home and we're going to tarp your trailer."

"What?"

"All you have to do is lead me to your car. Trust us, we're going to follow you and help."

In the middle of a blinding thunderstorm, we followed this woman home. Think about mobile homes for a moment: they're comprised of metal. Does it not seem that every time you watch the news following a natural disaster of some sort, that the mobile home communities are demolished, lucky to be in the same location? There we were, on her roof working in the presence of active lightning. We tarped the top of her entire trailer and got as much water out of her place as we could, so she could at least stay there without worrying about standing water. While the weather conditions created risk, we felt exhilarated, working together under urgent circumstances. It gave us an opportunity to be of service to someone in the local community who had no other recourse. It's just one of thousands and thousands of examples because that's what Home Depot does. The associates and store teams do these things for the right reasons, yet I never felt that the public understood all that we did. During any given week, storm or no storm, numerous community events are held throughout the United States, Canada and Mexico. Giving back is one of the eight segments of our culture and there exists a strong pride within the company relating to this. It is just what we do.

Three hurricanes kept my team and I busy, running all over the state to serve our fellow employees and customers. Just when we thought our work was done, toward the end of the season, Hurricane Ivan decided to close the season out strong. When it barreled into the Gulf, the first weather predictions put Tampa in its crosshairs. Due to the incredible storm surge, and a direct hit on Tampa Bay, we thought the city would end up under water. Weather analysts predicted massive damage, the likes of which we had not seen yet. We expected total demolition. Then, as we continued to monitor it, in the blink of an eye Ivan changed course and headed toward the Panhandle, creating mixed emotions. On the one hand, due to the density of its population, everyone felt relieved that Tampa was no longer taking a direct hit; on the other hand, those who lived on the Panhandle freaked out, *"Oh shit, it's coming for us!"* All the sudden, I remembered Tom Taylor's prescient words when Ivan inflicted $26.1 billion dollars in damages and killed 124 people. As the hurricane approached, it transformed into a catastrophic Category 3 storm that spanned the entire width of my district – 250 miles from east to west.

When it made landfall at the intersection of Florida and Alabama, it affected all eleven of my stores, to one degree or another. Most communities along the Panhandle were under mandatory evacuation guidelines. Ahead of the hurricane, I sent Pam, Jackie, and our dog to Iowa to stay with friends of ours who had family there, while I hunkered down in Destin with some of my store managers. We rode it out at the home of one of my managers Sabrina, along with her husband, Philip, an assistant store manager for Home Depot, in a mandatory evacuation area. Yes, we were in harm's way, but felt we were east enough of the worst effects (we were wrong). Regardless, it was expected of us to be in harm's way to react as quickly as we could to the post-storm damages and get the stores back open ASAP.

As I took shelter with my team, I participated in conference calls every hour on the hour with the command center. Prior to the storm, you get as much emergency storm product as you possibly can into the stores, with a laser focus on generators, batteries, flashlights, plywood, etc. I remember being in Destin with a clipboard (there's that clipboard again – no, not the same one I used in Fort Lauderdale!) and a legal pad, where I'd noted all the plywood trucks that were coming into the stores and their estimated time of arrival, with the home office pushing the logistics and transportation companies to the brink of their human capabilities to get the stuff in. It truly is an "all hands-on deck" necessity.

Outside of the Destin Store, a line of people formed that started at the lumber side of the building and wrapped all the way around the perimeter – all waiting for plywood. We set up canopies for shade, gave them water, and tried to keep everyone calm. After I got off the conference call, my job was to go outside – I took this on because I didn't want my store manager to have to do it. I wanted her to focus on general operation. These folks were yelling, screaming, and cursing their demands to know when everything was coming in. Keep in mind, we were two days out from the storm and everyone's nerves were frazzled. They just wanted to get back home with what they needed to take care of their families and homes. Given the volatility of the situation, we had sheriff's deputies on-site.

I approached two deputies and asked for their assistance. "I need two of you."

"What do you want us to do?"

"You need to stand on either side of me while I walk this line of people to communicate when we expect our plywood trucks. I'm going to inform them, but I want you guys by my side just in case something happens."

"Okay but understand something. Short of physically assaulting you, everything goes."

What that meant was, these customers could threaten me, curse at me, or do whatever...the deputies didn't want to make an unbearable situation worse. Everyone understood the raw emotions involved.

"That's all I'm asking," I assured them. "I can deal with all of that."

I walked the line to tell them when, how much, and the fact that we were limiting the quantities so we could assist as many customers as possible. I cannot count the curse words, threats of lawsuits, threats of bodily injury, threats of murder, and pronouncements that I was the anti-Christ I fended off that day. By the time we were through the entire line, I was completely drenched in sweat and in need of a strong adult beverage. To the credit of the Sheriff's deputies – big men standing about six-one and six-two, armed, and in full gear – they remained calm while these people had at me. I wanted so badly to help, but my hands were tied, having to supply 10 other stores too. Natural disasters reveal true human nature; you see what happens when good people are pushed to the brink. Of course, many folks expressed appreciation, but they never stand out like the ones who take their frustrations out on you. You know you're going to see them again in the store and you must let bygones be bygones. Adversity tends to bring out the worst in some and best in others. There's nothing like a Cat-3 hurricane to showcase both sides.

Exemplifying the amazing side of human nature, our Home Depot team remained dedicated and committed: associates refused to go home, and some associates worked 20-hour days. If I didn't need them on the cash register, they would go outside and help load up cars for customers. These employees were simply heroic. At that time, hourly associates were not eligible for bonuses, so their actions came from the heart. When I stood back to observe how the team reacted, I almost cried. I felt incredibly emotional, never once having to ask anyone to stay. They came to me and asked, "Where do you need me? What do you want me to do?" in lieu of going home, being with their own families, preparing for the storm, or whatever. This is yet another remarkable example of what the public will not understand about businesses and their employees, their personal sacrifices and response to a natural disaster of this magnitude.

With Pam, Jackie, and our dog evacuated, my teams knew I still had to button up my house, but I was in the stores and didn't have time to do it. *Why in the hell did I not put hurricane shutters up sooner?* One night, I put the word out that I was finally going home to board up some windows ahead of the storm. While in the process of prepping my house, suddenly I saw a caravan of cars pull up. A team of people from the Pensacola store drove over and helped me board up every window in my house with plywood because they knew I might ride it out alone in my house. Once they boarded me up to relieve my worry, they scrambled back. It was one of the most amazing experiences in my 33 years with Home Depot.

After the storm, I tried to get back to my house in Gulf Breeze, but because Ivan had damaged all the bridges, it was impossible. I returned to Sabrina and Philip's home, where I started drinking gin and tonics to calm my nerves and take a step back, while the Fleetwood Mac song, *Tusk,* pulsated in the background. Four gin and tonics in, just when I felt somewhat relaxed and a little buzzed, Paul called me to announce he saw Jim Cantore from the Weather Channel reporting on a fire raging near one of our Home Depot stores. Boy, that sobered me up faster than a pot of coffee and a B_{12} shot because Paul thought the Home Depot was on fire. I had already obtained intel that all our stores were intact, so I assured him, "No, that's a building close to our store, there's no danger, our store is good." When I hung up the phone, my heart was pounding...pour me another gin and tonic!

Time and time again, when danger lurks in the form of a tornado, earthquake, hurricane, or fire Home Depot is everywhere. You might recall one of our iconic TV commercials that featured a Home Depot delivery truck driving down a road, with a powerful storm ahead and to the left. As the truck approaches the intersection, it begins to turn right to its initial destination. It then stops, puts on its left turn signal, and heads into the storm. It's a stunning visual that affirmed what many of us felt.

ASSOCIATE TED'S TESTIMONIAL

Remember Ted, who shared a couple customer stories a few chapters back? While he worked nights in the garden department of the West Boca Home Depot, a big hurricane was coming. He recalls that his store manager took the time to speak with each employee to ask, "What do you need? Do you need plywood? How many sheets do you need? Are you able to get it to your property and hang and install it?" This was before all the plywood got taken by the customers.

Depending on where you were, they supplied that much help. Ted didn't have a truck, so they just dropped the sheet off at his house and when he got off work, he had time to put it up. For the older women who worked in the store as cashiers and were either widowed, single, or had no one at home to help, Home Depot sent off-duty crews to their homes to hang their plywood, so they could focus on their job and have some peace of mind when they got back home. Ted thought that was amazing. But that was only the beginning because he was about to experience Home Depot's genuine altruism on a personal level.

Notes Ted, "After hurricane came through, my house flooded. At the time, my wife and I had two little ones at home. She was nervous about my leaving before the insurance company came and the restoration place came to dry out the house. We were especially concerned about electrical issues. When I showed up for work, probably a couple hours late, I was freaking out and apologizing, 'I'm sorry I'm late.' I didn't think about my house that much. But one of the first people I ran into was the store manager, who said, 'Come in the conference room with me.'

"He had set up a table of chips, dips, sodas, etc. and calmed me down. 'I'll tell you what. We have a block of rooms at the Weston Hotel in Fort Lauderdale. I want you to go home, take your family, go to the hotel, stay there for four or five days, whatever you need. The meals are included. We'll see you next week, okay? So, just relax.'

"I was blown away. When I went home and told my wife, she started crying. We got the kids and we were able to relax. I could then just drive home to meet insurance companies and contractors during the day, then I went back to the hotel to eat dinner and use the pool with my family.

"That was my experience with Home Depot and I'll never forget it. You just don't see that in other businesses. I've been with companies, where, when the hurricane was coming, they didn't even tell you when you could leave. This was just one of many reasons why I appreciated my time at Home Depot."

Ted's story validates what I say about the company. Remember Captain Sully – how emotional he was to get a count of the souls after landing his disabled plane on the Hudson River? It's the same concern at Home Depot: our priority is ensuring the safety of all part-time and full-time associates. We don't rest until we know. My teams and I went through the rosters, enabling us to report to the RVP that we had accounted for all. During the execution of the task, the emotional toll is fatiguing, but the moment you confirm that all are well and accounted for, the feeling of pure joy and relief is indescribable.

EMPATHETIC LEADERSHIP IN ACTION

The smaller cities that sprawl across the Panhandle from east to west are connected by a series of bridges. Ivan damaged or destroyed full sections of bridges between the areas, inhibiting our access to the stores and communities. One of our first goals was to "lay eyes" on the 11 store sites to ascertain damage levels and needed resources. To accomplish this, Paul Raines commissioned a helicopter with two military pilots and flew from Tampa to our Fort Walton Beach store (just west of Destin), to pick me up and do the tour by air. Keep in mind, I had not yet been able to return to Gulf Breeze to check on my own house. Imagine the feeling of not knowing if your house is even standing, while you carry on with the obligations of your job – intense anxiety. All I knew was that Pam and Jackie were safe.

After visiting the team at the Fort Walton Beach store, we took off, bound for the Pensacola store. On the way there, Paul could have easily remained focused on our primary purpose, but, instead, he requested through the headsets that the pilots divert to my home. "Dardas, give the pilot your address. We're going to see your house." He always addressed me by my last name. I never received an explanation why, so I assumed he felt more comfortable with it. However, it did not work both ways as I discovered one (just one!) time, when I addressed him by his last name and he shot me a look as if to say, "Be careful."

With mixed emotions of excitement and dread, we flew to my house. I examined it for the first time as we circled, then hovered over the back yard, about 200 feet in the air. Thank God, it was still standing, but the backyard looked like it had been bombed. The screened-in pool – gone. All the landscaping Pam and I had planted – gone. It looked like a spaceship touched down, sucked everything up, and took it away. Ivan tore off the metal supports from the pool enclosure and turned them into javelins that pierced our Gunite pool. As we hovered over it, I remained nearly speechless, though grateful that the house itself was okay, minus a couple of shingles. Officially, a microburst had occurred and affected our house only, sparing our neighbors. Okay, back to work. From there, we traveled to the Pensacola store, which was five minutes west, and spent time visiting our team. I will never forget Paul for allowing me that opportunity. Simply put, he was a wonderful person, as well as a superb leader.

He hugged people, shook their hands, and promised, "We're going to help you. We're going to be there with you."

And he meant it. Paul made phone calls using the old GI Joe military satellite phones – eight inches long with a six-inch antenna. They were our only means of communication until the phone systems and cell towers were repaired. When we left, the entire group of associates came out to watch us take off in the copter. As the pilot started the engine, I asked, "What kind of Tom Selleck, Magnum PI move can you do with the helicopter?" (Again, for the younger readers, YouTube it.)

"Well, we can only do so much. What if we just swoop over the store really close?"

"That would be cool." Quick side note: if you ever have an opportunity to ride in a helicopter, do it.

With Paul and me in the back, we rose and hovered a bit, before the pilot almost turned the copter on its side as we swooped about 100 feet over the associates, who were all cheering and clapping. Next, we flew to Alabama, which sustained unbelievable damage. Throughout that 2004 hurricane season Paul exemplified incredible leadership. He and his region battled four hurricanes in the same year, which demanded coordination and dedication above and beyond the normal operations and functionality. He displayed calm, methodical, disciplined leadership. The crisis accentuated who and what he was – a key factor in our resiliency. His efforts to keep us focused and calm were nothing short of heroic, providing a foundation for all of us to follow. We were better having worked for and with him. He was rewarded not long after, ascending to higher leadership roles at corporate.

Would I have handled the 2004 hurricane season as well as Paul had I been promoted to RVP? I wondered. Inner confidence aside, I realized, "There's a reason why I didn't get the position. Thank God Paul did." His character and personality made all the difference. If leaders of companies and segments of companies truly understood their imprint on the teams they manage, they would achieve even greater success. More self-awareness results in more achievement.

TURNS OUT, I'M ONLY HUMAN

While in the Panhandle, Pam started to notice something odd about my behavior. Anxiety, mood swings and detachment exposed themselves to her and all those I cared about. Strangely enough, I did not recognize the symptoms. At my routine medical check-up (or so I thought) with our doctor, he came into the office and asked me to complete a behavioral survey with about 25 questions and multiple-choice answers. A random grouping, for example, "Name a color you don't like," or "What are you afraid of?" I was confused why my doctor asked me to complete this, curious as to what my answers would reveal.

After grading it, he informed me that, based on the results of my answers, I had a low level of anxiety and mild depression. WHAT!? He was able to form that opinion from my 25 answers? Pam was relieved because she'd noticed it in me; it wasn't a sudden phenomenon, but something that had been building over time. Depression and anxiety are hereditary in my family (aside from what Tom Cruise thinks). It was tough for me to accept. My self-esteem took a shot. In my mind, I was now mentally ill. I didn't want to see it in myself, yet it played a role through the rest of my career at Home Depot. My doctor prescribed Wellbutrin, a mild medication, and advised me to start taking it ASAP. For me, it felt odd and difficult to accept, given the pride I took in the way I interacted with others. I had to look in the mirror to make sure I understood how I was being perceived. Was this impacting my performance? Was it impacting my teams? Was this impacting my family?

Following the diagnosis, I stayed on the Wellbutrin for six months. Shortly after that, I announced to Pam, "You know what? I don't think I'm going to take these pills anymore."

"Why?"

"'Cause they're not doing any good. I don't see or feel any different."

"Are you out of your *flippin'* mind? Jackie and I have noticed an incredible difference."

Her unvarnished honesty blindsided me. I was looking for an excuse to get off the meds. Until then, the only pills I took were multivitamins or Advil. At that point, I still resisted my diagnosis, but Pam talked me through it and helped me reach a level of acceptance by describing the positive shift in my mood, demeanor, and stress level.

After the Wellbutrin, the doc decided to put me on Venlafaxine, something a bit stronger. My embarrassment about being on the medication led to a critical mistake. I should have been transparent with my supervisors and informed them of the situation. *"Why?"* you might ask. Even if you are on the appropriate type and dosage of medication, there are still bad days, along with the good days. Had they been in the loop, their understanding of who, and how I was would have been enhanced. It would have provided me a professional resource, a partner if you will, to put their figurative arm around me to assist me on those bad days. My failure to do so made an impact on the steadfast way in which I had to focus my relationships with those I worked with, and those who worked for me. It also created tense situations with officers at the home office. All due to my stubborn pride.

Even as I write this, I'm still on medication for anxiety. Later in my career when I was a regional manager, I finally confided in my supervisors the exact nature of my problem and its effects. Their first reaction was, "Oh, that explains it."

"What does that mean?"

"Well, we could tell by how you handled yourself from an emotional standpoint, in terms of your mood and behaviors. You were under control, yet we could see serious mood swings and behaviors."

What's the lesson here? Mental and emotional illness does not carry the same stigma it did many years ago. In fact, 16 percent of Americans today take some form of anxiety or depression medication, a 65 percent growth over the last 15 years. If you deal with a medical or mental condition, I strongly encourage you to let your boss or supervisor know about it. Communicate with them to forge a better understanding. While it is stressful to share such personal information, your boss or supervisor can assist you or at least understand your behaviors to a larger degree.

Referring to that human touch, I used my situation to help others. When I sat down with them to discuss their behaviors or performance, I shared my personal circumstance to reveal more of my understanding and empathy. Without judgment, I encouraged them to seek professional help, providing the time to do so. As a result, some of them scheduled doctors' appointments and got on medication...or at least talked to a professional. It is extremely tough to share something that personal, but if you understand your audience and possess a willingness to help, it can bring a relationship with a co-worker to a higher level. My sharing cultivated our mutual respect. Respect leads to trust, an invaluable commodity in any relationship. Proper, high-quality relationships provide an assurance of success for your organization.

A HEALTHY YOU IS THE BEST YOU

Hey, it's my book so let me channel my inner Bernie Marcus and get on my soapbox for a moment because I want and need to communicate something from my heart to every one of you. With all the passion of one who has learned from experience, I must urge you to take care of your health. It is your strongest ally for all you want to do in your life. On the job or at home, without it, you will not be living the dream to its fullest potential. Trust me on this, please! Take it from one who almost died because I ignored symptoms until it was almost too late. Assuming I had a chest cold, I finally went to the doctor. While she was doing her exam, she hesitated, then announced she was calling an ambulance to transport me to the hospital. It turned out I had two blood clots in each lung, requiring hospitalization and procedures. The medical team told me I had only two- to- three days before I would have experienced a major health event – a stroke or a heart attack – at age 52. There are more personal incidents I could share, but please understand that you, yes *you*, owe it to you family, your employer, your team and yourself to be the healthiest that you can be.

So, be proactive about your health and schedule your preventive medical, vision and dental appointments. Attention to these matters always yields better results. Do not wait until something happens, because then it could be too late. No, I'm not trying to be all gloom-and-doom here. I'm relating my experiences in the hope you will learn from them, because I am far from perfect when it comes to nutrition, well-being, and health. I'll be the first to admit, I am a dessert fiend. If sugar is in the house, I will find it. I'm also a fan of most wines and a great gin and tonic, but I work hard to eat and drink in moderation. The point is, I'm not imploring you to stop consuming your favorite foods and beverages...just to enjoy them responsibility, to paraphrase the old alcohol disclaimer.

However, I will recommend that we all need a release for the stresses our bodies endure and the mental gymnastics that take place upstairs, which affect us in various and profound ways. Therefore, we need two releases: one for the body and one for the mind. For me, it's working out and reading. If I go for any length of time without the ability to do both, my disposition devolves into negative territory. Consider this section a look-in-the-mirror moment: do you have similar releases to assist in countering the negative health impacts?

I hate hospitals...nothing against any personnel who work there. To me, just the thought of being admitted into one – which, unfortunately, has happened too many times – is enough to keep me on my health regimen. Oh, and if you are worried about the money, don't. Your family, friends, neighbors, employer, and co-workers would rather have you around. And now, I am done. Thank you for tolerating my thoughts. If they help just one person, then they were worthy of the time.

IS THERE AN ANIMAL IN THE HOUSE?

The classic *Animal House* is one of my favorite movies of all time. One week, I hosted a staff meeting at the Pensacola store to discuss a variety of topics. However, I wanted it to be fun and entertaining. I have always despised one-dimensional meetings, which I consider non-productive and unable to hold anyone's interest. With the help of my administrative assistant and store personnel, I incorporated media into the agendas, be it books, videos, or music. In the early days, we used overhead projectors only (yawn!). Nope, for this meeting, the multi-dimensional experience would be one that my audience would never forget.

I'd invited a couple ladies from our home office who were specialists in our special services business in the stores. I didn't have to twist their arms, because as you can imagine, everybody loved to visit us in the Panhandle. Thanks to the white-sand beaches, emerald-green water, sunshine, and palm trees, their visits, in a good amount of cases, turned into long weekends. In all, there were fifteen men and women assembled that day. My plan was to use a clip from the movie where the members of the Delta Tau Chi were in their frat house on double secret probation. John Belushi's character, John Blutarsky, tries to rally the fraternity by giving a great speech. He ends it by asking, "Who's with me?" and with that, he runs out of the room, but nobody follows him. When he comes back, Otter (played by Tim Matheson) supports him with a speech of his own, then everybody gets ready to go.

Prior to the meeting, I entrusted the store manager (very bad move) to set the movie right at that scene, so that when I clicked play, it would start with Bluto's speech. With it all set up (or so I thought) we proceeded through the agenda. At the end, I announced, "Just to reinforce my point, here we go," and asked the store manager to hit play. If you're in my age group, you may recall that there are many scenes in *Animal House* that are not suitable for children or mixed audiences – or to use today's lingo, NSFW (Not Safe for Work). Instead of the scene I described, my audience saw the scene where one of the cheerleaders was with her boyfriend in the car at Lover's Peak. When it started to play in my staff meeting, I couldn't get to the remote fast enough. I was horrified. Everything seemed to be in ultra-slow motion until we corrected. Everyone had a good laugh, more due to my discomfort with what was happening, than the movie itself.

Afterward, I approached the two ladies from the home office and said, "If you're going to turn me into Human Resources today, please let me know so I can get my statement together." We laughed about it again and I apologized a half-dozen more times. They told me not to worry about it...that they thought it was funny and enjoyed how the moment unfolded. I learned you must be careful with this sort of thing and sometimes, if you want a job done right (and professional), you must do it yourself. To this day, I don't know if the store manager sabotaged me, but I became more protective and diligent with my multi-media presentations from that moment on.

THE GIFT THAT KEEPS ON GIVING

At Christmas, we exchanged gifts with our bosses. Paul, with his creativity and personal flair, took gift exchange to an entirely new level. He liked to present us with unique, personalized gifts in the form of certificates. His assistant, Debbie, often told us stories of hearing Paul laugh out loud in his office, as she sat at her desk. When she knocked on his door to ask what was so funny, he told her he was generating the certificate titles for each member of his team. He could have easily delegated this task but chose to do it himself. One year, mine was named, "The Early Warning Radar Award," as Titled and Presented to Erik Dardas by Paul Raines." This was due to my effort to ensure that the region was always in stock on all items before the start of an ad or new catalog. If there were any issues, I would notify Paul, along with the merchants responsible for those items.

Paul would present the items to us at a staff meeting ahead of the holiday. It was a wonderful time, as you could see the enjoyment in his face and demeanor when presenting them to us. But, wait, there's more: he would find an accompanying item to go along with the certificate. Mine was one of those children's wind-up air sirens, filled with candy. Yep, he'd gone to the trouble of visiting a candy store. As we sat there, we were amazed that he would take the time to do is.

Enthralled, you couldn't wait to see what he'd do for everybody else. He was spot-on with each of the titles. It became special. During my career, I worked with other leaders who gave me the same book they gave other people. Sometimes that is okay. Paul's personal dedication and commitment impacted you to the point where you would do anything he asked, and then some. Leaders always have a choice: you can be like everyone else (status quo), or you can choose to be better, in a way that will positively impact your team.

True, on the surface it was just a silly little certificate and a toy, but with this seemingly simple gift, Paul recognized you for something and showed his appreciation. His efforts demonstrated that he was paying attention to what we did. When I agreed to make yet another move for Home Depot up to the D.C. area, he gave me another certificate at a staff meeting dinner, while we were in our corporate office in Atlanta. Before the dinner started, he made some general comments then he announced I was leaving for D.C. to take on another assignment. The award's name? "The Hate to Eat and Run Award." Brilliant and priceless. I still have those certificates, many years later.

By his words, action, and character Paul imparted countless values, lessons, and compassion on many, many people. He was an example of leadership, showcasing a consistent demeanor. I only saw him truly "lose it," one time while on a store walk. He had gotten angry over the condition of some of the store displays, which was shocking because it was so rare. I can tell you, though, it made you feel as if you had disappointed your father. It only happened once.

Unsurprisingly, Paul's leadership propelled him to a high-level officer position at corporate, second in position of running US stores before he became President and CEO of GameStop. Unfortunately, due to a terminal illness, he is no longer with us, though his legacy lives on. If you asked me, "Who impacted you the most at Home Depot?" My answer would be Paul Raines, right behind Larry Mercer. Paul came to anything I invited him to. We decided to do a reassociation with all employees who were with Home Depot over 10 years, wanting them to understand their obligation to be the best they could be. It was important to refresh them and help them understand how they could be role-models for the newer employees, per our expectations. I coordinated my team's event and invited Paul, who immediately accepted the invitation to share time with the associates. I found out later that he had prior commitments but had made changes so he could attend. Paul was younger than me, but he possessed a maturity and professionalism beyond his years.

Right before that memorable hurricane season, the company asked me to relocate to the Washington, D.C. Area. It was a difficult decision involving six conversations with the RVP, Gary. During the first five conversations, I told him, "no." I did not want to go, as life in Florida was going very well. But, as I've stated before, you rarely turned Home Depot down when the call came to relocate. In early days, diminished perceptions of allegiance to the company were the result. This time though, I didn't feel right about it, because I was backtracking on any desire to become an officer. We were in a lovely home in Gulf Breeze and we had good stuff going on: Jackie was attending a private, Christian school we were happy to get her into and Pam was all settled in and playing competitive tennis with some friends in a league. We lived in a great neighborhood. There was no reason for us to leave.

Still, my RVP kept asking. One day I was driving in the car when I got a call from Pam, who'd been talking to Jackie about the move. When Pam put her on the phone, Jackie announced, "Mommy talked to me about it and if you think we should move, it's okay." Based on that phone call, I called the RVP back and announced, "We'll go."

We worked out the logistical and financial ends of the deal, with Gary guaranteeing I would earn bonus as if I'd been in Florida the full year – which was extremely important. We were to be in our new area at the start of December. The overall bonus position of the new area was far less than the area I was leaving, which could have cost us significantly. The sales following an impactful hurricane are "off the charts" good – far beyond normal results. Those higher results continue for a length of time, due in part to the time it takes for the insurance companies to get checks back into the homeowner's hands. If I'm honest, although I kept telling Gary "no" at first, something kept nagging at me. Thinking back on Tom Taylor's words, maybe this relocation would not offer a vehicle for promotion, but since I was leaving the "country club" for one of the company's highest volume areas, maybe it would enhance my overall standing. Just to be sure though, right after Ivan I called Tom Taylor and offered, "If you want, I'll stay in Florida and you can get someone else for D.C." He replied, "Hell, no. I *need* you in D.C."

In all, we lived in Gulf Breeze for three-and-a-half years (longer than normal). Pam's standing joke with everyone was, "Every two years we move. As soon as I get settled and make friends, it's time to go." However, this time, she had one condition. "If we go up there, that's it. Once Jackie starts high school, we're not moving again." It was an easy promise to keep as I remembered how I'd been affected by my parents moving during my high school years; there was no way I'd do that to my kid, especially being female. Besides, we had lived and worked in the D.C. area before while I was a store manager in Gaithersburg, Maryland. The draw of the area to us was strong because we always had an awe for all that Washington, D.C. represented: the monuments, the history, the heart of the most powerful nation in the world. It never got old, when an event required your presence in the district, to drive by the Washington Monument or the Capitol. Majestic and powerful, at the same time. My return marked the beginning of a new chapter in my Home Depot career and the longest amount of time we would live in any one place.

Ladders & Learnings

- Become part of your company's culture as it pertains to volunteerism and community involvement. It enhances your personal and professional brand...and it will make you feel incredible.
- Identify a leader in your organization whom you consider

one of the best. Observe their behaviors as often as possible. Compare them to a leader who is not as highly regarded and note the differences.

EXECUTIVE MEMO –

Understand that your brand will be impacted more in adverse situations, as opposed to positive times in your business, by the way you lead your teams. Proactively work to validate high quality, collaborative communication with your direct reports on a regular basis, both as a group and as individuals.

12

ONE MORE TIME...AND GOD, PLEASE MAKE THIS THE LAST TIME

"He who would accomplish little need sacrifice little; he who would achieve much must sacrifice much. He who would attain highly must sacrifice greatly."

— JAMES ALLEN

The cost of living in the D.C. area shocked us, to put it mildly. The year was 2004, the pinnacle of the housing industry's high, over-inflated home values. This was move number six for us as a family! The relocation to Northern Virginia presented us with challenges we'd never dealt with before. The first time we lived in this region we had been renters, and it not been nearly as occupied by housing developments and new businesses. Suburban sprawl had saturated the "Beltway Area." The traffic became insane, with far more vehicles than the roads could accommodate, especially at "drive time." We were amazed at the differences eleven years had permitted.

The exorbitant cost of living is personified in the homes in the D.C. area. The median home price in Fairfax, Virginia is almost double that of Gulf Breeze, Florida. This makes sense, given the fact that out of the 20 highest-median income counties in the U.S., 10 are in the Mid-Atlantic area. The dirt there must have gold in it. My district included stores in Manassas, Fairfax, Arlington, and Falls Church – all in the high cost-of-living areas. Part of the relocation package gives you a week of paid time to visit the area and find a home. As we looked at houses, Pam and I wanted to stay within a budget of $550,000 to $600,000. Most people see those numbers and think, "Wow! That's an expensive house, probably a mansion."

Not in D.C.

We'd told our realtor we would like to live in Fairfax in a four-bedroom, two-bath home with a decent-sized yard and hard-surface countertops. I was stunned and speechless when she informed me over the phone that there were no homes in Fairfax in our target budget. Remember, I had committed to Pam and Jackie that we would be here for a while and I wanted something nice. I asked our realtor to provide the price we needed to be at to find our desired home in Fairfax. I will never forget that phone call. Being a man, I requested she give me the bottom line, in lieu of a detailed explanation. She said, without hesitation: $750.000. *SAY WHAT!?*

In my mind, I had a flashback to an earlier time when Pam and I turned down a relocation to the Hudson Valley/New York City area when I was still a store manager. After touring homes in Nyak, New York, I called my boss and advised him, "Listen, you can't pay me enough to move up there." It was not the move itself; we wanted to do that. It was the housing.

"Sure, I can. What are you looking for?"

At that time, we wanted a basic house, which I described to him. He offered, "Well, I can give you X amount of money."

"Vern, there's no way. I can't do it. I can't do this to my family." To quote Pam, we didn't want to be "house rich and life poor."

Now, here we were in Fairfax, with NOTHING available within our budget. Thanks to my déjà vu, I wondered if I should back-pedal on my agreement to move, which I did not want to do because I had committed. I couldn't do that to Gary after all the calls.

"What are we going to do?" I asked our D.C. realtor, dumfounded. I did not want us to go backwards in our lifestyle because of this move.

"Every mile further we get from D.C., the price of the house decreases by $10- to- 15,000 dollars," she informed us. At just 12 miles outside of D.C., the Fairfax housing market was out of reach. We traveled another 25 miles west to a small, historic town called Haymarket. We thought, based on our research and her formula, we could get an awesome house for less than $500,000 (uh...wrong again). After we toured 42 houses in four days, with no luck, we (I, mainly) panicked and raised our budget to $650,000. It was important to find a house we both could live with. The next day, we fell in love with one specific house. Unfortunately, the seller's realtor had forgotten to update us that the seller had accepted an offer the day before. When we walked in, it looked unkempt, with dishes in the sink and towels on the floor in the bathrooms – highly unusual for a home on the market. Then, as I was standing at the kitchen table, I noticed a document lying on the table with the term "sales contract," at the top. I picked it up, handed it to our realtor and asked, "What does this mean?"

She responded, "It means they accepted an offer. This house is sold."

Now I was furious; just beside myself. As we walked back to the realtor's car, Pam looked at me with apprehension. She knew I was ready to explode. Crushed, as I sat in the back seat of the car I lit into our realtor, "How could you take us to see this? You didn't make sure it wasn't sold. That was cruel. We're having such difficulty finding a house." My ninth move with Home Depot was proving to be the most challenging. I calmed down enough for us to go to lunch and strategize what to do next. Our next move? Wait for it...increase our budget to $750,000 to enable us to look at another grouping of homes. While I have never been in the ring with Mike Tyson for several rounds, I imagined this MUST BE how it felt. Exhausted and frustrated, we finally found our home near the end of the week at $689,000. At the closing, I thought I was going to have to administer CPR to Pam when she wrote the check for the deposit money. To this day, it's the most expensive house we've ever bought.

Compounding the issue, we wanted (Pam, more than I) a realistic monthly payment. Pam drew the proverbial "line in the sand." We ended up putting down 40 percent of the list price, and I said goodbye to my 1961 Corvette (Bernie would be happy). In fact, I didn't speak to Pam for three days because we diverted all that money into our house that could have bought me my dream car (yeah, poor me). Years later, it turned out to be one of our (her) smartest financial decisions. When we sold our house in 2018, we cashed in on the equity which enabled us to buy our house in Wisconsin and our house in Florida. *My wife is always right!* Why, of why, do I continue to challenge her. Men just stop – women are always right, even when they are not.

Aside from housing costs, we had to adjust to the sheer density of the population and the amount of traffic in the D.C. area, which competes with Los Angeles and New York City for the worst in the country. Making matters worse for me, our house was on the western edge of my district. This meant additional time in the car, even though my farthest store was only 35 miles east. Worst of all, the regional office was located north of Baltimore Maryland, almost 100 miles away. For all events and meetings, I had to drive there and back. Not whining, just saying. Some residents of the Mid-Atlantic area commute two- to- three hours EACH WAY to and from their jobs... and God forbid, there's an accident because that number will double. To put a decent roof over their families, they sacrifice time with them because there's just no other way to make it. I recommend that all companies that ask employees to relocate, provide adequate financial compensation – enough to allow them to live and work to the fullest.

I mentioned the importance of the family dinner when I talked about my new role as district manager in Houston, and how it affected my ability to get home in time until my little girl gave me a wake-up call. Well, to highlight my point further, thanks to Pam's Italian heritage, dinner is a big deal. Whether I was delayed in the stores or stuck in God-awful traffic, her biggest frustration was having cooked a nice meal and me not being able to get there, even when wrapping up the day at a decent time. It was defeating, just like that moment in our Houston home with Jackie before I took control. I knew some guys who tried to get into work at 5 a.m. to meet their goal of leaving the stores by two or three p.m. to make it home for dinner with their families. But if you left at that time, you missed an opportunity to interact with associates who came in to work after 2 p.m. These lengthy commutes take a huge toll on employees who must drive from rural/suburban areas to urban areas to perform their roles.

My recommendation to leaders in companies? If your employees deal with long, harrowing commutes, communicate with them to gain an understanding and determine what you may be able to do to make it as easy as on them possible. I must say, on behalf of all legitimate commuters who drive with respect, if you are a "rubber-necker" who feels the need to slow down for every accident and fellow driver getting a ticket, PLEASE, for the love of all that is good in this world – STOP! Your nosiness does nothing but compound the issue and delay everyone further.

One day I felt especially frustrated as I sat in my car, stuck in traffic due to accidents. It was so bad I couldn't even get out of Haymarket to travel to the Baltimore stores even after I tried every available side-road and option available. Exasperated, I emailed my VP, "I don't care what you do. I either want a helicopter or a jet-pack now."

"Turn in the requisition for the jet-pack but I don't think it's going to get approved," came the reply. It was a facetious exchange but yes, I was *that* frustrated. That's when I started considering, "What do I need to do to get out of here?" The job stopped being fun. I'd get home at night even more frazzled after the drive with its traffic and road rage, yet Pam wondered why I didn't use the time to "de-stress." Only after she drove in that traffic herself a few times did she understand.

"We don't know how you guys do this," Pam and our friend John's wife Heather remarked one day. "You have to do this every day; you have to sit in this crap. Now we know when you get home, the last thing you want to do is talk to a human being. You want to work out, get a drink, or take a nap." I'm sorry to admit that Pam and Jackie had to suffer my behavior because my commute was exacerbating my anxiety.

A prime example that highlights how bad it can get? One day, I was driving home and there was a small compact car beside me, filled with what looked like members of the brutal MS-13 gang. When they cut me off something fierce, it triggered my already precarious disposition and ignited a road rage response: I rode their ass and drove up to the side of their car, not fully understanding I was playing with fire. Yes, I was stupid. I made eye contact with the driver, screaming choice obscenities. In response, he yelled back, "I'm gonna show you something," as he appeared to reach under the seat, presumably for a weapon...maybe even a gun. His passenger in the shotgun seat put his arm on the driver and said, "Back off." All the sudden their car hit the brakes and went way behind while I prepared to dial 9-1-1. Were they really members of MS-13? I can't guarantee it but based on the markings and tattoos on their faces, it was highly likely. They had and continue to have a strong presence in the Manassas, Virginia area.

Start. Stop. Accelerate. Brake. Repeat. If you're doing it countless times on your daily commute, it's a problem. Aside from my mental and emotional state, the commute, damaged my physical health. Following three- to- four years of stressful commutes, I experienced a sleepless week, due to a strange tingling in my legs, which my doctor later diagnosed as restless leg syndrome. It makes you feel like your legs are moving when they are not and prevents you from sleeping until at least 2 a.m. My doctor prescribed the same medication used to treat Parkinson's, since restless leg syndrome is a movement disease triggered in the brain. I was already on anxiety meds and now I had to take another prescription. If I didn't take it daily, I didn't get to sleep until 2 a.m., but I'd still get up at my usual early time to get to that day's scheduled location. In the short-term it was a manageable solution, but over the long-term, I felt its dire consequences in the form of fatigue, short-temperedness, short-term memory lapses, and sore, aching joints.

Despite the unconquerable commute, I still loved my job and wanted to be the best in the region. However, I now had to manage another medical condition. I agreed to assume responsibility for the largest volume district in the region, which also needed a complete overhaul in the areas of service, standards, and results. The potential of this area was limitless. As I went into "attack mode" with my team, each time we took a step forward, we seemed to fall two steps back. The resurrection of the area would take more time and effort than I originally thought. Pressure from Gary, company officers and corporate resources was heightened, due to the sales volume, not only in the region but in the company, and its proportionate leverage. All these elements combined to lead to my own personal storm.

In fact, this is the first time I've ever publicly admitted it, but just ahead of my promotion to regional pro sales manager, I had a nervous breakdown. One day at home, Pam and I were in the middle of an argument when I just fell apart. I broke down crying with my head in my hands...almost completely numb and unable to move. The situation devolved to the point where I was not myself, not even close. It took a gargantuan effort to get out of bed in the morning – perpetuated by my increased separation anxiety from Pam. I will readily admit, for a brief time it impacted my job performance. Blessed is not a word I use lightly, but in this case, I truly was. Aside from visiting my doctor as quickly as possible, I began praying multiple times a day. I am not a "holy roller" by any stretch, but the need to reconnect with Him provided me with some peace and introspection. Pam's patience, support, and positive energy was unbelievable during this time, notwithstanding the fact that I was driving her crazy with the associated behaviors.

My doctor elevated the dosages of the medications I was taking. Although it took a couple of months, my behaviors corrected themselves Unfortunately, this is another example of my failure to communicate with my supervisors out of fear of their reaction. They had done nothing to create that fear in me; it was all my creation in my mind. I should have requested a leave of absence to appropriately handle it but felt confident I could work through it. After we came out on the other side of the crisis, I told Pam she deserved to be sainted for hanging in there with me. I truly meant it.

All the while, the pressure to perform continued. I heard more than once from my higher-ups that I was brought to the area for a reason, that they had elevated expectations for a guy with the surname "Dardas," and that the clock was ticking. Like an athlete who reaches the pinnacle, for example, the Super Bowl, the expectation is that you're going to repeat every year. If you don't, you suck, and the boos begin. At times, I believed that's how people looked at me. It motivated me to steadfastly continue. Financially, the stock was nowhere near where I needed it to be to retire, so more work was required. Besides, where would I go for another job? Lowe's? *NEVER!* I was not going to retire until I achieved the number recommended by my financial adviser, Reid, to enable me to never have to work again.

ACCENTUATE THE POSITIVE

Since my predecessor failed to train and lead associates and managers properly, I identified the need for direction and guidance. The priority was working first with the teams, then the stores. Stores in this area boast some of the highest footsteps (customer transactions) per week in the US. These Home Depot locations are also shopped the most...and boy, did they ever look like it. Remember the customer archetypes in chapter eight – our stores had a preponderance of all of them. They could look tight on standards and execution at 6 a.m., but by 5 p.m. appeared to be "trashed." The overnight recovery teams, along with the day teams worked their hardest, but frustration embedded itself into this vicious cycle.

In terms of profits, they remained the biggest cash cows in the company, but they were ugly. If you will, picture broken bags of concrete, trash all over the floors, packages ripped open, and merchandise thrown around and placed in the wrong displays. To put it bluntly, this was one of the biggest challenges I had faced, and we had our work cut out for us. I knew I could not address the presentation of the stores with any success unless I first sought the respect and buy-in of the store managers. I had to get them to believe they could do more than even they believed.

My efforts began on customer service. D.C. is one of the most diverse places in the United States, with residents from numerous countries, all over the world. The proximity to Washington, D.C. was mainly responsible for this, due to embassy personnel. Some of our stores employed people from 50 different countries, which presented an array of problems, from communication to homeland social protocols. For example, due to warring factions overseas, a native of one country could not be in the break room with a native of another country involved in the same conflict because of the urge to harm each other. Imagine the necessity placed upon the store manager to maintain the peace among their teams, while focused on improving customer service – it's heavy-duty stuff!

Such conditions created an enormous opportunity to improve and adjust communication to enable all different peoples to understand the meaning of customer service and other store-related tasks. Take, for example, the term "sweeping up." If you ask an associate to do that, do they really understand what you mean? I'm not exaggerating when I tell you, not everybody knew how to use a broom. You had to teach and show them. Thanks to my experience in urban centers like Philly, in addition to rural and suburban locations, I had real-world experience to guide me in my interactions with these distinct environments that presented unique challenges and demanded different approaches. Plus, at Publix, they taught you how to be a swift, high-quality sweeper. The goal was to sweep the entire store, sometimes with only two people, and do it efficiently, with no piece of trash left behind.

In the more difficult stores with higher diversities, leading by example became more important. They demanded much more time and effort on my part to spend time with all levels of management who knew I was a Home Depot veteran; I had to embed my experience in their DNA as quickly as I could and demonstrate standard through action. They walked with me and watched as I engaged with customers, then we critiqued the interaction afterward to ensure they took away the practical knowledge I wanted to impart.

Empowerment, defined as giving authority to by official means, became another weapon in our arsenal to satisfy our customers. For a lengthy period, our customer policies were very black and white, which created the need for a manager to respond to every situation that went outside the lines. At times, customers, became frustrated when they had to wait for a manager who had to conclude their present task before responding. At Home Depot, if an hourly associate engages with a customer in a situation, for example, an item out-of-stock or a damage issue, etc., the company empowers them up to $50 per incident to appease the customer, with no need for a manager. One of the most difficult challenges I faced? Conveying to my teams that Home Depot entrusted them with this privilege to prevent them from having to call a manager whenever dealing with a customer problem. Until we showed them how, they were hesitant. Once again, the solution was to lead by example, as evidenced by the following incident that took place at the Fairfax Circle store.

I was walking with the store team in outside garden by the plants, where the cash registers are open during spring, summer, and most of fall. A customer came with a chainsaw and a broken chain. With everybody watching, I engaged in a dialogue with him.

"Hey, how are you doing today?"

"Doing fine; just need to replace a chainsaw chain."

"Great! Come on, they're right over here."

Lo and behold, when we got there, we discovered we were out-of-stock on the one he needed. *Ah, a teachable moment.*

"Sir, we're out of that chain," I informed him. At the sound of my words, I witnessed his eyes droop and his overall demeanor transform into one of frustration. Let's remember, through all the issues we had with driving in this area, the same was true for customers. His thoughts probably centered on having to get back into his car and drive somewhere else, in all the lovely traffic. Other companies may allow their customers to just walk at this point, but not Home Depot. I knew he had something to do that day.

"What are you working on?" I asked.

"I'm trimming some trees and I have to get it done today. I'm on a tight deadline."

Normally, we would try to find a chain at another Home Depot location, and if it was convenient for the customer, ask them to pick it up there. Or, we'd drive and get it ourselves, then take it to their house. All these scenarios played in my head as we worked toward a solution.

"Tell me this: how old is your chainsaw?" I inquired.

"Oh, about four or five years old," he replied.

"Really? You could probably use a new one, couldn't you?"

"What do you mean?"

I took one off the shelf and handed it to him. "Here. Go get back on the job."

"What?"

"It is your lucky day. Not your fault we were out of stock. Get on the job. Just do me a favor, for everything else you ever need, please keep shopping at Home Depot."

"You're s******g me."

"No, I'm not s******g you. Now get back on the job before I change my mind," I joked.

We laughed, fist-bumped and he was on his way- very, very happy. After he left, the associates remarked, "That was the coolest thing we've ever seen."

"Now, I can do that at my level," I remarked. "What did you take away from that?" It led to a productive discussion about how they could use empowerment, at their levels, to solve a customer's problem on their own. While this example may seem over-the-top, it's not. That's how Home Depot rolled. Most customers on the receiving end repay that favor out of gratitude and loyalty. There are countless stories of amazing things we've done for our customers. We even purchased product at Lowe's that we did not stock, then deliver it to the customer. Of course, we didn't tell them where we'd purchased it. The chainsaw customer was just one of countless examples of ways in which we communicated our customer service standards to associates and managers. If I did it, I expected them to do it.

LIONEL RITCHIE SAID IT BEST: HELLO

Wanting to establish a healthy fear in my store associates, as Bernie and Arthur had done in me so many years earlier, I decided upon a customer service strategy. I would take a previous lesson concerning "inspect what you expect," and put it on steroids. I communicated my intention to do a combination of announced and unannounced visits to the stores, gauging customer service and store readiness. The initial goals were simple: look for greetings on the service side and pick up trash on the readiness side. Diversity can play the role of inhibitor relating to service, depending on people's comfort level with each other. Many diverse customers had a higher level of comfort speaking their own language, at times intimidating others from approaching. Wanting my team to overcome any obstacle, I "became" a customer for the unannounced visits. Donning a disguise of sorts, I wore clothes they'd never expect of me – no pressed khaki's, no wingtip shoes, no collar shirts. Instead, sweatpants or filthy jeans, a baseball cap pulled down on my eyes or backwards, sunglasses, and some dirt marks on my face became my uniform for the day, which consisted of three – to- four store visits. I walked each aisle and got within the ten-foot space (expectation to initiate greeting) of each associate. With reference to readiness, I also observed associates' initiative to pick up trash versus ignoring it in the hope that someone else would. Like the results in Houston, the first visits were downright depressing with few, if any, greetings and trash left on the floor. Following the visits, I provided the store managers my feedback, followed by a collaborative strategy plan. Along with that, we began to publicly reward the associates who had greeted me and offered their assistance.

Arthur had a great phrase when it came to actual results, often saying "Anything we tend to measure, always improves." Following his lead, we tracked sales on the days I secret-shopped (unannounced) versus the days of announced visits (in my business casual and apron). The best sales days were the announced, scheduled visits as the stores spent extra time and effort preparing the store (remember Bernie's Road Show comments). The store managers knew that they were ultimately responsible for the service and condition of their stores. Their efforts increased in these areas, validated by the customer service scores we received through customer surveys and my visits. As the process continued, it established a foundation. Of note, the unannounced visit results also improved as behaviors became consistent in both greeting customers and picking up trash. We were on our way. Just one (huge) problem – turnover. How do you establish standards that sustain themselves over time in a high turnover industry? The negative byproduct is the necessity of repetition. The things you emphasized thirty years ago remain constant today. A culture of standards, behaviors, and expectations demands constant reinforcement. Those who do it best win. Even in retirement, I shop in Lowe's and Home Depot and on occasion, I am very disappointed in level of customer service in both. It is evident that the war to win customers is still a daily battle.

People who don't remain with companies for longer lengths of time cannot fathom the commitment and resolve it requires. Those who do commit to a company long-term will endure the ups and the downs, proving their mettle. One must unequivocally love their company and what they do. The financial and stature rewards are there for the committed. For those of us who remained with the company through the best and worst of times, there is a palpable sense of gratification. Having already referenced the fear and anxiety in existence pending Bernie and Arthur's departures, December of the year 2000 began an extremely difficult seven-year stretch, thanks to a completely different approach to leadership. For those of you who ride rollercoasters, you know the feeling you have as you approach the highest point as you anticipate what awaits you on the other side of the track: either true excitement, or pure dread for what comes next. At Home Depot, we wanted to be excited for what came next, but an extreme feeling of dread loomed large.

Ladders & Learnings

Be completely honest with your supervisor as to anything and everything that is a concern to you personally or professionally. Awareness and understanding are powerful tools to assist you.

EXECUTIVE MEMO

As you relocate your team-members, please don't rely on a standard protocol only. Ensure that all factors involved are not detrimental to the team member and their family. Yes, there are sacrifices to be made moving up the ladder or doing what is right for the company. But if the move is mutually beneficial, the result will be greater allegiance and productivity.

13

SHINING A LIGHT THROUGH THE DARK AGES

"Corporate culture matters. How management chooses to treat its people impacts everything – for better or for worse."

— SIMON SINEK

Reading to this point, you probably think the demotion was the lowest point of my career with Home Depot. That is true. However, what I'm about to share is a close second – professionally, personally, and financially. Up to this point, I'd been blessed to work for two of the greatest business leaders on the planet, Bernie Marcus and Arthur Blank. In the not-too-distant future, I'd share a similar experience with company leaders Frank Blake and Craig Menear. Between those leaders, however, everyone who worked for Home Depot (including me), would have to endure the seven-year period from December 2000 to January 2007 that we refer to as "The Dark Ages." It proved to be the most challenging in the history of the company. Given the difficulty of the struggles I'm about to describe, reliving them for the purpose of this book was cathartic. This chapter represents *my* perspectives and opinions of the leadership team Home Depot put in place following Bernie and Arthur's departure.

Within those seven years, numerous transitions took place at executive leadership positions within the company. More than 90 percent of the original officer group left for greener pastures (of their own volition) or "sought other business opportunities" (were asked to leave). Having grown up at Home Depot, it was disconcerting for many of us to witness what was taking place. Toward the end of 1999, after that infamous 20th anniversary celebration that lulled the company into complacency, changes began to take place. Arthur left first (2001), followed by Bernie (2002), leaving many of us feeling uneasy and uncertain about the future.

Our new leader came on board as President and CEO and remained with Home Depot for seven years. One of the candidates considered for CEO of General Electric when Jack Welch, an icon in his own right, retired, Bob Nardelli accepted Home Depot's invitation after G.E. selected Jeff Immelt for the position. Once communicated, the decision created anxiety among veterans of Home Depot – from the officer level down – because he was not a known entity within the company, nor did he have "Big Box" retail experience. Bob was an outsider. The fact that he came from a massive, multi-faceted company like G.E. softened the blow somewhat, but still we wondered: *What was going to happen? Would Home Depot change and how? Who would fit in with these changes?* We'd cultivated an incredible culture under previous leadership that these fears loomed large, like a menacing thundercloud. After all, it was the first time we'd experienced a transition of this magnitude.

I'm going to be brutally honest: Bob was not a good fit from the get-go. If you don't believe me, visit Wikipedia, Forbes, or other resources for the full report about his tenure. During the Nardelli years, I moved from Houston to Pensacola, and from Pensacola to D.C. in my role as district manager. Admittedly, Bob did some positive things for the company along the way in areas of logistics, process, and technological advancements. However, we lost one of the most valuable aspects of Home Depot's culture: the focus on people. In fact, many associates and managers felt that Bob did everything in his power to diminish our culture, but then Frank Blake came along and reignited it with the force of a flame-thrower.

Our well-established identity was diminishing not only in the eyes of Home Depot's employees' perceptions, but in the eyes of others including our customers. Instead of embracing the tenured associates to gather information and formulate strategy, Bob and his team alienated the veteran group – and it was one of the biggest mistakes they made. In our eyes, they saw us as a roadblock to their plans, which they believed we would not embrace. We believed they thought our tenure indicated we were too set in our past, established ways. Rumor had it our new President and CEO never took the time to meet with Bernie or Arthur to seek their counsel on the culture and the best way to move the company forward. When I first heard that, I thought, "You've got to be kidding me; why would he not do that?" And I wasn't alone. Many of my colleagues had the same reaction: *How could the new leader not bother to partner with our two founders?* Among the Home Depot faithful, it created a defensive posture, rather than an offensive one. It forced us to start reconsidering everything we'd believed and known up to that point.

Employees wear tenure badges on their aprons showcasing the number of years they have been with the company. Most are very proud of them. About three inches around, you can clearly see them on the aprons. In fact, just the other day on Twitter, a young guy who hit his 11th anniversary explained in a tweet how proud he was of his time. He thanked three individuals – me among them – for helping him reach this milestone. While it filled me with appreciation for this hard-working employee and Home Depot, it also reminded me of the years 2000 to 2007, when highly tenured employees felt they had to hide the badges on our aprons; the same ones we'd once been so proud to show off as proof of our commitment to our customers and the company.

We felt if we dared display them, we made ourselves a target.

Whether in operations or merchandising, this fearful act of self-preservation seeped into the stores and affected morale. At all levels, the consensus was that if you had double-digit years with Home Depot, you hid it among the new officer group during store visits and at meetings, by removing your tenure badges from your apron. Long-term tenure created discomfort and anxiety, which was heightened in the aftermath of our stock plummeting in value. So much for our grand visions of extreme wealth as the value of our accounts tanked all the way down to a third of what it had previously been! At the district manager and field levels, many of us toughed it out (although many of us also had resumes ready-to-go) even as we watched many officer transitions continue. It was distressing to watch them go, especially the ones with whom I worked with directly.

Another striking example of the contrast in leadership styles between Bernie and Arthur and their successor involves Home Depot's Quarterly Earnings Calls to Wall Street. Every three months, we announce our fiscal numbers on a conference call at 9 a.m. with our officer group and all financial firms. The calls are the avenue for the company to announce results, discuss upcoming objectives and take questions from the financial community. Each call represents an opportunity to showcase the company and its people and forge relationships with financial firms. Salaried members of Home Depot were encouraged to listen to these calls, both for pride in execution, as well as understanding how others were perceiving the results. A tremendous amount of preparation goes into these calls, as the financial community can significantly impact the stock price, up or down. Early on in my career, I assumed your stock always got rewarded when your results were good and beat the expectations of Wall Street. I learned later that you get rewarded to an even greater extent for future results, providing the confidence for others to buy your stock.

From a leadership standpoint, I noticed that when Bernie and Arthur were with Home Depot, these calls were collaborative and characterized by mutual respect. Regardless of the news – whether we exceeded our numbers or fell short – every quarterly call had an engaging tone and a spirit of synergy. Fast-forward to when Bob Nardelli conducted the first few calls: after I hung up the phone I was disturbed. Instead of setting a collaborative tone, he spoke to the financial community in a patronizing fashion. It was not friendly but matter of fact, and direct; you could tell they were uncomfortable with his temperament. I remember thinking, *"That's* not good." Because financial folks will decide if they'll support Home Depot and to what extent by buying stock or recommending it to clients. There are many implications. Don't get me wrong: I'm not a whiz on the inner workings of Wall Street, but based on practical experience, I knew that the way you present yourself to others impacts your company either positively or negatively, as much as your financial results.

By all indications, our new President and CEO did not seem to be a people-person with strong relationship-building skills...or at the very least an understanding of how important our people were to our culture and brand. This was a detriment to him and how he was perceived. Even though he made some positive decisions at Home Depot, people do not view his overall time with the company as a success. For me, after experiencing the level of fandom for Bernie and Arthur, it was a huge letdown to witness quite the opposite for seven long years. As I mentioned, some of my co-workers including Sean Sites – who is among the top-100 tenured associates with Home Depot, hired directly by cofounder Arthur Blank – still get highly emotional when discussing it. When Bob Nardelli's departure was finally announced, employees joked that we all heaved a collective sigh of relief, while Home Depot people across the United States cheered. We needed a change, everyone knew it.

During his reign I only spoke to Bob once. At an annual meeting after the Florida hurricanes, we were assembled in a big ballroom when he walked in with his bodyguard. I approached him, held out my hand and introduced myself. At that time, my sister worked for Home Depot and lived on the west coast of Florida. Her roof had been severely damaged in one of the hurricanes and the Homer Fund allotted money to fix it. I walked up to him that day to thank him for the help they'd provided her. Rather than engaging in conversation, he offered a perfunctory, "You're welcome," as he stood there next to the man tasked with protecting him. He made no further attempt to converse with me. I walked back to my seat, wondering why I had approached him – there was no emotion there whatsoever.

By contrast, with Bernie and Arthur, numerous people would approach them, ask for a photo, shake their hand or discuss a topic with them. Bernie and Arthur were accommodating because they understood their level of celebrity and the effects of their accessibility. They had "rock star" status, yet each interaction with them was personable and engaging. They treated you as their equal. To be fair, they were the founders, plus they had more years with us than Bob. But when I think of how he squandered his opportunity to engage the veterans of Home Depot in meaningful dialogue, I can't help but believe that the seven years could have been very, very different.

STAFFING DECISIONS DIMINISHED THE BRAND

Under Bernie and Arthur, the company always had strong feelings about how we would staff our stores and the people we would hire. Countless times, at meetings or events, conversations centered on the topic and advocated the position to hire the best qualified person every single time, pay them well, train them, and then get out of their way so they could perform. Because expectations were higher for those with more qualifications and/or higher salaries, accountability discussions followed next. These employees would have to earn their money; if not, they would be released. When you read about the early days of Home Depot, when authors identified what distinguished us from our competition, what they cited most was the quality, effort, and knowledge of our personnel. The company even had names for two distinct teams that personified our beliefs in this regard. Bernie and Arthur understood how our team had to be different to attract the customers to us – not just once – but for life. Therefore, the teams were named in their honor.

The first was "Bernie Boys," comprised of older people, who carried with them the wisdom of their life experience. It did not matter what they had done before, so long as they possessed excellent people- skills, a servant's attitude, and a desire to sell. In most cases, they had retired from their previous job and wanted something to do to keep them busy. This was an effective strategy, as a mature employee carries the perception of wisdom, product knowledge, and professionalism. Many times, in my early career, I would be in an aisle with one of them and the customer would approach us, ignore me, and explain their need to them. The assumption of knowledge and experience ruled the day. Having those individuals in our departments strengthened our brand, especially in all areas related to customer service. To the point, we heard feedback such as "if you ever fire them, you will lose all our business." They generated fan clubs and clienteles, and customers requested them repeatedly. As a rule, Home Depot paid them more than the others, based on their experience and acumen in a given area. It was well worth the investment for the sales, service and results they generated.

The second was "Arthur's Army," comprised of tradespeople who had worked in specific industries: carpenters, roofers, flooring installers, painters, plumbers and electricians. Our goal was to hire them, place them in the appropriate departments, give them a set schedule to correspond with the times the pros and commercial entities shopped our stores (early Monday-Friday, and Saturday) and showcase their availability to our customers via marketing tools. This also proved to be a great strategy. Word of mouth advertising from one pro to another created tremendous brand enhancement, adding exemplary service to the product offerings and quantities we offered. Pros were extremely appreciative of this, and it provided them with the confidence to shop at Home Depot, knowing they had a qualified partner who represented their product needs in the store when they needed them. Because they'd been paid well as tradespeople, their wage was one of the highest in the store, an investment in their abilities and skills. We never wanted them to leave because of a wage when a project came up, so we compensated them to keep them. We employed each of the six trades mentioned above, which represented six employees among hundreds in the stores. Based on my experience, it was another wise payroll investment.

Payroll was our single largest overall expense as a corporation, both in dollars as well as percentage to total sales. Bernie's Boys and Arthur's Army represented a tiny portion of the overall store personnel, yet these individuals, along with the rest of our teams gave us tremendous leverage over our competitors and accelerated our brand with our customers. They justified their existence and ongoing emphasis. When Bernie and Arthur departed the company, the "Bernie Boys" program was discontinued and "Arthur's Army" was changed to "Master Trades Specialists."

One of the key staffing initiatives of Bob's team was to gain parity in the full-time/part-time mix of associates. At the time, stores were staffed with approximately 75 percent full-timers and 25 percent part-timers. The thought process was that achieving the goal of 50/50 would provide significant cost savings to the company in wage and benefits and make it more profitable. There was a functional goal as well: you could hire two part-timers for every full-timer and create a visual of more employees on the sales floor. Along with that, part-timers could provide availabilities to be scheduled at peak customer times, especially the weekends. It almost sounds good. It became a rigid discipline in the company, where stores stopped looking for quality full-timers because they had shortfalls in the part-time requirements. High-quality, full-time applicants were ignored because upper management applied intense pressure to the stores to achieve the goal.

The biggest error within this whole mess was the concern for the average hourly wage. To the new leadership it was too high, and therefore, it represented a quick method to impact the bottom line. Due to their backgrounds and experience, full-time associates were paid a significantly higher wage than part-timers. Corporate felt they could get more for less; subsequently, when a full-timer left our employ, part-timers were sought. In addition, when a Master Trade Specialist (MTS) left us, we were told to delay replacing them, to the point we never did. Today, there remains a small percentage of the MTS in select stores.

Under Bob Nardelli, our most valuable resource, our people, was being compromised.

As frustrated as the stores were, our customers also felt discouraged and demoralized. What they had come to know and expect from us about customer service was eroding. We began to hear comments from residential and pro shoppers, complaining of the lack of experts when they needed them and the quality of the associates' knowledge and professionalism. Despite pressure from the stores' communication to corporate and the customers feedback, Home Depot's direction did not change. Recollect, please, what I recommended earlier in the book: listening with an earnest ear to the bodies of people who influence and affect your business the most is not only prudent, but shrewd. I cannot think of two more important bodies to any business than the employees and the customers. Active listening to on a continuous basis is essential. Those who do not are doomed to failure.

MIA IN L.A.

At Home Depot's annual meetings, the President and CEO is introduced first, to huge fanfare, applause and a standing ovation. They kick off the meeting with their appreciative, positive and engaging comments, designed to energize the audience for what was to come. One year in Los Angeles, it was time to start the meeting...and no Bob. According to conjecture, he was backstage at some point when he allegedly decided he couldn't do it and left. As two of our EVPs (Executive Vice-Presidents) opened the meeting in his place, everyone was taken aback. Murmurs traveled through auditorium like the wave at an athletic event. Instead of focused energy on the content of the meeting, speculation ruled the day: where was our leader??? If you add up Bob's words, deeds, and approach to people during his time, it made an undeniable negative impact on an immense scale. Hundreds of thousands of associates, millions of customers and thousands of investors – no big deal, right?

It's a lesson for all businesses in every industry: it is imperative to place the suitable individual in the proper role. I include the President and CEO, along with the executive branch, in this philosophy. Analogous to a professional athletic team that chooses to replace their head coach, who then releases their predecessor's roster of assistant coaches and replaces them with his own team – the result is rarely a winning season.

How did Bob Nardelli ever become President and CEO of Home Depot? When he was not rewarded with Jack Welch's position, Ken Langone contacted him about replacing Bernie and Arthur. To be crystal clear, I don't dislike the man Ken selected; he was simply the wrong fit for the company and hastened into a role that was a mistake for both sides. Financially, it was a disaster. Not only had our stock price plummeted, but we also lost blocks of stock options. One year, as the expiration date expired, our share price was less than the strike price of the options, rendering them only as valuable as the piece of paper which held the data. I lost five-thousand four-hundred shares that year! Now, do the math: 5,400 shares multiplied by the current stock price. At a minimum, it was maddening to me and many others who lost their respective shares. You'd received them as a reward for the work you had done, and – poof! They were gone. Sean and I would discuss this on occasion, doing the math as the stock price increased. Mind-blowing was not the word, as we would look at each other and wonder, "What if........"

Despite the financial ramifications, we carried on. Store personnel and management did everything they could to support Bob. Once there was a corporate meeting in Atlanta with the financial community. At this point, his struggles to build a positive perception with that community were well known to the management team. Simultaneously, there was a meeting of officers and DMs also being held at the corporate office and they planned a surprise appearance at Bob's meeting. When Bob began to speak, a large gathering of Home

Depot people entered the auditorium to show their support with a rendition of the famed Home Depot cheer. A few even vocalized their support of Bob to show the financial community that so long as he was with us, we had his back. It allayed some fears on a temporary basis but didn't work out well in the long run. Rumor had it that the financial community thought the effort had been planned by Bob; they did not understand that it came from the heart of the team.

How did I keep myself and my team motivated during the Nardelli years? Along with many others, I went all-in on what Home Depot's culture represented to us, notwithstanding the destructive changes threatening its existence. People. This tough time forced us to bond even more with those who worked with us. When anyone asks me why I remained through this time, then on to 33 years total, I cite two things: one, the love of what you do; and two, the love of who you do it with. Tremendous, passionate, committed, hard-working, fun people. I always told members of my team, "If you do your job, you have nothing to worry about." If we were ever going to give it our all, it needed to be now.

Right before Bob left the company, I received a promotion to Regional Pro Sales Manager (RPSM). The promotion could not have come at a better time for me. I felt I had given the DM position my all and needed something different, something that would re-ignite my passion for the company. Being an RPSM afforded me the opportunity to impact the entire region, in one of the most crucial areas within the company. When it was announced that Bob was leaving the company, you could feel the relief within the stores. People were smiling and energized once again, no matter another upcoming change. It had to be better; it just *had* to be. Oh, but wait, there is more. When word leaked out that Bob had a "golden parachute" with Home Depot, the mood shifted to one of anger. A golden parachute is an agreement between an employee (usually an upper executive) specifying that the employee will receive certain significant benefits if employment is terminated. The anger was not at the existence of the agreement but levied at the amount of dispensation -

$210,000,000! During the seven-year period, our results and stock price lagged our archrival. Salaried members of Depot lost significant quantities of stock during that time, yet Bob left with a fortune. Still, we had to move beyond our resentment because it was time to go forward.

You could almost see and feel the difference immediately with his successor, who embodied the ethic and behaviors that accentuated our culture. We never gave up in the stores, but the period from 2000 to 2007 was a dark one for all of us at Home Depot. It felt like being in the locker room at half-time in despair because we were losing 45-0. Could we come back?

LIKE A ROCK STAR

When I was still a district manager in the D.C. area, we were scheduled to renovate the interior and exterior of a school in inner-city Washington D.C. as a community event. Among other things, the school needed landscaping, fencing, and concrete work. The entire project involved about 250 volunteer associates. I arrived early and received a call from my regional vice-president informing me that due to a last-minute "something," she wouldn't be able to make it. Mind you, she was supposed to captain the high-profile event; the media and dignitaries would be in attendance. It was now up to us to ensure a successful day. "Get with the other DM and handle it," she told me. "By the way, there's an officer from Atlanta named Frank Blake who will be at the event." *Wonderful.*

I grabbed a few things out of my car and walked into the school to set up a welcome area. As I greeted the few early people there and made sure everything was unfolding according to plan, I noticed a gentleman standing in the corner, not saying anything but just observing the happenings. Taking an educated guess, I walked over to him and asked, "Are you Frank Blake?"

"Yes, I am."

"Welcome," I said, extending my hand.

Frank had also come to Home Depot from General Electric. His first role was Executive Vice President for Business Development and Corporate Operations, reporting directly to Nardelli. He knew D.C. well because he'd been an Assistant Director of the Department of Energy for President H.W. Bush. At that point, all I knew was he was an officer from Atlanta. After I explained that my RVP couldn't be there and that I was the DM, he asked me to tell him a bit about me. Right from the get-go, he was personable, friendly and humble. He asked me what the game-plan was for the day.

"We're going to get everyone together, set the tone and start with a Depot cheer. We've got everybody divided into teams, going to be a very busy day," I continued.

"I heard about this and I just want to be here and help," he replied, before explaining his background.

Frank stayed with us from start to finish – close to nine hours – and helped organize one of the big storeroom areas. The man *worked*. He wasn't there exclusively for camera shots and glory moments. At the end of the day, he led the Home Depot cheer, as dirty and sweaty as the rest of us. It was amazing because I had no idea what was to come when he thanked us all and gave a nice closing speech. I thought that was it: Frank would go back to Atlanta and we would not see each other again. That was not to be the case.

Fast forward to the announcement of Bob Nardelli's imminent departure. Everyone wondered, "Who's coming now?" It was, "Okay great, he's leaving but who's coming next?" It's human nature to ask, "How will this affect me?" but we all exhaled when Frank Blake became Home Depot's next President and CEO. People who knew I'd worked with him at that community event called me to get some insight on his character. I was happy to express positive feelings and emotions with respect to Frank's character, leadership, work ethic, and approachability. In short, he was a direct contradiction to his predecessor; in one day's event, I interacted more with Frank Blake than I did in seven years with Bob Nardelli. There was a huge sigh of relief when Bob left, but with Frank's announcement, collective despair turned into happiness. People were thrilled by the news. It was time to put your tenure badge back on your apron. We were back. Frank lived up to our expectations: throughout his career with Home Depot, he represented the personal side of business and demonstrated wisdom and humility, along with a tremendous understanding. It was almost as if the sun came up again.

One of Frank's first acts was to engage Bernie and Arthur, to get their thoughts, concerns, and suggestions on opportunities for improvement, according to others in the know who'd informed us about it (we didn't hear it from Frank). Remember, the former President and CEO had never done that. Frank's simple, profound act earned him respect among Home Depot's faithful and demonstrated that he was going to respect the origins of the company and its culture and use that intel to help him move us forward. In my opinion, the difference between Frank and Bob was simple. Frank believed in the culture and utilized it as the foundation for all he did.

At our first annual meeting with Frank, we welcomed him to the stage with vigorous applause and a long-standing ovation, while chants of "Frank, Frank, Frank," reverberated through the auditorium. It only ended when he motioned us to take our seats. After making some brief comments, he paused, then started an introduction. Aside from a wicked sense of humor, Frank tends to be somewhat reserved when on stage. He knew the crowd would go berserk for the visitor, and we didn't disappoint: the place *erupted* when Bernie Marcus came onto the stage. We gave him a thunderous ovation while standing on chairs for several minutes, with everyone screaming at the top of their lungs. Frank stepped back to give Bernie his stage-front moment. From the beginning, Frank earned respect from the masses with his deference for one of the company's beloved founders. We knew then, things were going to be a whole lot different than they had been. Our culture was revived.

Post-retirement, Bernie built the largest aquarium in the world in Atlanta, which also featured a convention center. During one annual meeting, we attended an unforgettable event at the aquarium headlined by Bernie, Arthur, and Frank...but not Bob Nardelli. The company bussed us to the aquarium from our meeting location as we heard rumors of what was to happen. There were hundreds of Home Depot people in attendance, DMs and higher, and some of us had seen Bernie pull into the parking lot in his own vehicle. We knew then something special was going to happen, but what? The three of them had entered the facility through an entrance on the other side of the convention center, requiring a lengthy walk to get where we were all congregating. There were some stragglers among us, who were in the walkway where Bernie, Arthur and Frank walked towards us, side-by-side. When those in the walkway identified the three men, the cheering started. It transformed into shouting to alert the rest of us as to what was happening. The noise level got louder and louder and louder...and then, there they were, standing together within a small area that extended over the section where we were all assembled.

Moments like this are hard to describe to others who may not have had a similar experience at their place of employment. Following the "Dark Ages," we had been released from all that it represented. We'd put the world on notice – HERE WE COME! The deafening noise went on for a very long time; I felt like I'd been at an AC/DC concert. For two days afterward, I couldn't hear. What a powerful moment for everyone present. At the event, all three spoke with passion, honesty and conviction. From that moment on, Frank cemented his legacy within Home Depot, right up there with Bernie and Arthur. To this day, I believe we executed the most voluminous Home Depot cheer I ever heard. It was a celebration of one man's early, positive impacts, achieved by his embrace of all that Home Depot had been, and what it was going to become. The only complaint of that event from those in attendance? There must have been a problem with the air filtration system that night, which left dust particles in the air. How else to explain the serious watery eye problem most of us experienced, if you know what I mean?

Frank Blake not only understood how important Bernie and Arthur had been to Home Depot and the business community, he openly embraced it. In sharp contrast to his predecessor, he utilized

their philosophy and accomplishments as a foundation to take Home
Depot to a higher level. When he left the company in 2014, we
regarded Frank as highly we did Bernie and Arthur. During his
tenure, he brought us back from where we were (remember we were
losing 45-0 at halftime and we roared back to win the game by 52-
45). He was a catalyst for positive change, due to his demeanor,
behavior, and personal skills, a fact that was not lost on a lot of folks.
Home Depot's Board of Directors had learned from what happened
with the golden parachute of Bob Nardelli and implemented change.
When Frank's departure came upon us, we were flying – no, *soaring*
high again. The perception of our brand was at its highest level. Stock
prices were up to historic levels. The inner passion from the company
was at its peak. What doesn't kill you makes you stronger.

HONORING THE PAST, FOCUSING ON THE FUTURE

When your life is on the line and you are all-in – meaning totally
invested in your company even when it is experiencing rough times –
you engage in much soul-searching. You may get your resume
together, just in case, and look at other opportunities, figuring, maybe
this was it. Then Frank came along, and I heard employees say, "I'm
glad I stayed. I can't believe I was thinking about leaving."

Yep, a complete reversal. It is amazing what one person's influence can produce.

Among his many contributions, Frank gave us some excellent
phrases to accentuate his messages. One of my personal favorites was,
"I want you to have more dreams than memories." It was reassuring
to veterans of the company that the past would not be forgotten and
the best was yet to come. We started to believe again. We advanced
from survival mode to a thriving mindset once more – in opposition
to the naysayers. Prior to Frank's selection, plenty of folks lined up to
forecast gloom, doom, and our demise. From the financial community
to our competitors, and quite honestly, some of our customers – it got
downright ugly. Everyone sensed that there was "blood in the water,"
that we had experienced our "fifteen minutes of fame," and that it

was "game over." But they forgot one thing, one "little" thing – our people. Big mistake. Huge!

Please don't get me wrong: the seven years with Frank were not perfect. It took time to correct the opportunities for improvement he inherited: staffing policies, reversing acquisitions, re-establishing professional connections with Wall Street, the disconnection between the stores and corporate and, most importantly, our bond with our customers.

During the toughest of times, bellyaching, whining, and crying were an absolute waste of time. Negativity has nothing but an adverse effect on people. Yes, human beings are imperfect. You're going to have bad days. Harnessing all your energy into a positive force will produce the desired results. If we had done nothing but b*****d and whined during the Nardelli years, Home Depot could never have staged the recovery it did. Nothing happens anywhere, for any reason, without a committed, engaged team. Hour by hour, day to day, we fought hard for the customers and the business. Our hourly associates, who represent the largest number of Home Depot employees, provided the anchor for the resurgence. Under Frank's team, the urgency to hire the right people for the right role became the hiring mantra once again. The strength of an organization does not reside in the offices at the top floor of the corporate office. Instead, it resides at the level where the action truly happens – face-to-face with customers. With Frank's leadership, the hundreds of thousands of associates marched in lockstep and became a force to be reckoned with once again.

TWO-HUNDRED-TEN MILLION AND THEN SOME

With no idea of the amount of compensation Frank took with him at retirement, I hope it was a ton of money because he earned it... and more. Again, I feel zero angst about the pay and compensation of officers – so long as they earn that money by advancing their companies through their performance, while incorporating all levels of the organization. In my mind, Frank could have named his price. I will always believe that his presence at Home Depot was a "God thing." Our prayers had been answered, at just the right time.

LADDERS & LEARNINGS

- Stay true to yourself on your ethic, behaviors and performance, while you embrace your company's culture.
- Understand that your contributions will carry a company through the worst of times and enhance the best of times.

EXECUTIVE MEMO

Embrace your company's culture and people: the two indestructible facets of your business. Understand that when the people are with you, exceptional things will happen. Engage all levels of the organization with a humble, honest, and collaborative mindset.

1 4

ANOTHER RUNG UP THE LADDER,
MORE MILES TO GO BEFORE I SLEEP

"What got you here won't get your there."

— MARSHALL GOLDSMITH

The year 2007 ushered in extraordinary changes at Home Depot. Frank, of course, became our new President and CEO and I became a Regional Pro Sales Manager. When the Regional Vice-President offered me the position, I accepted it right away, with much enthusiasm. I'd worked as a district manager in three different geographic areas within the US, relocated for each one and, simply put, was burned out on the role. Given my mindset, the offer to become a Regional Pro Manager came at an opportune time. I still enjoyed working at Home Depot, just needed something different. The role afforded me the opportunity to wrap my arms around a specific segment of the company's business, one that was critical to its overall success.

Nineteen regional teams exist within the company, each comprised of an assemblage of subject matter experts in individual areas who report to the regional vice-president. The areas are operations, human resources, associate relations, merchandising execution, regional merchants, PRO and services (special orders and installation). Sean Sites accepted a Regional Merchant position at the same time. Both of us began our new roles with a fresh outlook, looking forward to new challenges. Regional roles had responsibility for all ninety-seven stores. The differences between a single district and an entire region, in terms of leadership, functionality and communication were significant. The opportunity to impact a larger entity in associates, sales volume and operational efficiencies provided a good amount of satisfaction. Maybe, just maybe, this would be my last position at Depot.

The gentleman who preceded me in the role, left me a clusterf**k. There was nowhere to go, but up. The region's sales in pro were well under plan, the team was performing in an individual manner, rather than as a team, and the coup-de-grace? My predecessor did not know and did not care. Rather than embrace and own the role, with an understanding of its importance to the company, he was a placeholder that existed in the position, for far too long. Faced with the above, it become apparent that pro could and should, lead the region to financial success.

If you surveyed 25 contractors for their feedback on Home Depot, most of them would say we were resident-centric, that is, more focused on homeowners. Yet if you assembled the same number of homeowners for the same survey, they'd tell you the opposite. It's funny that one side always thought the other side had more representation, but truth be told, without pro customers, Home Depot and Lowe's financials would be very similar. The Pro business at Home Depot is one of the top three differentiating factors for the company, versus its number one competitor. Simply stated, pros shop Home Depot more frequently and spend far more per transaction. If Lowe's ever made inroads into our dominance in this area, the rivalry would take on a much different dynamic.

It was exciting to take a regional position in the Mid-Atlantic, one of Home Depot's highest volume sales regions. The performance of our region, due to its contributions to the overall company financials, could leverage the results for the company, positively or negatively. No pressure or anything! When you transition from a district role to a regional one, you come to understand that you make less of a direct impact and become more of an influencer. As a district manager of 10 stores, I had direct oversight of the people who worked with me. It was simpler to ensure things happened within those stores. Now, with 97 stores and the demand to execute something – whether a training class, a new product, a staffing solution, or an operational process, I learned quickly that my communications skills must excel beyond my previous capacity. Author Marshall Goldsmith's book advises, *What Got You Here Will Not Get You There*. Why? To that point in time, my behaviors were tailored to a specific district, grouping of stores, management hierarchy and team of associates. Assuming the regional role, just increased my area of responsibility to eleven districts, ninety-seven stores, a broadened management hierarchy and up to fifteen thousand associates. Not a small task. The foundation of ethics, behaviors and standards I maintained as a DM, would need to be augmented, focused on clarity, efficiency and follow-up.

OWNERSHIP OF SITUATIONAL AWARENESS

When a scheduled visit took place within the region, the regional team was expected to be present with the RVP. Whether it was the Divisional President, EVP of stores or the President and CEO, each member of the regional team had the responsibility to know the pertinent financial results of the entire region, store by store. Oh, and by the way, even though we had detailed reports, it was always better if you did not have to refer to them. You needed to *know*, not just be able to read. If a store or department was exceptionally successful or decidedly underperforming versus their peer group, you had to be able to explain why. The reason? The causal factors of the successful store may need to be replicated in the other stores, and conversely, the negative elements in the non-successful store may necessitate training or accountability. You had to have the back of the RVP and be ready to provide input at a moment's notice. Oh, and like the Secret Service for the President, on occasion, you might have to take a metaphorical bullet for a deficiency.

Honesty: a short word with a BIG meaning. When interacting with executives and officers at the highest levels, you do not need to play games. Wherever they take place, those engagements are designed to be collaborative, honest, direct, real, and non-personal. But when challenged for information, there will always be those among us who choose to be defensive, vague, deflective, or even deceptive. As I mentioned earlier, thanks to Arthur most of my peers and I learned early on that honesty was the best policy.

QUALITY COMMUNICATION IS KEY TO HIERAR-CHAL RELATIONSHIPS

One of the hardest things I had to do was assume a partnership position with the district managers, versus a true peer relationship. As peers, we had perceptions of each other, and at times they inhibited the growth of the new relationship. Not all eleven district mangers thought Sean and I deserved the promotions we received, creating roadblocks we managed to overcome. As a partner in their success, the role of my teams was to optimize their results with pro as the leading contributor. Responsibilities included visits to their stores, interacting with the store teams, celebrating successes, identify areas that needed improvement, and training.

Recommendation is a key word in the realm of a regional manager. Aside from the teams that report directly to you, you do not have direct oversight or authority over the store personnel. In lieu of delegating actions, you must instead be influential – a compelling force on the actions, behaviors, and opinions of others. My goal, therefore, was to help all levels of personnel understand the potential of the PRO business and their role its success in terms all available tools.

With the support and partnership of the 11 district managers, the regionals could accomplish much in their efforts to assist all stores. If, however, you had not earned that partnership or the district manager was non-cooperative, then the results could be quite different. Earlier in the book, I spoke of not judging others in your own perception – a grave mistake. To achieve maximum success with eleven individuals with their own set of beliefs, ethics, behaviors and personalities, you must forge one-on-one relationships.

For example, it was not good enough for me to explain the importance of PRO because within the group, each person had a different interpretation of what that meant. I had an initial expectation that my renowned passion would result in their automatic acceptance of every recommendation I made. Yeah...I was just a little off (more sarcasm). Now, remember, you are never going to make everyone happy; I certainly did not. There are various leaders who don't like others meddling in their business, cannot accept constructive criticism, or have higher priorities than your focus of responsibility within the company. What I'm about to share is not a judgement of them in comparison to myself. When I was a district manager in Texas, Florida, and the D.C. area, the teams under my supervision rolled out the red carpet when higher-ups came to visit us to see how we were doing. I learned that you can never gauge when you will need a specific resource at a pivotal moment, which is why I embraced every opportunity to build a cohesive relationship. Beyond the early interactions, doing yielded many advantages. What was another quality that distinguished me from some of my peers? I never wanted a pat on the back or recognition about all the excellent things we were doing for my own edification. Yet I recognized how it important is was for my teams...and rightfully so. But on a personal level, I wanted the executives, officers, board members, and other VIP's who came to visit to tell me what they saw, felt, and heard in terms of our opportunities for improvement. I wanted them to give it to me straight, with no sugar-coating. Acknowledgment of what I already knew was working was much less valuable.

At first, I partnered with the eleven district managers and approached each one in a unique way. I learned what made them tick, and how I had to understand, interact, and communicate with them. Between the eleven, they had different motivations, career plans and perceptions of themselves. Out of all the district managers, I enjoyed tremendous relationships with half; I experienced okay relationships with one-quarter; and with the remainder...well, let's just say the relationships were not good, necessitating additional efforts and time. I developed action plans to include conference calls, district visits, and written summaries to enhance each one.

In my new role, I now had two bosses: The Regional Vice-President, who oversaw all stores in the region and their overall functionality and the Divisional Pro Director, based in Atlanta, who reported to the Divisional President of the Northern Division, the RVP's direct boss. Both demanded honest feedback about the stores and PRO teams, which at times placed me in awkward situations and put pressure on other relationships. I learned quickly to be proactive and communicate with my DM partners first, before relaying any information to my supervisors – especially if the info was negative or could damage the DM or their stores. No one wants to receive a phone call from their boss inquiring about a situation when they are not prepared or informed. Your direct reports could construe this as back-stabbing or grandstanding – and as a leader, you do not want to be perceived that way. Rather, you want to be the "trusted advisor" to the DMs in a two-way relationship built on confidence and trust. They must know that you will entrust them with all necessary intel *before* it goes to the next level. As a Regional Pro Manager, my DMs understood that I had to be honest in reporting to my supervisors, but they very much appreciated the time I allotted them to prepare a strategy or communication to the Regional Vice President or Director of Product Development.

YOU ARE ONLY AS STRONG AS YOUR WEAKEST LINK

As I mentioned, when I was a Regional Pro Manager, my team consisted of salaried employees called Pro Account Representatives (PAR), along with a smaller team of hourly associates in support roles. This is the only team whose roles and responsibilities are outside the four walls of a Home Depot store. PARs spend 95 percent of their time meeting with institutions and government facilities, charitable foundations, and contractors – from property investors to remodelers to property managers and tradespeople. They maintain a portfolio of clients, with numerous financial goals.

Managers and leaders tend to forget that the teams they assemble and influence are reflections of themselves. That effect can be either positive or negative. Having said that, through my almost ten years in the role, I was fortunate to have surrounded myself with the best available. Of course, there were transitions through the years for a myriad of reasons, but the nucleus of the team was solid. At the time of my retirement, they carried a brand and perception as one of the highest producing, effective teams in the company. I am proud of all their accomplishments.

One of my longest serving team members, Zsa Zsa (Zsanitta) King, embodied the strength of the team. She begain her career at Home Depot in the stores in an hourly capacity, where she worked tirelessly and earned herself a promotion to supervisor of her store's PRO Team. Her performance, personality, ethic and beliefs led the company to promote her to the PAR Role. She "owned" it from the beginning, exhibiting high quality relationships with her portfolio of accounts, a relentless need to succeed, and the production of financials. More members of the team could be celebrated as well, but you get the idea. If I could have cloned her, I would have. They made me look good. We all had to work very hard to get to the point they were when I left. The key to success was the relationships we formed, knowing what made each other tick, and how it all came together. I've used the puzzle analogy before, but it bears repeating: no matter how many pieces you put together, if just one is missing, the puzzle is incomplete, representing failure.

Home Depot provided another benefit to me in my Regional Pro Role: an administrative assistant named Gidget Jones. Like Zsa Zsa, she excelled in all she did on a consistent basis. Gidget was just as valuable as any other team member. She handled everything that I threw at her, and then some. Proactively, she kept many things off my plate, allowing me to devote my time to other matters. Plus, she took a rigid stance on company guidelines and processes such as expense controls. She kept me in line when I ventured outside of standard protocol. Wednesday, April 22 is Administrative Professional's Day. Put it on your calendar and make sure you do something wonderful for them; they deserve it.

Home Depot's secret sauce to our success? The people you surround yourself with and the relationships you form. The performance, execution and results will take care of themselves if you manage people properly, consistently, and fairly. Remember the "Dark Ages" I referred to in the last chapter? Well, there you go.

IF I HAD TO DO IT ALL OVER AGAIN, I'M TAKING THE TRAIN

The position had a downside: an expanded geographical territory. As I mentioned, we purchased a home in Haymarket Virginia, about 40 miles west of D.C., which was very close to the westernmost side of our region of 97 stores. As a district manager with a much smaller territory, I thought my daily commute was a nightmare, but when I became Regional Pro Manager, I added Philly and its suburbs, down to the eastern shore, the entire state of Delaware and Maryland, D.C. and its suburbs, Northern Virginia and one store in Ranson, West Virginia. Pull up a map of the United States and locate the area I just described. It appears to be the smallest physical area on the map. But it yields some of the largest traffic headaches.

In terms of population and car-count, this is one of the densest areas in the U.S. It features several transportation modes including trains, buses, airplanes and automobiles. Although I love to fly, I hate getting caught up in weather delays and sitting at an airport, nor do I enjoy riding on buses due to the close environment and the out-of-control situation where someone else is driving (that's just me). I decided to drive my own car, knowing if done right, I could get there and back in the same day. If I left at 4 a.m., I could get to Philly by about 7:00 a.m. During the first couple of months in the role, I'd drive up there, spend time with the teams, and then drive back that night. It made for a long, nonproductive, 18- to- 20-hour day with half of my time spent in the car. *Advil time! WTH was I thinking?!*

The extended commute, in both miles and time, took its toll on me. Here I was, on the road with my iPhone and iPad, texting people, attempting to be productive, and multi-tasking. It wasn't safe. Even with a Bluetooth talking on the phone hands-free, I can't tell you how many times someone nearly killed me, or I almost caused serious harm to others. With an accident, driving from Virginia to Baltimore could turn into a three-hour or more ordeal. By 2009, all this stop-and-go traffic was starting to get to me. I'd arrive home in a bad state-of-mind. Pam and Jackie would be home awaiting my arrival, looking forward to spending time with me. As soon as I came through the door, they could tell what my drive home had been like. It was extremely difficult to turn off that traffic impact and let it go. I would go to the basement and work out to release my frustration.

Most of our stores are in high-population areas because we want that density of houses and foot traffic to guarantee business volume. Home Depot's Real Estate Department does analysis and surveys before approving a new store location. If the figures align and reveal a specific profitability in a certain amount of years, the store is "green-lighted." If not, the store is a no-go. When my Regional Vice-President offered me the role of Regional Pro Manager, she said, "We're not going to move you again. We're going to give you some more money because of the expenses," meaning drive-time and impact on my car. However, there was never any consideration of an apartment in a central location to make it easier to get around and come home for the weekends. It was just assumed that I would do whatever it took to manage my obligations.

If you spend more time sitting or driving than standing in your job, my advice is to get a good, no, an *excellent* chiropractor. Living in Haymarket, Pam worked for a chiropractic practice so whenever I could, I went in for adjustments with Dr. Joanne Hutton to complement the blood pressure meds and blood thinners I was already taking. I was hurting every day. After arriving home some days, I hesitated to get out of the car. I knew when I stood up, the pain would overwhelm me until I moved around for a bit. I began to have a deeper empathy for elderly folks who were dealing with arthritic conditions. I believed I now knew what I might be dealing with in the future.

To alleviate the problem, I adopted a two-pronged solution. First, Gidget helped me schedule my visits a month out, making reservations at hotels two- to - three nights a week. Only problem with that? More time away from family. However, Pam and Jackie remained supportive, even when it felt we were living separate lives. Second, I took one day a week to work from home. It blew my mind how much I accomplished and how much better I felt.

The commute played an integral role in my decision to retire. Yes, I loved the position, but I just couldn't deal with the traffic any longer. When I got up in the morning and took my prescriptions, only to get home at night and take more, I knew it was a problem. "Man, how much worse is this going to be if I continue?" I wondered. As I've said, I have a high amount of empathy for businesspeople who have a significant commute. It is not easy getting up at 4 a.m. to travel to a job requirement; it's always fun if you are going fishing. When you find yourself plotting each location of Dunkin Donuts and Starbucks within the region for that necessary caffeine fix, something has got to change. A good friend of mine, Chris, has a great phrase he uses when saying goodbye, "Drive fast, take chances." Well, I took that advice, racing my GPS to every location, doing anything and everything to make up time. I managed to do that well for the duration of my time in the region and my driving record was in good standing. That is, until the last two months. What happened? As I started to relax, confident in my decision, all the sudden I started getting pulled over by Virginia and Maryland's finest. I escaped a ticket the first few times, but my luck ran out on the last few, rendering me one ticket from suspension – yeesh! I hate Sammy Hagar!

From associates and store managers to district and regional managers to officers and Board members, all the way up to the President and CEO, honesty is the best policy. However, it is incumbent upon those in leadership positions to foster a work environment in which all opinions – positive and negative – are welcomed and considered. If action is necessary, follow-through is a must to ensure your integrity. Remember, communication involves both active listening and talking to reach a resolution. Once you pose an open-ended question, remain quiet while the other person speaks to obtain all the information you need to reach a mutual agreement about what to do next. By involving your employees in the solutions, you'll earn their respect, retain their loyalty, and reach even greater levels of success for your business or organization.

Ladders and Learnings

This is purely a personal request from me to you: schedule and keep all health-related appointments, including doctors and dentists. Be proactive about your health; don't maintain the attitude, "It won't happen to me." Never, ever ignore physical symptoms because they can be a warning of something serious. Where's there's smoke, there's fire.

Executive Memo

Ensure that all managers and leaders implement regular, two-way, collaborative communication sessions with their team members to discuss performance and other topics that are important to them. Schedule individual sessions too.

15

GO HIGH OR GO LOW?

"Leadership and learning are indispensable to each other."

— JOHN F. KENNEDY

When it comes to productivity and performance, most leaders adhere to one of two schools of thought. Neither one is right or wrong; it's all relative to where a leader believes he or she can make the most positive impact based on their allotment of time and effort. In my role, I had to decide on a proper course of action based on financial data that 80 of my 97 stores were performing well and exceeding their numbers while 17 of them were underperforming.

The dilemma? Given that I was responsible for the region's pro financials in total, which strategy would I choose to optimize my efforts and the numbers?

The first school of thought is the most common – devoting time and effort to the 17 underperforming stores. As leaders and managers, we are conditioned to fix things, and fast. While it may appear to be a commonsense solution, you must do an analysis before acting. Even if you could repair all 17 stores, what would be the numerical effect on the region's overall numbers? Would the total volume and realized gains impact the region's totals to a measurable extent? True, this would be management by exception, but only you can determine if you would gain total leverage.

This course of action would then dictate overall analysis of behaviors, as well as financial reports. A game plan, developed with the teams, focused on scheduled visits, staffing, training, executables and follow-up would need enacted. Mending these stores would certainly be a success, but would it be as large a success as the second course of action?

The second action plan? Focus on the 80 over-performing stores, with the intent of optimizing their results. The thought here? Although successful, are they as successful as they could be? And, would the cumulative gains in this group, far outweigh those of the 17 others, justifying more time and effort? Many questions arise as to this being the right choice. Do the stores have easy sales plans or are they truly earning their numbers? If earning, what are their behaviors and actions? Could said discoveries be shared in the other stores, as best practices?

Regardless of choice, there are human elements to either one. Focusing primarily on the 17 could alienate the 80 and vice versa. Choosing the 17 could cause a morale diminishment in the 80, who might feel that they are not garnering attention for their positive performance. Choosing the 80 could also cause a morale loss in the 17 stores, which could develop an attitude of abandonment. I could be taking a huge risk if I lead this way. Are those 80 stores going to hit the proverbial wall, where they can't produce increases any longer? Earlier, I discussed comp increases, a method by which many businesses measure results, where the current fiscal period is compared to the same period in the previous year. In what some refer to as "Performance Punishment," these businesses then put pressure on their best performing stores, regions, and divisions to exceed their highest numbers the following year. In response, I've heard many managers remark "S**t. We're going to have to kill ourselves to hit these numbers again. What about the non-performing stores? When will they push *them* harder? Why can't they pull their weight?"

Not only does that attitude become contagious among levels of management, companies that engage in this school of thought remain mired in a comfort level. They assume they can count on their top areas to carry their entire organization. As a Regional Pro Manager for the Mid-Atlantic, one of the highest-volume regions in Home Depot, it seemed the corporate office always gave us one of the highest growth targets year after year. While we felt we were up to the challenge and focused on the actions that would produce the expectations, it became successively difficult to attain or exceed them. Memories of conversations, year after year, in the conference room of the Baltimore office with the team shaking our heads, trying to understand why other regions consistently had lower plans than we did. Have I already mentioned, "What does not kill you, makes you stronger?"

Given the two schools of thought and my own practical experience, my recommendation is to strike a proportionate balance between the two. The Pareto Principle, more commonly known as the 80/20 rule applies here. Heck, it almost applies everywhere. When analyzing the data at my disposal, manipulating it every which way, it became apparent that 80 percent of the sales volume was coming from 20 percent of the stores, including some of the underperforming stores. The best leaders don't ignore either side of the equation; they coordinate their schedules, goals, and expectations to attain their objectives, using all intel. Pertaining to the region's numbers, they exposed a cross section of stores that became my priority to engage. Notifying my bosses of my action plan, they were pleased with the direction and the thought process. Then, I developed the second priority group, and so on. On the weekly and monthly conference calls with the teams, I explained what the strategy was, how it was developed and how it would be carried out. It was actionable and teachable.

. . .

BE ON THE LOOKOUT FOR YOUR MOST IMPORTANT CUSTOMERS

In the Pro business, there's a standardized industry code, or SIC assigned to each type of pro customer, for example, a plumber, painter, or electrician.

At Home Depot, we have five main pro customers:

1. Property Investors- House Flippers & Commercial Property Owners
2. Property Managers / Apartment Complexes, Condos, Groups of Hotels
3. Specialty Restoration / Insurance Industry (Fires, Floods & Natural Disasters.).
4. Remodelers/ Small- to- Large Contractors with Trucks or Vans Who Do House Additions, Remodels & Assorted Smaller Projects.
5. Tradespeople- Roofers, Carpenters, Painters, Plumbers and Electricians

These five types represent over 90 percent of our pro customers. If you happen to be in Home Depot at 7 a.m., you'll be amazed how many people are walking around wearing ballcaps, hoodies, tee shirts, or sweatshirts emblazoned with their business name on it. The pro customer takes an enormous amount of pride in their work, a characteristic that makes them identifiable. Whenever conducting walks with groups of people, I would silently count all customers wearing something that distinguished them as a pro. At the end of the walk, I'd ask, "Hey, how many pro customers do you think are in here today?"

They'd kind of look at me funny. "What? You want an actual number?" And I would respond, "Sure! How many pro customers do you think we've had since we've been walking around the store?"

While they threw out numbers, I had an actual count in my head – which was always five times higher than the amount they thought. Then, I would explain why, using it as a teaching tool for awareness. Typically, at Home Depot, pro customers spend three- to- four times the amount of money than a homeowner does per each transaction. Further enhancing their importance, the pro customer will visit a Home Depot 80- to- 90 times more per year, on average, than a home-owner. My point? This information is public to Wall Street and to our associates at Depot. Within the company, we communicate and share this information as often as possible, accentuating the pros significant impact on the company's results and continued dominance.

The challenge continues to be the daily reinforcement and emphasis of this information to each team member their role to assist, starting with excellent service. Here is my question to you, the reader: In your business, do you have a designated customer segment impacting your results like Home Depot does? If so, how do you accentuate that with your teams? If not, are you sure? You might want to go back and take another look. Home Depot does many, many things to showcase their appreciation for the pro – from desig-nated parking and cash registers, to volume discount programs and fuel rewards and the list goes on and on. What does your company do for yours? Customers who feel appreciated for their patronage, whether a homeowner or pro will frequent that business most often.

Here is a true example. One of the most powerful moments at Home Depot occurs when an officer group visits a store and the associates can introduce a customer and share the relationship. It's a thrilling experience for the employee to receive accolades and appre-ciation from company officers, highlighting their efforts on service. The customer, in this case a pro, also feels the appreciation from the store because they are made to feel as if they are the most important person in the building.

Once, there was a gathering in a store with the President of the Division, the Regional Vice-President, the entire team from President's office, all their functional support team members, including my boss and all his support team members...truly, it was an entourage of over 50 people. One of our hourly associates at the pro desk in the store had discovered a new pro customer in the aisle, a man with a key ring dangling from the top of his pants that held nearly 300 keys. No, I'm not exaggerating. We were impressed from the get- go, amazed he could even keep his pants up.

Our associate had approached him and asked, "Man, what's going on with the keys?"

It turned out that each key belonged to a different property he managed. As a property manager, part of his job entailed running around to make sure his rental properties were not in disrepair. He'd come into Home Depot that day to buy a couple of items, but thanks to our associate, he purchased three carts full of merchandise right before the officer team arrived. I'd gotten there early. The associate called me over to introduce me and told me all about him. I thanked him for coming in and gave him a 10-percent discount.

"Hey, a favor," I continued. "If you don't have to leave right away, we are expecting some people here in about a half-hour. I would love to introduce you to them and showcase what you do because they are going to be in awe. You're the customer that makes Home Depot tick these days."

I watched as the biggest smile spread across his face. "Let me go get a cup of coffee and I'll be back. I swear, I'll be back," he promised. And he returned, a half-hour later.

Our entourage had arrived. Discussing their plans for the visit, I added, "I know you've got a tight agenda today, but you have to meet this guy. You will not believe his story." I brought him over to introduce him. Filthy dirty, he was the typical pro customer with the ripped shirt and ballcap on...and here is this grouping of 50 people standing there in business casual with orange aprons on. It could have been intimidating for him.

"I want you to meet, Brian," I began. "After you shake his hand, look down at that keyring." They all looked down and I asked him to tell the officers what he did for a living. He told them his full story.

"Tell them how much a year you spend on all these businesses," I requested.

"Well, we spend probably close to one-and-a-half million dollars," he stated.

Then I brought the associate into the conversation. "I want you to meet Jim. Thanks to him doing what we ask them to do, he approached Brian today, struck up a conversation and now we are building a relationship." After I gave Jim accolades, the customer interjected on his behalf.

"I gotta tell ya. I just came in for a couple things today, just wanting to get in and out...and now I'm walking out with three cart-loads of stuff. I hate when you guys do that to me." Everybody laughed. "But I gotta tell ya, he told me about stuff they can do for me as a pro that I never knew before."

At the end of the day, the officers gave the associate an Executive Homer Award (worth $50) in front of everybody, to a huge round of applause while pictures were taken. It was a win/win for everyone – our customer, our associate, the store team, the district, the region and the officers, who left knowing our team was on top of the pro Home Depot business. The overall day was terrific, as I recall. But the only specific circumstance I can remember was the engagement with Brian. One-and-a-half million dollars of potential spending – just because Jim approached and engaged. Yes, daily reinforcement of your culture and expectations can and does become monotonous, but it does not matter. Your employees and your customers deserve your best in this area.

SHIPLAP, BARN DOORS, SOCIAL MEDIA AND HOME IMPROVEMENT NETWORKS

These days, networks like DIY and HGTV are wildly popular. Talk to any human and they will tell you, without hesitation, which show is their favorite, along with which one they cannot stand. Though I have not seen a direct correlation between the success of these networks and the financials of the home improvement industry, they have influenced customer demands noticeably. When barn doors started popping up on HGTV on the show *Fixer Upper*, everybody and their mother wanted them. In fact, I had to install two of them for my mom in her new house and became quite proficient at it. Yes, I did buy them online, from Home Depot. That's one example of the evolution of products you see in home improvement centers and distributors. We have come a long way, baby – from paneling in the 60s and 70s to shiplap (thank you, Joanna Gaines) and barn doors in the second decade of the new millennium.

Home improvement reality shows are influential, and many viewers take them at their word when they promote a design trend. Between HGTV, DIY, Pinterest, and other social media sites, it's a treasure trove of ideas. Years ago, it was *Better Homes and Gardens* magazine, but times have changed thanks to rapid advances in technology and social media. The networks were smart enough to diversify their portfolio of shows quickly. For example, HGTV features *Flip or Flop* in California, *Hometown* in Mississippi, *Fixer Upper* in Texas, *Love It or List It* in North Carolina, and *Property Brothers* in Westchester County New York, just to name a few. On the flip side, these shows put pressure on all retailers, wholesalers, and distributors to make these products available to customers. The requests come in by the hundreds, via phone, e-mail, website communication and, yes, regular mail. Many, many people need to have the latest and greatest. The good thing for us? It creates an appetite for our customers to move forward with the remodel or addition they had been thinking about for a while.

Point of explanation: the home improvement industry and construction business are almost indestructible. Regardless of the state of our country's economy, the global economy, natural disasters, weather or political climate, our business is a safe place to be. Of course, it can vary somewhat, closely watched by the economic community. When the economy is good, most everyone's morale is high. And when morale is high, spending goes up. Home Depot is one of the beneficiaries during these times. Take for example, the housing industry. When home values increase, it enables a higher usage of home equity loans where Home Depot, Lowe's and others realize an uptick in spending. Oh, and by the way, all workers within the trades and construction benefit mightily because projects get scheduled well into the future, providing job security and income.

Here's a funny thought to ponder: have you ever just sat in your favorite chair, with an adult beverage and contemplated the impact to the entire business world if a specific segment is successful? Stay with me for a minute on this. If confidence in the economy is high and consumers spend copious amounts of money at Home Depot, what other businesses will reap the benefits? The simple answer is ALL of them. From development to manufacturing to logistics to hospitality to retail in general, and on and on. The only people (seemingly) unhappy about it are those in the opposite political party not in control of the oval office or Congress (just saying). The far-reaching tentacles of the effects generated by one business's success or failure are often misunderstood by many.

GIVING BACK

What happens in the aftermath of a national crisis? Nesting, defined as "settling into something." Referencing September 11 again, I want to be completely respectful; I mention it here to illustrate my point about its impact on business. And not in any celebratory fashion, either. When it happened, we were in collective shock as a nation for months, if not years, continuing till today. We can NEVER FORGET because "those who don't learn from history are doomed to repeat it." In the aftermath of 9/11, people "nested" more. They did not want to leave their homes, travel, or spend money on vacations: all they wanted to do was stay in their safe zone or home base. For these reasons, they proceeded to spend more money to make that environment cozier and more comfortable. Many businesses realized positive impacts, while others suffered. At the time, and ever since, Home Depot wanted to be there for their customer base in any way they could.

No matter what's going on in the nation, the world, or the economy, this industry remains. With hurricanes, somebody must sell plywood. Somebody must remain open because of supply and demand. While it may vary or fluctuate, there is always a demand. Coming out of the housing boom of 2004, when values of homes reached their pinnacle, then collapsed, we experienced a fluctuation. Home-buying decreased for a period, but then people started nesting again. Now we're back in a cycle where home sales are picking up, it's stabilized, and people are taking HE loans and spending money on their homes again. Drive down any street in a populated area and you will see at least one house in the process of renovation in one way or another. Bernie and Arthur probably realized this when they founded Home Depot: regardless of the economy, the company was built to help customers, no matter the circumstances. But when there's a crisis like a natural disaster or a community need, Home Depot shifts into a higher gear. It's amazing – almost as if we inject our employees with caffeine, Red Bull, and B_{12} vitamins.

That brings me back to social media, a mixed blessing in the modern technology age. One day it can be a friend to business, the next a detractor – which can be frustrating. Quicker than an ex-spouse who claimed at first that the divorce was going to be amicable, it has a "what have you done for me lately?" quality. Through the years, Home Depot has been both the darling of the media for all its growth, beliefs, and success *and* the devil for our competition intensity, lawsuits, tendency to put small businesses out of business (allegedly), and causes we support through our philanthropy. Regardless of the industry, all businesses must maintain a constant awareness of their standing within the various platforms in existence. As technology advances, these will become bigger, faster, and more interactive. Companies can either take advantage of this opportunity or choose to let it happen...which could be disastrous.

Think I'm exaggerating? Here's an example. While I was a regional pro manager, one of the accounts we owned within our portfolio happened to be one of the world's largest charitable organizations. We enjoyed a good relationship with them, supplied them with huge quantities of product, expedited their deliveries and assisted with efficiencies. One day, a few members of my team and I were privileged to take a tour of their headquarters. As they led us through the complex, they introduced us to members of their staff before we arrived at their "command center" of sorts, where they monitored events and situations the world over. We ooh-ed and ahh-ed, over-whelmed by the sheer potential of what we could do together in part-nership. When we moved to the next location, we passed a gigantic room filled with a massive amount of technology and staff: numerous computer terminals, phone banks, printers and more. I asked our guide what those individuals did and was shocked when he told me they were the media monitorization team, whose mission was to iden-tify all negative press and social media mentions and communicate and strategize appropriate responses. I was blown away. It bothered the h*ll out of me that one of the world's greatest organizations would be the subject of this type of activity, and the scope of operations necessary for a complete team.

Now, I am sure many corporations may have these teams at present. I am not advocating for them. My point is that the awareness must be there, and certain things can and should be communicated. I will be one of the first to voice my distaste for the "keyboard cowards" on Instagram, Twitter, Facebook, LinkedIn and more. You know what I am talking about – those who cannot or will not engage a person or organization. Instead, they choose to vent (most of the time in an irrational manner) on their faceless computer. However, much like a problem customer within your physical environment there is value in the middle. Or, to put it another way, the devil is in the details, if you can get beyond the emotion. To sum it up, media of any sort must be part of any organization's strategy. Let's look at the posi-tive effects.

Ellicott City Maryland, located in DM Jim Emge's district, expe-rienced horrific flooding for the second time in two years. From the minute it happened, Jim rallied supplies and teams to get needed product into the affected area, the moment authorities gave people – including the Red Cross – access. I remember standing along Main Street, wondering what the people were going to do to recover. Even after witnessing the devastation of many hurricanes, my mind was blown as to what I was seeing. Twice, in two years. Although he runs a large grouping of stores, Jim is that "boots on the ground" guy who can respond faster and better than anyone to disaster by mobilizing his team to come to the community's aid. He shows a great aptitude in not only being aware about what's going on his stores but also in his communities. Those who work with or for Jim have a powerful example of leadership. When he leaves Home Depot, his legacy will encompass not just how he ran his stores, but the way he engaged with the community. In my mind, there's no one better at it than him, although I'm sure there are other Home Depot's across the country and in Canada and Mexico that would beg to differ because they have that guy or gal...and they probably do. But in my world? Jim's the man. He received a well-deserved award from our regional vice-president on behalf of Home Depot for his relief efforts and representation of the company in the community. Several media pieces cited the efforts of Jim, his team, and Home Depot. That is the kind of press that you want. I hear the city of Baltimore needs a mayor – I have always told Jim he should run.

While it's a core value of Home Depot to serve its communities in countless ways (something embedded in our DNA), we're terrible about telling the world about it. Part of our community service involves the police and fire departments, EMTs, and hospitals...organizations with whom we partner at the local level. At times, we built small sub-stations for the police in our parking lots, as was the case when I opened the Roosevelt Boulevard store in Philly. During the month of October, every Home Depot store hosts a Fire Safety Day, with various events for families. You'll see helicopters in the parking lots, EMTs with an ambulance, and fire-fighters with their rigs, interacting with kids, who love to climb all over the fire trucks. Every year, we donate countless smoke alarms to local fire departments – millions of units – because we have an appreciation for the fire-fighters, some of whom work part-time in our stores for extra income. There are numerous articles, videos and mentions on all media of our relationships and combined efforts with EMTs, Firemen, Police. Positive impact.

It bothers me terribly that our society, today, tends to devalue and disrespect our first responders. One could argue about the role of media in forming people's opinions as they continue to feature the negative situations and the inappropriate actions of the few. What would happen if the media, instead chose to focus on the daily innumerable accomplishments and highlight the acts of heroism? People often disparage those who choose to go into a role as a fire fighter, police office or EMT, yet these are some of the smartest and bravest people on the face of the planet whose only goal is to help others, make a living, and take care of their families. Funny how the same people who malign them count on them when they're in grave danger. The hypocrisy of it all makes me ill. Home Depot holds the utmost respect and admiration for first responders and did everything we could to collaborate, donate, and employ all we could. There was never a time that they were never there for us, always responding and assisting, keeping us and our customers safe No matter your organization, one of the best relationships you can cultivate is with municipal resources in the local area where your store, business, or company resides. It's vital. It's right. It's what we should all do because we need them. They are us.

Another example of where social media can be a positive or negative influence involves corporate giving. Remember that "Giving Back" is one portion of the overall culture at Home Depot. Yet many consumers and members of the public have no idea. Since its inception, Home Depot has battled perceptions of being one of the "large evil corporations," when in fact, the good things Home Depot has done for its employees, communities, first responders, military and other organizations are incalculable. The public often forms opinions based on limited narratives they find on media sites or only sees what it wants to see. If they took the time to explore what the big orange box represented, there would be an astounding response: "I had no idea." This is not just a "Depot thing." There are many self-governing, socially responsible companies who do not need government oversight to mandate where and how their efforts and monies are utilized. Let's be honest; free enterprise does a much better job of leading, managing, and regulating itself. I am not disparaging the government; however, there are enormous opportunities for improvement in many local and federal government-run programs. In free enterprise, change can be enacted more efficiently and urgently.

In case you are wondering why, as I once did, corporations do not spend more time publicizing their efforts in the above areas, it is because they are too busy executing their efforts, managing their businesses and moving forward.

The Homer Fund: For Employees Only

Back in 1999, aside from providing unforgettable entertainment at the 20th anniversary celebration, Home Depot founders Bernie Marcus, Arthur Blank, and Ken Langone made an important announcement concerning the establishment of a new program called the "Homer Fund." Each of these men contributed five-million dollars of their own money to this philanthropic venture, which benefits Home Depot associates in times of dire need or circumstances such as an unexpected illness, a death in the family, or a natural disaster.

The procedure requires applications to funnel through human resources to a committee that determines which ones are approved and to what extent. Anywhere from hundreds to thousands of dollars will be disbursed, based on the financial needs. The Fund is a shining example of leadership initiating something which will begin to sustain itself based on the actions of others. The self-sustainment is due entirely to the employee base at Depot. They choose an amount that they would like to come directly out of their paychecks to support the program. The Homer Fund is a testament to the culture of the company and how the employees truly believe in its content and their role. At present, Home Depot employs somewhere north of 400,000 employees. I read a post on social media stating that over 93 percent of all employees were donors this year. That just doesn't happen everywhere.

Given the generosity and thoughtfulness of the company, the Homer Fund and the Home Depot Foundation (community grants), it saddens me how our company, other large companies and their executives are viewed by many in our society. I recently shared an article on social media extolling Bernie's charitable work and his magnanimous nature. In my post, I stated how this has always been a core value of his. Some knucklehead responded, "Oh yeah, I can just imagine how much he's given instead of buying another house, car, or private jet."

I countered, "Hey, I understand how you might not know what you're talking about, because you don't know him as well as I do, but please do your research and then let me know how you feel." I never did hear back from the guy. That interaction bothered me because people make perceptions that are not true and stereotype the lives of the rich and famous. Yes, Arthur Blank owns the Atlanta Falcons, but most people have no idea all he does for the city of Atlanta and its surrounding communities. They don't know that Bernie started the Marcus Foundation, a medical foundation that helps children with medical and behavioral issues. Even though people are ignorant about such things, Bernie and Arthur are never going to crow about them, because it's just not their style. But the Homer Fund is an example of what they put in place to benefit Home Depot associates, and part of their philanthropic legacy that helps associates in need to this day.

"One of the most important actions, things a leader can do, is to lead by example. If you want everyone else to be passionate, committed, dedicated, and motivated you go first!"—Marshall Goldsmith

Please tolerate one more example about leading by example. This one is somewhat different. You can never tell when an opportunity presents itself to reinforce what your company and you, are all about. I can never, ever walk into a Home Depot and not shag a few shopping carts because it was such an integral part of what I did early on as a part-timer. Even as a store manager, district manager and regional manager, if I got back from lunch and noticed a bunch of stray carts strewn across the parking lot, I'd gather them and return them to their rightful place. Some members of management would have gone inside the building and asked others to respond. That wasn't my style. Remember, I had to work all those desserts off.

I remember one day I was pushing carts. Because I had an appointment that afternoon, I was nicely dressed in pressed khakis and dress shirt, wingtips, and my Rolex. I saw a couple get out of their car where there was a cart nearby, so as I went up to retrieve it, I greeted them.

"Hey, how are you folks doing today?"

They first looked at me, then down at my shoes. The gentleman noticed the watch on my wrist and asked, "Who are you?"

"Ah, I'm just shagging some carts today. This is what we do."

"There is no fricking way," he retorted. "That's a Rolex on your wrist and those are wingtips. What are you doing?"

"Well, okay, I'm the district manager. This is one of my stores and this is what we do. We lead by example. My employees are obviously busy elsewhere, so I wanted to gather these up."

They just looked at me like I was a lunatic: I'm dressed like I own the place and I'm out there, shagging carts. Just then, I saw three employees coming out of the door. "What are you guys doing out here?" I asked.

"Oh, someone saw you in the parking lot and told us we can't have our district manager shagging carts alone."

I looked at the couple and asked, "Pretty cool, huh?"

And he just smiled and agreed, "That is good."

"That's Home Depot. That's what we are," I told him as I kept pushing them inside. It was wild. They knew something was up. They stereotyped who was supposed to be outside, engaging in a lower-level job. In those situations, I always impressed what we were about upon the customer, never forgetting where we started and that we never asked our people to do what we would not. I carried those lessons forward like a figurative backpack. I never forgot them because that's all I had. I grew up at Home Depot and once invested, took these philosophies with me to every level I climbed. While it blew some people away, it made others uncomfortable. If I was with a group of officers and all the sudden, I started shagging carts they'd be like, "Oh, God." Because then they felt they had to do the same.

However, I invariably received validation for my efforts when the lot guy or girl came running out the door and announced, "Ah, thanks man. I really had to go to the bathroom."

"Don't worry about it. I got this," I'd reply.

When they tried to grab the carts from me, I'd tell them, "No, I got these. Go get some of the rest." And I'd stay out there with them for 10 minutes and they'd thank me for the help.

"Don't worry about it. This is how I started," I'd assure them.

"Really?"

Any time you can interact with another human being you have an opportunity to make an impression, and you can choose to make it good, bad, or ugly. As this story illustrates, my recommendation is to make the best impression possible. Whether in your professional or personal life, it's excellent advice for everybody because 1. it's the right thing to do, and 2. you never know who's watching. Case in point: Pam and I took a road trip to Wisconsin and on the way stopped in a restaurant, where we sat down at a booth. Next to us were three attractive, well-dressed people: two guys in suits and a lady in a nice dress. Two of them were younger and the older one was obviously their boss. It turned out they were from a law firm, where the older man was a partner.

During their conversation they made fun of other people, utilizing curse words. Profanity doesn't bother me, but there's a time and a place for it. When you're in the middle of a restaurant with families around you? Yeah, it matters. They got their meal, ate, and finished before we did. As they got up, it looked like a family of 12 kids had been eating there, with stuff all over the floor and the table, yet they made no attempt to clean up their mess (probably figuring it was a job for the "little people"). Pam and I just looked at each other and asked, "Wow, what kind of representation is that?" It was certainly an example of a negative impression. If I had needed a law firm, I would not have hired them because I had no respect for them, based on their behavior. Just because somebody is wearing an Armani suit, or a Donna Karan dress doesn't mean they have class. Oh, and that leader's example? Pathetic.

LADDERS AND LEARNINGS

Never forget where you came from. Each level you rise in the organization increases the importance of showcasing the behaviors that differentiated you from others. The foundation that you built along the way is very important for others to see.

EXECUTIVE MEMO

Strike a balance between your top-performing and low-performing entities, to fully engage with all and avoid alienating anyone. This will ensure improved and increased productivity and help you achieve your desired results. Always communicate your forward-looking strategies to your teams to help them understand your expectations.

16

MY HOME-GROWN LEGACY

"I get asked a lot about my legacy. For me, it's being a good teammate, having the respect of my teammates, having the respect of the coaches and players. That's important to me."

— PEYTON MANNING

Remember my stated goal of retiring from Home Depot at 50 to be available for my daughter as she started high school? Yeah, well, despite my keen awareness and desire to make it up to Pam and Jackie for all the times I either could not be there for them or hadn't been as present as I would have liked, it didn't happen. I'd made stupid decisions on money. In some instances, I spent versus saved. Whenever I earned options and compensation for my performance, instead of buying a new car or putting a chunk of change into landscaping for one of our houses, maybe I should have waited until we moved into our end-all-be-all house...or at least carefully considered what I was doing.

My dad retired from Home Depot at just over 50 years old. Not too shabby, right? As the story goes, Arthur was less than ecstatic when Dad submitted his resignation. To convince Dad to stay two more years, an offer of additional stock was offered. Without divulging the exact quantity of shares, just know it was substantial. At its current price, the package represented seven figures in value. But Dad was done, so he turned down the offer and moved on with his life. Even though I served as executor of his estate at one point, he refused to disclose to how much money he retired with. His lips remained sealed when I joked, "Don't worry, I plan on making my own," to assure him I wouldn't need his money and was simply curious. As I was coming up through the same channels in the company, I wanted that information to provide perspective, but for whatever reason, Dad never felt comfortable sharing it with me.

As I approached 50, the dreaded "mid-life crisis" reared its ugly head. The influence, however, may not be what you think. Back in my younger years, I never had an affinity for tattoos and had a negative perception about people who had them. That is, until the year I turned 50 and went to Vegas for Home Depot's annual meeting. One day during our free time, five or six of us walked through the Miracle Mile Shops by Planet Hollywood. Out of curiosity, we stopped in *Club Tattoo*, a famous tattoo parlor. As we looked at all the available tattoos on their computer system, I saw one I really liked in the form of an eagle. I have appreciation and respect for eagles, their behavior, and what they represent to the United States. I wanted it. I called Pam and said, "Hey, um, we're in a tattoo store and I found one I really like. I'm thinking about getting it. What do you think?" Of course, all the guys made fun of me because I had to call her for permission, but I didn't want to go home with ink on my body somewhere without her knowing. "What do you mean, you have to call your wife? You're 50 years-old, for God's sake."

"I'm calling her," I insisted.

After about three or four phone calls, asking the artist who had been assigned to me many questions, I decided to get my eagle tattoo, along with another gentleman in our group who selected a tattoo he liked. I was such a baby, asking where the least painful area was to get one. When all was said and done, I returned home with an eagle on my right shoulder. The next two years when we went to Vegas, I scheduled appointments ahead of time with the same artist. Everybody teased me because I was 50 before I got my first tattoo, asking, "Why are you getting them now?"

"I guess I just know what I want."

Today, I sport two eagle tattoos and an American flag. The American flag and eagle tattoos were symbolic of my mindset at that time, when I started thinking differently about everything: work, home, and life. Despite my mid-life crisis, I never wanted to go out and buy that $300,000 car but I had other considerations, like "Where are we going to live?" and "Where's that end-all house going to be?" Pam and I had always dreamed of living on the water, whether by a lake or the ocean.

For a five-year-period following my 50th birthday, my enthusiasm for getting up at 4 a.m. every Monday, staying at out-of-town hotels two- to- three nights per week, and driving in the horrendous Mid-Atlantic traffic started to wane. Once I noticed it, I became concerned because it fed into the notion of, *Well, I'm 50 now. Is it time to try something different?* I wasn't ready to retire, mainly due to finances; most of my financial holdings were in Home Depot stock, which was thankfully on the rise again. Yet, even though the stock was going back up and the company was on a winning streak, I wasn't where I needed to be just yet on the monetary side.

It created an internal struggle: *Do I stay at Home Depot or seek employment with another company while there's still time? Do I go for a different position at Home Depot?* When I reached my milestone birthday, I'd been a Regional Pro Manager for seven years. I loved the position, my team and what the role did for the company. Still, my inner dilemma persisted: *Either Home Depot is going to be my everything for the rest of my life, or while the getting's good, maybe I need to try something else?*

To answer these questions, I conducted some research into businesses and companies, which caused me to consider my options carefully. When you hit the age of 50 and over, you're in a protected group – *mature citizens* – if you will, but at the same time, you're older than what companies consider for higher level positions. It's been proven that companies tend to select employees in their late-20s through their late-30s to be officers. There are exceptions, of course, but at some point, you've got to play the odds. Due to my actions, the goal of reaching the same position as my Dad was out. It became about the enjoyment of the role and preparation for my departure.

I've always had a tremendous amount of respect for Home Depot's officers in terms of who they were and how they functioned. Larry Mercer provided an early window into the leadership perspective by the way he worked with people, then years later, Paul Raines. When Paul was selected for the role in Florida, I took note of his words, deeds, and actions and realized he embodied everything I would have wanted to be. Both Larry and Paul demonstrated the qualities every officer should have. With genuine humility, they worked WITH people and knew how to utilize their resources to do their jobs well.

As I stated, I had two bosses, one in Atlanta, Tony Drew, and one in the regional office, Que Vance. There were times when I drove them both nuts by making a decision that was more emotional than professional. Or, I showed empathy for individuals when I should have fired them sooner. In the moment, I thought I was making the right decision, but in some cases I was writing checks I could not cash. At times, my decisions exceeded my autonomy and authority levels a bit; then, I had to justify my actions to them, taking up their valuable time. Toward the end of my time, I developed a fear for my job. I always had a healthy fear with respect to my job, either trying to live up to Dad's reputation or produce the best results in the company. Every day I went to work with a positive attitude, motivated to be my best and to bring out the best in others. Yet one of my bosses informed me, "You know what, Erik? We feel like maybe one day you are going to make such an emotional or detrimental decision that we are going to have to hold you accountable." That made me nervous. There was no sugarcoating that statement – if I made one more mistake, serious enough in nature, I would be terminated, regardless of all that I had done prior. I went from a having a healthy fear to thoughts of, "If I can't change who and how I am in my 50s, if I get an opportunity, I may have to get out under my conditions, not theirs."

This is hard for me to admit. I always thought I took constructive criticism well. There was never a time when somebody sat me down and b*****d me out for anything that I never gave them a high-five, a fist-bump, or a man hug at the end and said, "Thanks, I really appreciate this." You know why? I deserved it, always owning the good AND the bad (someday, maybe the politicians and celebrities will do the same thing). But I started to think: *if I put myself in harm's way, would it force their position?* Did I really want to be that person who, after spending decades with the company, left to "seek other business opportunities," as they phrased it on conference calls? I didn't want to be the subject of a call where they'd announce, "Hey Erik Dardas is no longer with us. He's seeking other business opportunities." I decided that I was going out on my own terms. And, I was going to do all I could to not put myself in harm's way.

Having been with Home Depot this long with the family name always at stake, I wanted to go out on a high note. I had my pride. God bless my two supervisors, Que and Tony for their honesty, because they provided the very latest update to where I was at, and their concerns. They were not forcing me out of the company; instead they did not want me to put myself in their cross hairs.

The next step was to seek guidance on all financial matters. Fortunately, in working at the chiropractor's office, Pam discovered information about a financial advisor in Haymarket with an excellent reputation, so we decided to visit the father-son duo of Gary and Reid Howard of Ameriprise. Reid had just graduated from school and returned from England when we met them.

"What is your goal in relation to your job?" they asked.

"One day soon, I want to walk into this office and hear you tell me that, without risk, I can retire," I answered. For two years, we followed their advice and employed their techniques to achieve our retirement dreams.

THE SOUNDTRACK OF MY LIFE

I can sum up hitting my 50s with three songs: "I Want It All" by Queen, "Peace of Mind" by Boston, and "What Are You Waiting For?" by Nickelback (yes, for all you Nickelback haters, yes, I like Nickelback). When I first reached my fifth decade in life and failed in my primary goal of being retired for Jackie's formative high school years, I took it hard. I considered myself a failure, even though no one else did. I would come to realize that some goals are unrealistic. Referencing the Queen song, I wanted everything: money, glory, and appreciation but I reached a point where I wanted what Boston sang about in "Peace of Mind."

At many Home Depot meetings and workshops, we began with an icebreaker like, "If you were deserted on an island and could only have one album to listen to, what would it be?" I always answered, "Boston." I love them. The years go by but their music never ages; it just resonates with each new generation. The day I decided to retire, I listened to the Nickelback song, "What are You Waiting For?" repeatedly. Those three songs wrap up my 50s and my mental state which centered around thoughts of finances and what I wanted to do, be, and have during my next phase of life.

Even as the Regional Pro Manager for the Mid-Atlantic, I never felt an attachment to the geographic area. To me, it was never my "be all, end all" place; it was another stepping-stone to lead us in the direction of where we wanted to be. All Pam and I talked about was being on the water somewhere, even though she and Jackie loved living in Haymarket because of its proximity to significant, historic areas. Oh, and the Mid-Atlantic area has amazing scenery, populated with incredible wineries in the suburban and rural areas.

As I mentioned, the Home Depot stock price prevented me from retiring at 50. When we met with our financial advisers to formulate a plan, they conducted a survey akin to taking an SAT course to prepare for college. It was a questionnaire that covered every aspect of your life – financial habits, goals, current resources, and expenses. Gary and Reid produced a result to take us through what our situation would look like from the present moment all the way through age 95 (I just hope to live that long). At first it was disheartening to realize we were not yet where we wanted to be; it felt defeating that I had to keep working. I had hoped one of them would look at me and say, "Hey, you can retire." Instead, they guided us through the two-year process of analyzing and working on our goals, bills, assets, and expenses. As a typical male who's interested only in the bottom line without much regard for all the details in-between – like how you're going to make it to retirement and how you're going to maintain it – I'm blessed to have Pam on my side. She provides the balance I always talk about in everything else. If not for her, I would have probably taken that money and spent it a whole lot faster.

Aside from a spouse who grounds you, when it comes to planning for retirement, a good relationship with your financial advisor is key. I cannot describe the level of commitment and empathy Gary and Reid showed us as clients, which led to us becoming good friends. It wasn't just a business relationship about the numbers and money; truly, it was care and concern for us as people. Pam and I never went to a meeting where we didn't spend hours talking and sharing. Gary and Reid built a solid trust with us, providing the comfort I needed to make the decision to retire once they gave me their approval. Without that trust, I don't know if we could have made the leap when we did.

As important as trust is to me, it's even more critical to my wife. In our case, when I retired, I had a certain amount of money in various resources; barring additional sources of income, that's what we had to live on, forevermore. Anyone who has been through the process knows it's a daunting decision that you cannot take lightly. Pam and I sure didn't. I'll never forget the day we walked into the Ameriprise office – a little over two years after forming our relationship – knowing Gary and Reid had arrived at a conclusion. As my wife will attest, when we walked through the office doors, I barely made it into the foyer before looking at Reid and blurting out, "Well?"

"You can go," he replied.

It was such a moment, hard to describe. A tidal wave of emotion consumed me as those three rock songs reverberated in my head, my eyes watered, and my entire body experienced an adrenalin rush. After overcoming countless trials and tribulations throughout my Home Depot career – most notably that harrowing day in Arthur Blank's office when I walked away with a demotion and not a termination – it felt surreal. I did not know what to do next. Pam and Jackie had stood by my side the entire time through nine relocations and the countless demands and palpable stress my work put on all of us. At last, we were all reaping the rewards of my home-grown legacy. Not bragging, but it blew my mind that I could retire well before most other people can – many with college degrees or higher. On the way home, Pam and I prayed, thanking God for the privilege, asking for his blessing on what we wanted to do. We did not want to go it alone. The decision proved to me that there are multiple pathways to success but there is no substitute for a solid work ethic, self-motivation, and resilience. Knowing I could stop working with a certain amount of money to enable me to do what I really wanted to do? That's a milestone moment. It is difficult to explain how it made me feel, but I felt such a comfort and relief that we'd arrived at our goal. I was still employed at the time. I asked Reid, "Is there anything, *anything*, that you can think of, that would derail this?"

"Aside from a geo-political conflict or a major world war, we have nothing to worry about."

Funny, not too long after our meeting, the North Korean dictator, the little s**t, started throwing his weight around and it bothered me. I can't say I didn't sweat my retirement decision a bit when that happened as the stock market dipped over the initial panic that a major conflict could take place. Other than Pam's parents and brother, who is a genius with numbers and financials, I didn't tell anyone I was retiring. I kept it quiet, not wanting it to affect the remainder of my time with the company. At that point, I had not decided when my official last day would be. Doing research, I wanted to attain my next anniversary date, which would afford me additional financial rewards.

Once your financial adviser tells you it's okay to retire, it blows doors wide open that were only cracked open before. I was about 55 years-old, rationalizing that I could do something else besides Home Depot. Although I continued to work for a brief time beyond that fateful conversation at Ameriprise, it changed my demeanor. Through honesty, oversight, and direct communication, Home Depot had let me know I was probably at the highest level I could climb in the company: there were no other options beyond my current role as a regional pro sales manager. I was one step below an officer, and I knew my age. All these thoughts and considerations began to over-take my consciousness.

"Blood, sweat, and respect. First two you give. Last one you earn." —Dwayne Johnson

Tony made it crystal clear to everybody that I didn't retire just from some country club or low-volume area; up to the last day, I ran one of the most powerful pro regions in the company in terms of volume and revenue. He coached me to the end, his words and guid-ance showing appreciation. The relocation from Florida to the Mid-Atlantic was validated. Instead of people thinking that I bided my time in one of the simpler geographies, everyone knew that I was a "driver" to the very end, with my teams contributing a significant amount to the company's renewed success.

At retirement, Pam and I had been living away from her family for 23 years. We'd settled in cities and towns all over the country. Pam's family was always one-hundred percent supportive of our relocations. Her parents, along with her brother Jay, from day one, treated me like I was a member of the family. Through all the tough times at Home Depot, they remained some of my strongest supporters. But now that our parents were getting older and experiencing medical issues ranging from mild to serious, we wanted to be closer to them. It's ironic, wherever I went in Home Depot, because my dad had been an employee during the largest and fastest growth of the company, I ran into people he'd hired, worked with, or just knew. They always asked about him and I sensed that they expected to hear glorious details about him traveling the world and doing something spectacular. But Dad was low-key. All he wanted was to live on a lake, take care of his yard, hunt, fish and play golf. When he got ill with dementia and I told people he was battling medical problems, they expressed profound and sincere empathy, just as he had done for them. I'm incredibly proud of him for the family legacy he established and nurtured at Home Depot.

It meant so much to me to walk away a winner in terms of my own legacy. Recently, Pam and I traveled to Michigan to support my parents with some medical appointments and projects at the house. While Mom and I met privately with her doctor, Pam stayed in the waiting room with Dad. Another "gentleman" sitting nearby discovered that my dad and I worked for Home Depot and made some disparaging comments about the company. In response, Dad stood up for Home Depot and for me and what I did there. He told this guy how proud he was of me. When Pam relayed the story to me later, it made me feel great that even with all his problems, Dad could feel that way about me and verbalize his feelings. Given what I experienced during the demotion and my fears about tarnishing the Dardas' name, it was especially gratifying that my father could hold that mindset.

I mentioned it before, but it still amazes me how much my life in retail mirrored my dad's. Neither one of us had college degree; we moved everywhere on behalf of the company and worked our asses off, but in the end, we retired in our 50s, though Dad was a few years younger than I was. It is stunning when I think it through. These days, Pam and I are looking for ways to better protect our long-term finances, take better care of our health, and spend quality time with family and friends, splitting our time between our houses in Florida and Wisconsin.

LIVING THE AMERICAN DREAM

Whenever I did presentations, I always added music. During breaks, I'd select certain songs to play because I wanted people to hear a message. Don't get me wrong, I have ZERO talent in this area. I'm tone-deaf and musically challenged, if you will. I still remember a bad choir tryout in school, but think I sound great in the shower. Lack of talent aside, music has been symbolic and meaningful throughout my life. Three months after Reid gave me the greenlight, I typed up my resignation note and retired from Home Depot. On the way to work that day, I played the Nickelback song over and over. When I got there, I greeted everybody, then went back to the training room to set up my laptop as usual. As I sat there in silence on that winter day, somewhere around the end of January, I contemplated the contents of my note to my bosses Tony and Que, wanting to be thoughtful and specific.

I began by saying, "I've made my decision, based on careful consideration. I would like my last day to be March 31." Why March 31? It gave me my five weeks of vacation time (working through my anniversary) and tenure on stock options when I divested and transitioned to Ameriprise. In all, I gave them two-months' notice. My bosses acknowledged my email right away, remained supportive and understood how difficult a decision it had been to make. I wanted to be fair to the company as well. Due to our promotional guidelines, replacing anyone at a management level takes weeks to accomplish. The spring season would be upon the company quickly. No room for downtime.

My bosses announced my retirement on a regional conference call. Many people were surprised; others, not so much. Some employees expected to hear the news, due to the rise in our stock prices – thanks to the leadership of Frank Blake followed by Craig Menear, and the rest of us working our asses off. It's a testament to the right leadership that Home Depot stayed in its wheelhouse (culture).

Back in the early 2000s, when our stock went down to $19 per share, people asked, "Dardas, what's it going to take for you to retire?"

"If it gets back up to $50, I might start thinking about it."

Well, when it got back up to $50, they were like, "Are you ready to retire?"

And I answered, "Nah, I'll wait until it gets to $75 per share."

We repeated the same conversation when the stock hit $75 per share. Finally, the stock price rose high enough for me to say, "Okay, great, now it's at a point where I can hit my number." That's a credit to Home Depot's management; they rallied the company and included every single employee in the solution. The most successful entities, regardless of segment, win by teamwork. Take the lot guys, who shag carts. I would go up to them and ask, "Do you know how important you are to Home Depot?"

They would just look at me like, "What do you mean?"

"If you don't greet those customers when they're walking in the door, they might not spend as much money. They may go somewhere else the next time." Some of our customers consider these employees legendary because of how helpful they are outside. Home Depot appreciates them, but I've seen companies treat hourly employees like s**t. To use a military analogy, generals are not always on the front line. When American soldiers stormed Normandy in World War II, there were no generals on the beach. God forbid, if I ever came out of retirement and went back to do it all over again, I would advise all new employees, "Go into your job with the greatest of attitudes that you are willing to do everything and anything, no matter what it takes. If you don't know what 'work your ass off' means, you'll never be a success."

It takes a lot of money to hire, train, and assimilate employees. Nobody wants to waste anybody's time. At Home Depot, regardless of your position or whether you came from another company, had a college degree or worked in management, you had to have a positive attitude, a strong work ethic, and the ability to thrive in a teamwork atmosphere. As I've stated before, I admire people who have the resolve to get a four, six, or eight-year degree; when it came to schooling, I didn't have the discipline. My forte was applying myself at a job, like I did with sports. You can't lean on having a degree as your primary platform because your education level is just one part of an entire package for an individual. A college degree does not guarantee your success. Degree or no-degree, it comes down to self-motivation and work ethic, so apply yourself and work hard.

Contrary to the popular misconception, Home Depot employees are not losers of society working a last-resort job: they are people who want to help others and enjoy being around people. In fact, many of them are military legends, doctors, nurses, first responders, and tradespeople...all unbelievably talented. I consider myself blessed to have worked with amazing people at Home Depot at all levels. I've witnessed their humanity during hurricanes, floods, and tornadoes. I've seen them sacrifice their personal needs for the benefit of their community. In my 33 years, there was never a time during a crisis when I wasn't blown away by my team's and Home Depot's response. I may be retired, but my feelings for Home Depot remain as strong as they were when I was there.

If I died today, I would have lived an excellent life filled with incredible experiences. I've skydived, ridden in helicopters, white-water rafted, and visited many countries. Because of how I was raised, the way I looked at life (even with all its problems) and worked my ass off for a company that rewarded me, I had the resources to take cruises to Spain and Italy and travel wherever I wanted. Yet I couldn't have done any of it, if not for working my ass off for a company that appreciated it. I'm forever grateful to God for my home-grown legacy.

EPILOGUE

"Don't go around saying the world owes you a living. The world owes you nothing. It was here first."

— MARK TWAIN

Many folks feel defeated because they set themselves up for failure with unrealistic goals characterized by irrational ambition. Remember how angry I was when I didn't receive the promotion to store manager of Daytona when I thought I should? Learn from my experience: focus on being the best you can be in your current position while envisioning where you want to go and how to get there. Whether you are a short-order cook, a busboy, a janitor, fry order cook, or bagger at a grocery store, excel in your job performance at every rung of the ladder. Take pride in your work, no matter how menial you or others perceive it to be.

As a junior in high school, my parents pushed me to get a job. I applied for a part-time position as a dishwasher at Ponderosa Steak House, where I made $1.90 per hour in 1978. Aside from the big money, the required uniform was blue polyester bell-bottom pants, a red-and-white checker polyester shirt, and a stupid, blue Ponderosa Cowboy hat. The worst part? Thanks to all the grease I got on my uniform, I smelled terrible when I got home. On a positive note, our high school baseball team practiced baseball in a field behind an elementary school that was right next to Ponderosa, so right after baseball practice, I ran across and got to work.

When I arrived at five p.m., all the dishes from the entire day were saved up for me on rolling carts. I had to wash them as quickly as possible for the dinner crowd. But before I could even get to the dishes, I had to wrap hundreds of baked potatoes, every day, in tin foil, preparing them for cooking. At first, I freaked out, "OMG! I am never going to get to the dishes. I have to wrap potatoes!" It bothered me until one day I walked in and said to myself, "You're an athlete for goodness sake. You can figure out a system and get on it." From that moment on, I made it a game in which I could wrap potatoes faster. On my own initiative, I came up with processes to make my job easier and more efficient.

As I stood among the big washtubs in the back with the potatoes, I figured out schemes. I brought in my own radio and got a beat going. I arrived at work and wrapped up all the potatoes, then moved on to the dishes in an orderly fashion, clearing dishes on specific trays. Soon, it became a game and a competition to do whatever I could to keep up. Even then, I took a lot of pride in my work ethic and creativity. However, I'll admit I hated that stupid uniform and the fact that I was forced to wear it, even as a kitchen employee. It didn't help that customers laughed at it, but I did what I had to do. By the way, my shift didn't end until every dish was done and put away, and the rear kitchen area spotless.

Today, I talk about my Ponderosa Steak House experience with pride. It was a job I executed well, once I found a way. It formed one of the building blocks in my life that made an impact and set me up for success. Of course, I didn't realize it until I got older and thought, "Wow!" Sadly, these days there's a lack of pride in what used to be commonly known and revered as a "solid work ethic," and a "first job." Unlike my parents, many parents today do not have the mentality that their teenage kids get a part-time job. There isn't the same desire for a high school or college student to join the workforce while in school. Maybe it is due to affluence or to the fact that they'd rather stay home playing with all the technology options. Many young people have told me, "My mom and dad said I didn't have to get a job. It's not like it was in their day."

I disagree.

Not getting a job in high school is a missed opportunity for our young people to find more out about themselves and what they are made of and build a foundation for the future. Case in point: I have special empathy for younger kids who are looking to start their careers. As I ask them what they are looking for or what their goals are, many do not know. Today, with or without a college degree, I hear thoughts of "not wanting to work for the man," or "I am waiting for my dream job." To the point of inaction, or procrastination. Another comment I hear frequently, "Well, I don't have any experience."

Symptomatic of many young people: if they can't come out of the gate with the perfect dream job, they just won't do it. One could blame societal pressures, an upper education system that doesn't always deliver on what it promises, or immigration impacts on the trades and general workforce. However, I wouldn't change a thing about the jobs I worked in my early life...whether I loved them or not. They formed a foundation within me, exposed me to the inner workings of businesses, and helped develop self-discipline. If I hadn't taken these jobs, my foundation would not have been nearly as strong. As a kid I thought I was *Joe Jock*. In my mind, my athletic prowess was going to land me a scholarship, and then I would go on to become a pro ball player. When I was young, there were no ifs, ands, or buts about it. But then, I began to suffer injuries and realized it wasn't going to happen. Without a work-related foundation from my parents and my early experiences in the workforce, there is no way I would have achieved the success I've had. I cannot overstate the importance of a strong work ethic.

Recently, I was up in Wisconsin with Pam, and everywhere we went we saw signs saying, "Part-time help needed," or "Help wanted." How sad that these businesses are struggling to find good employees, in some cases, for extended periods of time.

To parents reading this book with kids in high school or college, please collaborate with them, if they are not employed. Recommend, for all the right reasons, that they should have a job, even if part-time. If you're a young person reading this book, take the initiative and get yourself a job, even if your parents are not pushing for it. There is absolutely nothing to lose, but SO much to gain. Get out there and experience the many positives you stand to gain from the experience: interacting with others, collaborating as a team, and understanding how business functions. As my own experience proves, you cannot receive that kind of an education in the classroom. I heard a term the other day while discussing the book with a friend, which I am owning, based on my experience. He said I had attained a "Street Degree." Although my friend has his college degrees, he admitted that my unique degree could be more powerful in many situations. Once again, I am not anti-college; instead I am into efficiency and productivity. If only 27 percent of all college graduates attain a job within their field of study and carry student debt in the hundreds of millions of dollars, it makes perfect sense that opportunities exist...with or without a degree.

We must set up our kids and younger people, for a higher level of success. Getting into the business environment as quickly as possible will yield many learnings and life lessons that they will carry for the remainder of their lifetimes. For example, when I worked at Ponderosa, we had three managers who wore ties. Two of them were great and the third was an a*s. One night in the kitchen, I made some negative comments about him to one of the waitresses in a strictly confidential exchange between the two of us – or so I thought. I didn't realize there was a small glass window by the dishwashing station that allowed the managers to view the kitchen area AND overhear conversations. The next day, he called me into his office to tell me that he and another manager heard the whole exchange, in what can only be described as a "Come to Jesus" moment. At first, I feared he was upset enough to fire me, but we cleared the air...after he chewed me out, but good.

What was my lesson?

Do not speak ill of your boss in a public setting. After that meeting, our relationship improved because we had an honest dialogue. I respected him for letting me keep my job, clarify why I felt the way I did, and changing things in response to my feedback. Afterward, I received a promotion to cook, if you want to call it that. Still had to wear the same goofy outfit. I got out of the back area and learned how to prepare steaks and meals. If not for my Ponderosa job, I would not have learned how to manage conflict at a such a formative age. My story is just one example of the countless benefits of getting a part-time job while still in school or deciding what to do with your career. It's an invaluable experience and it beats sitting at home and doing nothing about your lack of money and resources to do anything fun or interesting.

To keep our country and our people strong, we need to encourage a return to the work ethic that made our country exceptional. In Wisconsin, while renovating our home there, I interacted with many tradespeople. Almost to a person, they complained about the low quality of their hires, in some cases, due to the available workforce. It's tough for them to find qualified people, but that opportunity is not quarantined to just Wisconsin. It currently resides throughout our country. The situation is so dire, to the degree that Home Depot and Lowe's have now publicly announced programs, involving large sums of money, with the goal to train people on the building trades. Think about it for a moment: how many high schools still teach shop class? We do not have the foundation for workable skills that we once did.

Our educational system doesn't teach hard skills anymore to

introduce teens to power tools, show them how to build things and give them the satisfaction of working with their hands. Some of those jobs remain unfilled because of the mindset of our current youth and their parents, who look down on such jobs with disdain. It's as if "trade" is almost a dirty word. Thank God for Mike Rowe and all the work he does to highlight the dignity and importance of so-called "dirty jobs." Yet, how many people watch and listen to him? How many parents and kids hold a negative stereotype of employees of Walmart, Lowe's, and Home Depot and believe, "It's beneath me to work there." Instead of thinking that way, keep an open mind and understand that a job like that could be one of the most significant stepping-stones for your growth and future. As I said in the beginning, whatever you do, be the best you can possibly be; the most successful leaders and executives started at entry-level positions somewhere, doing a menial task.

Think about a kid in high school or college who forms everything they know about business, ethics, and communication from all their time spent on social media and what they learned at school, then goes for that all-important job interview. Do you think that will work out? Maybe, maybe not. I am trying to not preach, but if I was a parent of a high schooler today, he or she would get a job, just like our daughter Jackie did. Working 20 hours per week at a job is much more valuable than spending 20 hours a week on Snapchat, Twitter, Instagram and Facebook. And since I'm on this rant, politicians who know nothing about business should cease and desist with their insistence that the government transition minimum wage to a living wage. A minimum or "living" wage of $15 per hour is counter-productive to job growth, competitiveness and entrepreneurial spirit. An entry-level, hourly wage is NOT meant to be a living wage; it is meant to be a starting point. Meritocracy, not socialism, produces growth, competitiveness, efficiency, inventiveness and ethic.

Pam and I had dinner recently at PF Chang's, where we were the first customers for our waiter, on his first day on the job. He was just an outstanding kid. We watched how he handled his responsibilities as a server still in training, taking pride in us as his first table. I hope he carries that attitude forward because the lack of initiative and work ethic is a huge concern for me. If it doesn't adjust itself, we're in deep trouble. But it must start in the home. As parents, we have an obligation to our kids. Our roles are not supposed to make life so easy for them that they do not know how to function on their own. Instead, it's to give them the opportunities to build a life for themselves. Our pride should rest in our kids getting a job to build their own foundation and personal brand. Your personal brand begins from the moment you are born, with your attitudes and behaviors and how you are perceived. As parents, while making life better for our children, we also need to think about how we are preparing them for this wacky, crazy thing called life.

I thank God every day for the opportunities and blessings in my life. There have been plenty of days where I may have taken that for granted, only to have a "something" present itself in my life to provide a quick course correction. As Americans, we live in the land of opportunity. It is up to every one of us to earn the optimum that can be produced as a result. Tomorrow is never a given, nor should anyone hope to thrive by being given everything versus earning it through effort and perseverance.

If you take away nothing else from this book, I hope it's the realization that – despite what society dictates – there are multiple pathways to success. That is, if you cultivate a solid work ethic and a dependable personal brand, have the willingness to do whatever it takes, and remain receptive to constructive criticism and use it for never-ending improvement in your personal and professional life. We are blessed to live in a country filled with endless pathways for advancement. Keep your vision, work hard, remain humble, and be thankful every day for the chance to start over.

A Few Testimonials from Fellow Home Depot Veterans

"Hey Erik, you probably don't remember me, but you hired me at Home Depot #2550 in Gaithersburg in 1993 as lot attendant. I eventually got promoted to a lumber supervisor, then the paint department before you left. I just want to thank you for all your teachings. I am now an operations manager for a HVAC/Electric Services company. You instilled the "Customer Service #1 Priority" in me, and I carry that attitude to this very day. When I counsel an employee or hold training classes, I always refer to some of the lessons you taught me. Believe it or not, I still have videos from our store meetings. Well, I don't want to write a book, here. I just wanted to reach out and thank you." – Trevor Moore

"I have known Erik for his entire career at HD. His attention to detail and execution at all levels was exemplary. His work ethic was nothing short of excellent. He also developed outstanding relationships with his customer base and associates alike. In short, it was my honor to work alongside him." – Daniel McDevitt, Merchandising Director, Cross-Functional Retail Operations and Teams

"Erik is a hard charger that understands what it takes to lead and motivate any size team to a goal. He is someone worthy of following and leads by example when appropriate. He makes work fun, but consistently delivers results with no excuses. One of the top mentor's I ever had the privilege to work for. Any company would be incredibly fortunate to have Erik as a leader." – Matt Salerno, Senior Project Manager at the Mayo Clinic

"Man, I just realized I hit 23 years with my company today. I was a 14-year-old who got a call from my uncle needing help at his job filling beer and soda orders. I even had to go on deliveries into some of the roughest neighborhoods delivering beer to sandwich shops and Chinese food restaurants located at 52nd and Lancaster, Wayne and Wyndrum, Broad and Girard, to name just a few. I then landed a job my junior year of high school fixing copy machines – just maintenance; easy stuff, filling paper and toner orders for a place in a neighborhood called Juniata Park. When I graduated high school, the owner offered me a job full-time and to put me through school to learn about the equipment. I was thinking about, it but wanted to explore more options. The Sears building was torn down and I filled out an application in a trailer meeting a few people. I came across a guy who was high-energy, fast-talking, serious, and respectful. I learned he was the general manager. After an interview for a full-time job, the guy gave me a shot.

Although it was $3.00 less an hour, and I had zero experience for the company, I wanted the job. One day a call came to my house. The manager asked for me to come in for overtime, then he was told I was at my part-time job. The next day, this manager sat me down, asked a few questions, and said, "Quit the part time job. I will give you a shot. We need you inside." I agreed and told the owner from the printer company. The owner, Jack, smiled, understood, and wrote me a business check for $1000.00 and told me to buy a reliable car to begin my life! With my jaw on the floor I was on cloud nine. I couldn't accept the check but was told it wasn't an option; I was taking the check. I went to my new job and told the manager I put in my resignation. The manager filled out paperwork, gave me a substantial bump in wage, and challenged me to learn a sales department, moving me right inside. I bought my first car for $1,200.00 and broke by butt for the company since. I give all the thanks and appreciation to Erik Dardas who took a chance on not only me but many of us who still work for the company today." – George Elwell

ABOUT THE AUTHOR

 Michigan native Erik Dardas began his career with Home Depot as a part-time associate in the company's Fort Lauderdale Florida store in 1983, following in his father's footsteps. When he first donned the signature orange apron, he had no idea that what started out as a second job for extra income would soon transform into a 33-year career with the world's largest home improvement retailer. He wrote *Home Grown Legacy: Life, Ladders and Learnings in the World of Home Improvement* to highlight the service and dedication of retail employees and leaders, affirm the value of a strong work ethic, and express his gratitude to company associates, managers, and officers for helping him grow into a better man, leader, husband, and father. He is currently retired with his wife and fellow Home Depot veteran Pam, splitting time between New Smyrna Beach, Florida and Two Rivers, Wisconsin.

ACKNOWLEDGMENTS

To Pam, without whom this book would have never happened, or been this good. Your undying support meant everything to me.

To Jaq, for her directness, honesty and advice. And, for helping me understand what life is all about.

To Daria DiGiovanni, my ghostwriter, who tolerated me for a year and a half, working tirelessly to help me complete my dream.

To Reid Howard, for your honesty, input and direction along this book's entire journey and evolution.

To all the people named in the book, for their interaction and impact on my professional life. Special people doing special things, day in, day out.

To the Home Depot Legal Team, for their collaboration and insight, helping to produce the final product.

To Logotecture, for their terrific work on the design and formatting of the book.

To Magnetic Social Clips, for producing a wonderful portfolio of marketing videos, enabling exposure of the book on social media.

To the hundreds of thousands of associates at Home Depot and

Lowe 's, who toil every day, to elevate our Specialty Retail competition.

To the millions of retail workers in total, across all companies. Thank you for what you do.

And to the incredible customers I interacted with over my 33 years. I hope I treated you well.

REFERENCES

BOOKS

Built from Scratch: How a Couple of Regular Guys Grew The Home Depot from Nothing to $30 Billion, by Bernie Marcus and Arthur Blank

What Got You Here Won't Get You There: How Successful People Become Even More Successful, by Marshall Goldsmith

ARTICLES

Home Depot Creates 3,000 Multimillionaires, Co-Founder Says
https://www.foxbusiness.com/features/home-depot-creates-3000-multimillionaires-co-founder-says

Bob Nardelli at Home Depot: $223 Million
https://www.forbes.com/pictures/ehii45khf/bob-nardelli-at-home-

depot-223-million/#6462c088269b

Glossophobia (Fear of Public Speaking): Are You Glossophobic?
https://www.psycom.net/glossophobia-fear-of-public-speaking

The State of Mental Health in America 2018
https://www.mentalhealthamerica.net/issues/state-mental-health-america-2018

50 Years On, Moore's Law Still Pushes Tech to Double Down
https://www.wired.com/2015/04/50-years-moores-law-still-pushes-tech-double/

The Highest and Lowest Divorce Rates in America by Occupation and Industry
https://qz.com/1069806/the-highest-and-lowest-divorce-rates-in-america-by-occupation-and-industry/

Average S & P 500 Company CEO Makes 273 Times Median Employee Pay
https://www.foxbusiness.com/business-leaders/the-average-sp-ceo-makes-273-times-that-of-the-average-employee

The 10 Richest Counties in the U.S.
https://www.usnews.com/news/healthiest-communities/slideshows/richest-counties-in-america?slide=2

From the Archives: Going for Gold
https://corporate.homedepot.com/newsroom/home-depot-going-for-gold

The Homer Fund Celebrates 20 Years of Giving
https://corporate.homedepot.com/newsroom-community-posts/homer-fund-celebrates-20-years-giving

67170142R00189

Made in the USA
Columbia, SC
23 July 2019